Writing Jazz

Writing Jazz
Conversations with Critics and Biographers

SASCHA FEINSTEIN

excelsior editions

Cover credit: Trombonist Slide Hampton. Photo: Steven Sussman, used by permission.

Published by State University of New York Press, Albany

© 2025 State University of New York

All rights reserved

Printed in the United States of America

No part of this book may be used or reproduced in any manner whatsoever without written permission. No part of this book may be stored in a retrieval system or transmitted in any form or by any means including electronic, electrostatic, magnetic tape, mechanical, photocopying, recording, or otherwise without the prior permission in writing of the publisher.

Links to third-party websites are provided as a convenience and for informational purposes only. They do not constitute an endorsement or an approval of any of the products, services, or opinions of the organization, companies, or individuals. SUNY Press bears no responsibility for the accuracy, legality, or content of a URL, the external website, or for that of subsequent websites.

Excelsior Editions is an imprint of State University of New York Press

For information, contact State University of New York Press, Albany, NY
www.sunypress.edu

Library of Congress Cataloging-in-Publication Data

Name: Feinstein, Sascha, 1963– author.
Title: Writing Jazz : conversations with critics and biographers / Sascha Feinstein.
Description: Albany : State University of New York Press, 2025. | Series: Excelsior editions | Includes bibliographical references and index.
Identifiers: LCCN 2024025594 | ISBN 9798855801071 (pbk. : alk. paper) | ISBN 9798855801064 (ebook)
Subjects: LCSH: Music critics—United States—Interviews. | Musical criticism—United States—History—20th century. | Jazz—History and criticism.
Classification: LCC ML403 .F45 2025 | DDC 781.6509—dc23/eng/20240702
LC record available at https://lccn.loc.gov/2024025594

for Lynne Miller—
if you want

And, as you can see, I lived long enough to get this down onto paper, knowing well that—like notations on musical score paper—it'll go on being strictly dead stuff, an artifact, until another human being runs it through that most marvelous of instruments, imagination, and transforms the look of it into sound by breathing sense and meaning and feeling back into these blues.

—Al Young, *Drowning in the Sea of Love*

Hey, Rudy: Put this on the record—*all* of it.

—Miles Davis, Hackensack, New Jersey, December 24, 1954

Contents

Acknowledgments		ix
Introduction		1
1	Whitney Balliett / Poetic Prose	5
2	Bob Blumenthal / Hitting Your Mark	19
3	Stanley Crouch / If You Can't Do Better, Might as Well Just Stay Away	49
4	Linda Dahl / Breaking Down the Gates	71
5	Maxine Gordon / Maxine Calling	87
6	Farah Jasmine Griffin / The Culture of Jazz	109
7	John Edward Hasse / Living Archives	125
8	Willard Jenkins / Taking It Back	145
9	Hettie Jones / But I Know What Time It Is Now	169
10	Robin D. G. Kelley / Evidence	185
11	Laurie Pepper / The Artist's Way	207

12	Tom Piazza / On the Record	223
13	Ricky Riccardi / The Archival Mind	241
14	A. B. Spellman / Don't Give It Up	261

Index — 285

Acknowledgments

All the interviews first appeared in *Brilliant Corners: A Journal of Jazz & Literature* (lycoming.edu/BrilliantCorners). Founded in 1996, the journal has been sustained largely because of David Rife and Gary Hafer, my friends and colleagues at Lycoming College; as I have noted many times before, their editorial work has been invaluable.

I extend profound gratitude to the whole team at SUNY Press, especially senior acquisitions editor Richard Carlin, production editor Caitlin Bean, and copyeditor Dana Foote, whose astounding eye for detail tightened up the manuscript immeasurably.

The reprinted texts preceding the interviews, as well as previously published work that appears elsewhere in the collection, add enormous substance to these conversations, and I am extremely grateful to the authors, estates, and publishers who granted permission to reprint these works:

Whitney Balliett. Excerpts from "The Duke's Party," "Three Pianists," "The Prince of Jazz," and "The Natural" from *Collected Works: A Journal of Jazz, 1954–2000* by Whitney Balliett. Copyright © 2000 by Whitney Balliett. Reprinted courtesy of the estate for Whitney Balliett.

Bob Blumenthal. Excerpts from the liner notes for *Coltrane: The Classic Quartet* by Bob Blumenthal. Copyright © Bob Blumenthal. Reprinted courtesy of Universal Music Group. *The Complete Argo / Mercury Art Farmer / Benny Golson / Jazztet Sessions* by Bob Blumenthal. Copyright © Bob Blumenthal. Used by permission of the author. Excerpt from the liner notes for Jackie McLean's *Let Freedom Ring* (Blue Note Records RVG Edition) and Horace Silver's *Song for My Father* (Blue Note Records RVG Edition) by Bob Blumenthal. Copyright © Blue Note Records. Reprinted courtesy of Blue Note Records.

Linda Dahl. Excerpts from *Stormy Weather: The Music and Lives of a Century of Jazzwomen*, *Morning Glory: A Biography of Mary Lou Williams*, *The Bad Dream Notebook*, and *Haunted Heart: A Biography of Susannah McCorkle* (all by Linda Dahl). Copyright © by Linda Dahl. Used by permission of the author.

Maxine Gordon. Excerpts from *Sophisticated Giant: The Life and Legacy of Dexter Gordon*, liner notes for *BOPland: The Legendary Elks Club Concert L.A. 1947*, and liner notes for Dexter Gordon's *Tokyo 1975* (all by Maxine Gordon). Copyright © Maxine Gordon. Used by permission of the author.

Farah Jasmine Griffin. Excerpts from *If You Can't Be Free, Be a Mystery*, "Literary Lady," and *Harlem Nocturne* (all by Farah Jasmine Griffin). Copyright © Farah Jasmine Griffin. Used by permission of the author. Excerpt from *Clawing at the Limits of Cool* by Farah Jasmine Griffin and Salim Washington. Copyright © by Farah Jasmine Griffin and Salim Washington. Used by permission of the authors.

John Edward Hasse. Excerpts from *Beyond Category: The Life and Genius of Duke Ellington*, "The Swing Era" from *Jazz: The First Century*, "We Saw Jazz through His Lens" from the *Wall Street Journal*, and "The Team Sport of Jazz" from *Discover Jazz* (all by John Edward Hasse). Copyright © by John Edward Hasse. Used by permission of the author.

Willard Jenkins. Excerpts from the arranger's preface to *African Rhythms*, liner notes for the CD reissue of *Dizzy's Big 4*, "What's Your Take: Is Racism Still an Issue in Jazz?," and introduction to *Ain't But a Few of Us: Black Music Writers Tell Their Story* (all by Willard Jenkins). Copyright © by Willard Jenkins. Used by permission of the author.

Robin D. G. Kelley. Excerpts from *Thelonious Monk: The Life and Times of an American Original* as well as an unpublished manuscript from *Thelonious Monk: The Life and Times of an American Original* (all by Robin D. G. Kelley). Copyright © by Robin D. G. Kelley. Used by permission of the author.

Yusef Komunyakaa. "February in Sydney" from *Pleasure Dome: New and Collected Poems* © 2001 by Yusef Komunyakaa. Published by Wesleyan University Press. Reprinted with permission.

Laurie Pepper. Excerpts from liner notes to *Atlanta: Unreleased Art Pepper, Volume 11* and *Art: Why I Stuck with a Junkie Jazzman* (both by Laurie Pepper) as well as *Straight Life: The Story of Art Pepper* (by Art and Laurie Pepper). Copyright © by Laurie Pepper. Used by permission of the author.

Tom Piazza. Excerpts from *The Guide to Classic Recorded Jazz*, *Setting the Tempo*, *Understanding Jazz: Ways to Listen*, and *Blues Up and Down: Jazz* *in Our Time* (all by Tom Piazza). Copyright © by Tom Piazza. Used by permission of the author.

Ricky Riccardi. Excerpts from liner notes for *Columbia and RCA Victor Live Recordings of Louis Armstrong and the All Stars*, *What a Wonderful World: The Magic of Louis Armstrong's Later Years*, liner notes for Louis Armstrong's *Pops Is Tops: The Verve Studio Albums*, and liner notes for Ella Fitzgerald and Louis Armstrong's *Cheek to Cheek: The Complete Duet Recordings* (all by Ricky Riccardi). Copyright © by Ricky Riccardi. Used by permission of the author.

A. B. Spellman. Excerpts from the introduction to *Four Lives in the Bebop Business*, liner notes for Eric Dolphy's *Out to Lunch*, and liner notes for John Coltrane's *Ascension*, as well as the poem "On Hearing Sonny ('Newk') Rollins in the Park on a Hot Summer Night" from *Things I Must Have Known* (all by A. B. Spellman). Copyright © by A. B. Spellman. Used by permission of the author.

Al Young. Excerpt from "Straight, No Chaser" in *Drowning in the Sea of Love: Musical Memoirs* by Al Young. Copyright © by Al Young. Used by permission of the Estate for Al Young.

Introduction

Perhaps I've told you this story before. Manhattan, 1976. I'm thirteen. The Beatles had been the beloved soundtrack of my youth, but my taste in music had devolved. On this particular afternoon, I enthusiastically decided to share my latest soporific pop LP with my father and godfather, Thorpe Feidt. The first cut concluded. My father said nothing. Thorpe offered a strained smile—a clear and painful loss for me—and then my father announced he was going to hip me to jazz.

He put on an album by Dixieland trombonist Kid Ory, but I just raised my eyebrows, so he quickly switched to *The Hawk Flies High*, a 1957 session led by tenor sax genius Coleman Hawkins. The opening cut, "Chant," had a bouncy-enough head, but it was Hawkins's entrance that made my head snap. I'd never heard tone with such teeth, such *authority*. As much as his horn filled the living room, it entered my entire being. I could not quite comprehend how a wordless instrument could elevate my spirits to such a degree. I suddenly wanted to hear everything he'd ever recorded. Put more simplistically: I knew this music eclipsed the dross that had been entertaining me.

My father left the room with the record playing, but Thorpe saw my fire. He knew the music very well and started sifting through albums in the record cabinet, transforming the dullness of that afternoon into one of the greatest days of my life. We heard Art Blakey's *A Night at Birdland, Volume One*, with Clifford Brown devouring "Split Kick" and Lou Donaldson ripping up the break on "A Night in Tunisia." (Bird's still-more classic rendition would soon be in my life, too.) He spun Duke Ellington's revelatory performance at Newport in '56, with Paul Gonsalves creating a frenzy with his twenty-seven hip choruses. Ella Fitzgerald and Billie Holiday. We listened to another Hawkins album, *The Hawk Relaxes*, which opens with "I'll Never Be the Same," a tune that spoke to the whole experience. In the weeks that followed, jazz became the center of my life, an unfailing balm, a kind of religion.

It would be years before I embraced writing as an equal love, but even in my early teens I turned to literature as another way of understanding this soul-stirring music. Leonard Feather's *Encyclopedia of Jazz* offered tantalizing biographical snapshots (as well as addresses and phone numbers!), and Joachim Berendt's *The Jazz Book* helped to put the music in chronological perspective, an education I badly needed. My father alerted me to pieces by Whitney Balliett in the *New Yorker*, and I found his prose more musical than anyone else's, although I was so green as a writer that I didn't even realize I should be jealous. Most of all, though, I loved the oral histories, such as those found in Robert Reisner's *Bird: The Legend of Charlie Parker*, with transcribed interviews about Charlie Parker from roughly eighty friends and fellow musicians, and the brilliantly edited (by Nat Shapiro and Nat Hentoff) *Hear Me Talkin' to Ya: The Story of Jazz by the Men Who Made It*. Biographies and autobiographies followed, among my favorites, Duke Ellington's *Music Is My Mistress*, Charles Mingus's *Beneath the Underdog*, and Art and Laurie Pepper's *Straight Life*. And I leaned on liner notes (this being the pre-CD 1970s, when they were prominently presented and easily read). In some cases—as with A. B. Spellman's liners for avant-garde releases—the writers provided avenues into the music that my young ears could not begin to navigate without a seasoned guide.

The distinguished writers interviewed in this collection obviously share a passion for jazz, and each has produced a hefty amount of literature that illuminates both the music and its practitioners. To sum up their contributions would be ridiculously reductive; it is enough, I hope, to say that their writing has been invaluable for jazz-related scholarship. These interviews first appeared in *Brilliant Corners: A Journal of Jazz & Literature*, which I founded in 1996 and still edit, and took place from 2006 to the present (except for the one with Balliett from 1999). Others from the first ten years of *Brilliant Corners* were published in *Ask Me Now: Conversations on Jazz & Literature*, and in many ways, these books speak to one another, although *Ask Me Now* heavily emphasized poets inspired by jazz.

The first interview I ever conducted with a writer took place in 1985, when I was a nervous undergraduate with a cheap tape recorder. My honors thesis focused largely on the poet Michael Harper, and I managed to obtain funds to bring him to campus for a reading. As a reward, I was allotted about half an hour with him in the privacy of my mentor's office. I didn't get to ask many questions; anyone who knew Michael knows he commanded any room he walked into. But at one point I noted that much of his poetry demanded a knowledge of jazz, and I asked if he worried about his work not being understood because of national ignorance. He replied:

> Well, yes and no. The yes part of it is that every poet would like to be understood, and I don't think that many of my poems can be understood without a little work. I don't set out as a modus operandi to confuse my readers, but at the same time jazz music is so indigenous to American culture that even if you have a predilection not to like it, you have to really be informed about it if you want to be informed about American culture. And so I have a bias.

It seemed to me then, and much more so now, that such a bias should not only be encouraged but celebrated, and I hope these varied conversations do exactly that.

1

Poetic Prose

Whitney Balliett

Whitney Balliett (1926–2007) joined the staff of the *New Yorker* in 1951 and became its jazz critic in 1957, remaining there until 2001, during which time he wrote over 550 articles. Starting with *The Sound of Surprise*, his seventeen books include *American Musicians II*, *American Singers*, *Collected Works: A Journal of Jazz, 1954–2000*, and *New York Voices*. He received many awards and honors, including a 1996 Academy Award in Literature from the American Academy of Arts and Letters. During his lifetime, Balliett interviewed hundreds of musicians, and his experiences have been well documented in his essays.

The following excerpts from Balliett's writings have been reprinted with permission. The interview took place in his Manhattan apartment on January 7, 1999.

"The Duke's Party" (excerpt)

When the room was full, the President and Mrs. Nixon, followed by Ellington and his sister, entered, and everyone stood. I can't resist such fillets of melodrama, and I got a lump in my throat. The President, moving in a quick, wooden way, jumped up on a platform in front of the bandstand and, in his deepest rain-barrel voice, said something to this effect: "Sit down, please, ladies and gentlemen. This is a very unusual and special evening in this great room. Before the entertainment begins, we have a presentation to make. I was looking at his name on here and it says 'Edward Kennedy'"—he paused—"'Ellington.'" Laughter. "For the first time during this Administration I have the honor of presenting the Presidential Medal of Freedom." Ellington, standing pensively beside Mr. Nixon, was reading the citation over his right shoulder. "In the royalty of American music, no man swings more or stands higher than the Duke." The President handed Ellington the medal. Everyone stood, and the applause was thunderous. "Thank you, Mr. President," Ellington said, and, taking Mr. Nixon by both arms, he conferred *his* celebrated award—the classic French greeting of left cheek against left cheek, right against right, left against left, and right against right. The President blushed and took a seat in the front row. Ellington said thank you again and listed the four freedoms that Billy Strayhorn had lived his life by—freedom from hate, freedom from self-pity, freedom from fear of possibly doing something that might help someone else more than it would him, and freedom from "the kind of pride that could make a man feel that he is better than his brother."

"Three Pianists" (excerpt)

Cecil Taylor packing them into the Five Spot for three solid weeks! Cecil Taylor playing *encores* to get off the stand! Cecil Taylor—iconoclast, super-avant-gardist, mysterioso pianist—a matinée idol! Incredible but true. When Taylor first came up, the thought of such acclaim would have caused jigging hilarity. There was nothing accessible or even especially attractive about his music. It operated completely on its terms; to join in, the listener did the work. Little has changed about Taylor. He is still tiny and muscular and solemn, and he still performs like a wrecking crew. He stabs and pounds and hammers the keyboard. His enormous glissandos skid heavily. He plays staccato arpeggios so fast they become ribbons of sound. His arms are blurred pistons, and he rocks in wild irregular circles. He comes very close to making visual music. And so his new popularity is suddenly understandable. His music, though totally dissimilar in content and construction, has all along been a forerunner of electronic music, of hard rock, and so has his way of performing it. The music around him has simply caught up to Taylor, and everything he does is now apposite. One can easily imagine turning on to Taylor, drifting down through his polyrhythms and dense harmonic tongues, through his massive chords and thundering arpeggios. Taylor's first number tonight at the Five Spot was the first set, and it lasted almost an hour and twenty minutes. It was vintage Taylor and it consisted of several immense Taylor solos spelled by somewhat shorter statements by the alto saxophonist Jimmy Lyons, an indefatigable cohort of Taylor's and an eclectic who spins out variations on the thoughts of John Coltrane and Ornette Coleman and Eric Dolphy. Perhaps Taylor's instrument no longer matters. He has become obsessed with blocks of sound, with sequoias of sound, and if he could not produce on the piano what he hears in his head, he would do it by other means. He would gather about him whales and jets and cascades, and make them sing and roar and crash. And we'd listen.

"The Prince of Jazz" (excerpt)

Perhaps [Wynton] Marsalis will write a jazz opera, a jazz symphony, a concerto for jazz trumpet. Whatever, it will be adept mimicry, adept synthesis. So go out into the jazz fields and listen to such true contemporary voices as those of Kenny Barron and Roy Haynes and Tom Harrell, of Joe Lovano and Bill Charlap and Sean Smith, of Leon Parker and Brad Mehldau and Steve Wilson. They have long since run with the past, and are now spreading their own singular organic beauties.

Blood on the Fields was, astonishingly, awarded a Pulitzer Prize. Duke Ellington, the master of us all, was notoriously denied a Pulitzer in 1965, which caused him to say, "Fate is being kind to me. Fate doesn't want me to be famous too young." Marsalis, of course, is already what the Duke was afraid he might become. Fate, contrary to all indications, has not been kind to him.

"The Natural" (excerpt)

There is a secret emotional center in jazz which has sustained the music since it outgrew its early melodic and rhythmic gaucheries, in the late twenties. This center, a kind of aural elixir, reveals itself when an improvised phrase or an entire solo or even a complete number catches you by surprise. When these lyrical bursts happen in nightclubs or at concerts, their afterimages inevitably fade. Caught on recordings, though, they last forever. So here, in no particular order, are some classic recorded beauties: the first twelve or so bars of Louis Armstrong's second solo on both takes of "Some of These Days," played in a revolving halftime in his low register and unlike anything else he ever recorded (Columbia; 1929); the eerie, almost surrealistic melody that Paul Gonsalves fashions on the first bridge of a "Caravan" done with Duke Ellington (Fantasy; 1962); Charlie Parker's stunning two-chorus solo on "Funky Blues," replete with an opening now-listen preaching figure, a shivering, sotto voce run at the start of the second chorus, and a dodging, ascending climactic figure (Verve; 1952); the cluster of soft, keening notes that Joe Lovano plays near the end of "Lament for M," a dirge by Gunther Schuller written in memory of his wife for "Rush Hour" (Blue Note; 1995); the Sidney de Paris-Ben Webster-Vic Dickenson-James P. Johnson-Sid Catlett "After You've Gone," certainly as close to a flawless jazz recording as exists (Blue Note; 1944); and all of the remarkable pianist Bill Charlap's "Turnaround," an Ornette Coleman blues that he fills with huge, stuttering chords and sailing-along-the-tonal-edge single-note lines (Criss Cross; 1995).

Interview

SASCHA FEINSTEIN: When you interview musicians, do you have a set agenda—written questions, a particular angle?

WHITNEY BALLIETT: I just begin talking, and then I try to shape it. But of course it depends on the person. If you get someone like [pianist] Joe Bushkin—he almost drove me crazy. He never stops talking. He gets started and it's just stream of consciousness. He goes on and on and on. I was with him for six straight days, and it almost killed me. *Finally* I stopped him and said, "Now Joe, you've got to stop. I want you to talk about such and such." But then he'd start again and go sailing off into the blue.

I try to edit the essay chronologically. After relaxed talk and that kind of stuff, I'll say, "Well, let's go back to the beginning. Talk about your parents. What was your father like, what was your mother like—," all of which, I think, is important.

FEINSTEIN: And then you edit your questions?

BALLIETT: Oh yeah. Sure. [Balliett points to the tape recorder.] I've never used one of those.

FEINSTEIN: Really? Why not?

BALLIETT: I don't know. When I started interviewing people, I just took notes.

FEINSTEIN: Bushkin is obviously one extreme, but many musicians must need to be drawn out, no?

BALLIETT: Yes. People like [trumpeter] Jabbo Smith. He was really semi-articulate and it was difficult to get him to talk. Many of the older fellows are that way. Some are just difficult. [Pianist] Dick Wellstood was very hard to speak with, very sharp-tongued. He offered almost nothing, and finally I had to say, "Look, Dick. Either we do this interview or we don't, but if you want to do it, you'll have to answer my questions and really talk." And then he opened up.

When I visited Ray Charles in his building in California, he made me sit in the waiting room for three hours. Maybe he thought I would disappear. I don't know. When we did speak, he said a lot. But he said all sorts of wonderful things about his father, and, years later, when I read David Ritz's book [*Brother Ray: Ray Charles' Own Story*, cowritten with Charles], I found out his father had been mean, that he'd been an alcoholic. That's why I added a footnote when I reprinted the essay [in *American Singers*]. I really got taken.

FEINSTEIN: Most of your interviews, though, seem to have been a joy. I'm thinking now of your piece on Mary Lou Williams.

BALLIETT: She was terrific. I used to see her in later years and she'd say, "You know, that's the *best* piece you ever did." [Laughs.]

[At this point, the batteries in the tape recorder died, and I had to replace them.]

FEINSTEIN: I bet you're as pleased as ever that you don't use tape recorders.

BALLIETT: [Smiles.] You know, I was thinking just that.

FEINSTEIN: You play the drums, and so you know that—in terms of sharing an experience—there's nothing in writing that quite compares to playing jazz.

BALLIETT: No, that's true.

FEINSTEIN: When did you decide to spend most of your energies writing?

BALLIETT: After I graduated from Cornell, I was lucky enough to get a job with the *New Yorker*. When I came down here, I thought I was going to be another Edmund Wilson. [Chuckles.] I can't remember exactly how it happened, but in the early 1950s, while I was at the *New Yorker*, I started to do little pieces for the old *Saturday Review*. I did more and more stuff for them—profile-like things—and somebody showed these pieces to [William] Shawn [editor of the *New Yorker* from 1952 to 1986]. One day he asked me if I'd like to start doing a column on jazz.

FEINSTEIN: So you realized your whole professional life that you would be a writer but that you'd keep your hand in drumming?

BALLIETT: I knew I didn't have the ability to be a professional drummer, and I didn't play much in college. I started again in the late fifties and early sixties. Daphne Hellman, who's a harpist, has a house over on Sixty-First Street, and she started to have these musical evenings. Dick Wellstood would show up, and there were a lot of *New Yorker* people. Lee Lorenz, the cartoonist, played trumpet. (He's a good trumpet player. Still plays.) Warren Miller, who also played trumpet, really kept his chops up. He sounded kind of like Frankie Newton. Paul Brodeur played the clarinet, but you never knew what he was doing. He'd take a solo and end ten bars before the end of the chorus because he thought it was over, didn't know where he was. Anyway, that went on for a couple of years. We left her place and played at studios here and there, about once a month.

And I've sat in at various places at various times. As I mention in that *Atlantic* piece ["Sitting In," January 1998], Barney Josephson had a New Year's Eve party at his place—Marian

McPartland played, Eddie Heywood, others—and I sat in with them. [My wife] Nancy was there, and my old editor from the *New Yorker*, Popsie Whitaker, was sitting with her (he had a tongue like a viper!), and when I came back to the table, he looked at me and said, "We wondered where you were." [Laughs.]

Once at the Cape—at The Columns on Route 28—I was sitting in with [pianist Dave] McKenna, who hates drummers. (He doesn't need a drummer with that left hand.) So in comes [Bobby] Hackett, and he goes over and starts talking to McKenna, telling this funny story. Well, I started laughing, and Hackett leaned over to me and said, "Hey, Whit. You're on one and three." [Both laugh.] I had lost the whole time!

FEINSTEIN: Do you see crossovers between writing and music?

BALLIETT: Well, if you're going to write about jazz music, I think it helps a tremendous amount to be able to play because you really understand what it is to play that music, to be in a group. The exhilaration and so forth makes some sense. If you had never played—didn't know anything about that—I would think it would be a real drawback.

FEINSTEIN: I feel exactly the same way—about any art. Once, when I became very interested in sculpture, I started hitting stone just to get the feel.

BALLIETT: Is that a sculptor's term, "hitting stone"?

FEINSTEIN: Not that I know of.

BALLIETT: That's nice. [Smiles.] I like that.

FEINSTEIN: What's your opinion of Leonard Feather?

BALLIETT: Leonard was okay. I mean, Leonard had ears. He was a musician. [Pauses, then chuckles.] We were once at a Monk concert in 1958 or '59, when Monk still hadn't really hit. Leonard was sitting in front of me, and he turned around and said, "Do you think he's any good?" [Both laugh.] Well, I *did* think he was good . . . I didn't trust Leonard very much. There was a time when he was in on everything. He would write a blues tune, and then he would record it with him playing the piano himself, and he would organize the thing—and then he'd review the record label. [Laughs.] I mean, Leonard was a very oily character.

FEINSTEIN: Are there individual jazz biographies or autobiographies that you particularly admire? When we first met, I remember having a memorable conversation about [Art and Laurie Pepper's] *Straight Life.*

BALLIETT: I thought that was a terrific book. I've just started this huge book of Dick Sudhalter's about white jazz musicians [*Lost Chords*] that's coming out in the next couple of weeks. Thousand pages. And that's good. I'm glad he did that. I mean, even Martin Williams, who had a pretty level head on his shoulders, slighted so many white people when he compiled the *Smithsonian Collection of Classic Jazz.* People like Bobby Hackett, [Jack] Teagarden—he just left them out. I mean, you can't do that. So this is good that Sudhalter has done this. Because there was a lot of [racial] interchange, but that's gotten all out of whack. What did Jim Hall say to me in that profile? "I've always felt that the music started out as black but that it's as much mine now as anyone else's. I haven't stolen the music from anybody—I just bring something different to it." Hall worked with Sonny Rollins for a long time, but when they were on the cover of *Down Beat*, Rollins started getting all of this flak from black musicians—"What are you doing with this ofay?"—and Rollins fired him. Later on he apologized. But that was the beginning of it—Miles Davis and others—the whole reverse racism thing.

When I first wrote about Wynton [Marsalis]'s concerts in the early eighties—before there was any Lincoln Center orchestra—I noticed there was *one* white player in the band. And I thought, "Gee, that's weird," and I mention it at the end of my piece in a very discreet way. [Pause.] Have you listened to [Marsalis's] *Blood on the Fields?*

FEINSTEIN: Yeah.

BALLIETT: [Rolls his eyes.] God. I wrote a review of it, but Tina Brown [editor of the *New Yorker* from 1992 to 1998] never ran it. (I later learned she had a deaf ear for music.) I thought the music was terrible. [That review later appeared in *Brilliant Corners*, and then in Balliett's *Collected Works*—SF.]

FEINSTEIN: That's probably why she didn't run it—she didn't want to criticize the only jazz composition in history to receive the Pulitzer Prize.

BALLIETT: [Rolls his eyes again.] Pulitzer Prize . . .

FEINSTEIN: Where do you find the limitations to be?

BALLIETT: I liked some of Cassandra Wilson's singing, and some of the blues sections were pretty good. But I found it to be pompous, and shallow. It didn't swing. And it went on and on and on. Three hours long. Exhausting.

∼

FEINSTEIN: You wrote an essay for the *Atlantic* in 1953, and the bio says you were "a poet and essayist."

BALLIETT: I had published a few poems in the *New Yorker*.

FEINSTEIN: Jazz-related?

BALLIETT: No. [Pauses.] Someday I'll publish a book of poems. Let's see—how many do I have now? Seventeen. [Laughs.]

FEINSTEIN: How often do you turn to poetry?

BALLIETT: Oh, I haven't written a poem for three or four years. My last experience—[chuckles]. I turned it in to [the poetry editor] Alice Quinn at the *New Yorker*, and I didn't hear anything and didn't hear anything, and I finally went to her and said, "Alice, what happened to that poem?" And she said, "What poem?" She had moved her office, and Tina Brown had come in. Anyway, out of embarrassment or whatever she printed it.

FEINSTEIN: I think I know that poem—"Back"—with two cats named after [the jazz club owners] Barney Josephson and Max Gordon.

BALLIETT: Yeah, Barney and Max. They had the right colors. [Laughs.]

FEINSTEIN: The poet Philip Larkin praised your work so highly—"Balliett is a master of language"—and you've used that as a blurb. How do you come to terms with the fact that he hated modern jazz?

BALLIETT: He was a real moldy fig. But if he wants to say nice things about me, that's fine. Who's going to know he was a moldy fig? Most people don't know what a moldy fig is, anyway. [Chuckles.] He was a strange guy.

FEINSTEIN: Terrific poet.

BALLIETT: Wonderful poet. But *strange*.

FEINSTEIN: You have a profile on [pianist] Cecil Taylor in which you quote one of his poems. What do you think of Taylor's poetry?

BALLIETT: That's the only one I remember seeing. It's way out.

FEINSTEIN: Taylor's so very different from most of the people you write about.

BALLIETT: He's very different from most *people*. Actually, the very first column that I did for the *New Yorker* was about his first record [*Jazz Advance*], and I wrote about it in glowing terms, that I thought he was very important ["Progress and Prudence," 1957]. And I've seen Cecil a million times. He's unique. He's certainly on the furthest boundaries of jazz music—I don't know what you could call some of what he plays.

I remember the jazz concert they threw at the White House when Jimmy Carter was president. They had a wonderful lineup, everyone from Mary Lou Williams right up to Cecil. We were all sitting on the grass, the piano was about twenty feet away, and after Cecil finished he got up and headed for some trees. Jimmy Carter was seated beside me on the grass, and he jumped up and *ran* after Taylor to thank him. [Laughs.] It was such a funny sight to see him race across the lawn after Taylor and have them disappear into this clump of woods.

FEINSTEIN: That was the concert when [Dizzy] Gillespie sang "Salt Peanuts" with Carter, no?

BALLIETT: He taught him "Salt Peanuts." They sang it together. And Carter was very funny. Dizzy asked him if he would like to go on the road with them, and he said, "I may have to after tonight." [Both laugh.]

FEINSTEIN: Was that the only White House concert you've attended?

BALLIETT: No. We went to [Duke] Ellington's seventieth birthday party in 1969. It was a lot of fun. Good group. I'm so sorry the recording's never been released. [The CD appeared three years after this interview, *Duke Ellington: 1969 All-Star White House Tribute*—SF.] Wonderful band: [Paul] Desmond was in it, Jim Hall. [Gerry] Mulligan had done the arrangements. [Pauses and chuckles.] Nixon played "Happy Birthday," and Duke gave him four kisses. [Laughs.] It was unbelievable.

FEINSTEIN: That must have made him nervous . . . Did the musicians enjoy themselves? I mean, how do you think politics enters in a performance like that?

BALLIETT: It was a very cheerful evening. Everybody danced, and then Nixon disappeared.

FEINSTEIN: Yeah, but Nixon wouldn't have disappeared in the woods to chase Cecil Taylor—

BALLIETT: You know, I feel sorry for anyone who never heard the Ellington band live. Records are one thing, but that band, when they were on . . . You heard them, right?

FEINSTEIN: No. I was ten or eleven when Ellington died.

BALLIETT: Oh.

[There was a pause. It seemed that Balliett wanted to say something, but nothing arrived.]

~

FEINSTEIN: Your book *American Singers* includes many portraits of cabaret singers, the kind some jazz-heads feel are far removed from jazz singers.

BALLIETT: It depends on the singer. Mabel Mercer was one of the great performers. She was wonderful. Now, she was not at all a jazz singer, but she influenced jazz singers. Billie [Holiday] used to listen to her all the time. Sinatra used to listen to her—he was crazy about her because of the phrasing, the articulation. She could get a lyric across in a way that was just fantastic. Some cabaret singers are right on the edge—very close to being jazz singers.

Have you seen the Smithsonian five-CD collection of jazz singing?

FEINSTEIN: Compiled by Robert O'Meally?

BALLIETT: [Rolls his eyes.] Maddening, the way he did it. He just didn't do it right. He's got Ella Fitzgerald singing "Until the Real Thing Comes Along," and the great version of that was done by Julia Lee, a Kansas City singer, which was on juke boxes, for God's sake, when I was in college. Wonderful. Really *down*. And in his blues section he doesn't have Joe Turner. Doesn't have Robert Johnson. That's just insane.

FEINSTEIN: He was also responsible for the CD that accompanies *The Norton Anthology of African American Literature*, and I was very surprised by his choices. King Pleasure singing "Parker's Mood," but nothing by Bird himself. Nothing at all by Coltrane—although that might not bother you as much. You seem to have had reservations about Coltrane's music.

BALLIETT: Oh yeah, that piece [from 1968]. But I did another piece about three years ago where I tried to be absolutely evenhanded. I think I put down some of the later stuff because it simply goes beyond me. I don't understand the shrieking that he was doing—and a lot of musicians didn't, either. I love the work Coltrane did with [singer Johnny] Hartman, and what he did with Ellington. Wonderful, and moving.

FEINSTEIN: Given his music from the end of his career—and what, say, Cecil Taylor has done since—do you feel that the boundaries of jazz have been defined?

BALLIETT: Yes. The abstract jazz—the New Thing, as they used to call it—has been taken as far as it can go. After that, it turns into a different kind of music. And all of these kids now are just aping the hard bop players. The exception, I think, are in the piano players: [Brad] Mehldau, and certainly [Bill] Charlap.

FEINSTEIN: You're currently working on a piece about Charlap.

BALLIETT: He's terrific. Whew. [His profile later appeared in the *New Yorker* and his *Collected Works* as "The Natural"—SF.]

FEINSTEIN: In general, though, you've been a little tough on the "young lions" who have been getting a lot of attention in the last few years.

BALLIETT: Well, I haven't written much about them.

FEINSTEIN: True, but the little that you have hasn't been all that favorable. You're the only one I know, for example, to question the intonation of [bassist] Christian McBride.

BALLIETT: Well, it's true. On the record I heard, he lost his time on his solo. You can't do that. I mean, if you're going to do far out things, that pulse has got to be going.

FEINSTEIN: Who else do you find overpraised?

[It was now noon, and the grandfather clock behind us started to strike very loudly, making it impossible to hear each other.]

FEINSTEIN: I guess they've been saved by the bells.

BALLIETT: [Laughs.] The next time, it'll only be one.

2

Hitting Your Mark

Bob Blumenthal

Bob Blumenthal began writing jazz criticism in 1969 for *Boston After Dark* (later known as the *Boston Phoenix*) and afterward became a jazz critic for the *Boston Globe* until 2002. During this time, he worked as an attorney, primarily for the Massachusetts Department of Education, and contributed to such publications as the *Atlantic Monthly*, *Rolling Stone*, the *Village Voice*, *Down Beat*, and *JazzTimes*. He also wrote the liner notes for many albums, and continues to write notes for new and classic recordings, including the RVG reissue series of Blue Note Records. He received Grammy awards for best album notes in 1999 for *Coltrane: The Classic Quartet / Complete Impulse! Studio Recordings* and 2000 for *Miles Davis & John Coltrane: The Complete Columbia Recordings 1955–61*. His other honors include the Jazz Journalists Association Excellence in Feature and Review Writing award in 2001, and their Lifetime Achievement award in 2005. His book *Jazz: An Introduction to the History and Legends Behind America's Music* was published after this interview.

The following excerpts from Blumenthal's writings have been reprinted with permission. The interview took place in Dennis, Massachusetts, on August 21, 2006.

Liner Notes for *Coltrane: The Classic Quartet* (excerpt)

Some music can conjure an era years later, echoing the values and concerns of the surrounding culture. When we hear such music, we marvel at how it reflects its times. John Coltrane's quartet music did something more. It defined the period in which it was created, revealing and setting in motion energies that resonated throughout jazz and American society in the first half of the 1960s. When we hear Coltrane's quartet recordings today, over 30 years after their creation, nostalgia is the least of the experience. This is organic, living art that retains the illuminating burst of discovery.

What continues to set Coltrane's legacy apart, above and beyond its sheer brilliance, is its constant evolution and sense of direction. Coltrane's refusal to stop and savor any one of his many triumphs, his dedication to pushing forward and finding more, made him the focal point in a critical period of jazz history. He did not make this journey alone, however. With the support of pianist McCoy Tyner, bassist Jimmy Garrison and drummer Elvin Jones, a unit universally recognized as the classic Coltrane quartet, the saxophonist brought closure to his investigation of chord-based improvising over standard material, perfected the modal approach that he as much as any single musician made a common part of the jazz language, and crossed the threshold of even freer expression that he would explore in his final two years with his last ensembles.

Liner Notes for Horace Silver's *Song for My Father* (excerpt)

This album, the most popular in the lengthy Blue Note career of Horace Silver, is also the most oddly assembled. Silver was one of the most efficient jazz artists of the period. He had a knack for producing well-balanced, conceptually coherent programs of 12-inch album length; and, given his extensive output, he left amazingly few alternate or unissued performances. *Song for My Father* had more of a cut-and-paste appearance, with four titles recorded in October 1964 by a new Horace Silver quintet, plus a quintet and trio track made a year earlier. A jumble of this type, while not unheard of at Blue Note, was hardly Horacian. . . .

Song for My Father turned out to be a triumph for both the leader and Joe Henderson, who did two things here that are indicative of his contributions to various Blue Note sessions of the period. He brought in a great original, "The Kicker," which he would also record three years later on the Milestone album of the same name; and he blew a solo on the title track that stole the show. Efforts of this quality explain why Henderson, like Silver, came to be viewed as one of the definitive Blue Note artists.

Liner Notes for Jackie McLean's *Let Freedom Ring* (excerpt)

In a sense, Blue Note got two alto saxophonists when it signed Jackie McLean to a contract late in 1958. One was a master of the bebop vernacular who had helped usher in the more caustic and percussion-driven hard-bop era, and who can be heard to best advantage on Freddie Redd's 1960 masterpiece *Music from "The Connection."* The second was a more restless, exploratory soul attuned to where contemporaries such as Ornette Coleman and John Coltrane were headed, who sought his own path into the new music. This renegade side of McLean's personality is well described in the memorable liner notes the saxophonist wrote for the original release of the present album, and could be heard in embryo as early as his first date as a leader for the label, when the version of "Quadrangle" that McLean describes was recorded. . . .

The final two compositions [on the album] are both related to the blues; but while "Rene" employs the standard twelve-bar structure and harmonic sequence once the solos commence, "Omega" abstracts the form to arrive at a three-part modal structure. Both compositions inspire superb performances, with the parade of tart blues licks in the former recalling André Hodeir's description of Thelonious Monk's treatment of pop songs as an "acid bath."

Liner Notes for *The Complete Argo / Mercury Art Farmer / Benny Golson / Jazztet Sessions* (excerpt)

By the end of 1962, the Jazztet had been disbanded. "We had reached a crossroads," Golson says. "Each of us wanted to go in a different direction, and it was impossible to pursue both in one band. The jobs had fallen off as well." Two decades would pass, with Golson turning to studio writing and Farmer relocating to Austria, before the partners would reconvene under the Jazztet moniker, often with Curtis Fuller, for occasional tours and recordings.

Golson's memories of the Jazztet experience remain positive. "One word comes to mind when I think of those years—adventure," he emphasizes. "We went to the same forest every day, but never touched the same trees. That's what you call anticipation, which music has to have to progress."

And progress clearly remains at the top of Golson's agenda. "Since each of us is imperfect, there is always something to shoot for, and any musician who's satisfied is in trouble. When people tell me that I don't sound like I used to I say 'thank you,' because everything changes, so why shouldn't music? My eyes are always on the horizon, and who ever arrives at the horizon?"

Interview

SASCHA FEINSTEIN: I want to concentrate on the art of writing liner notes, but since you've been writing for over thirty-five years, I should first ask how jazz entered your life.

BOB BLUMENTHAL: Ray Charles is to blame. I was born in 1947 and grew up in a suburb of St. Louis—Clayton, Missouri. I loved the radio, and one of the things that I find very fortunate when I look back was that there was more black pop radio than white pop radio. And what really drew me in was a song that crossed the lines: "What'd I Say" by Ray Charles. After my bar mitzvah in 1960, I took some of my bar mitzvah money and said, "I want to buy that song." As luck would have it, I did not buy the two-part "What'd I Say" 45; I bought *Ray Charles: In Person*, which had a live performance that was done in Atlanta. To my surprise, half of the music on that album was instrumental jazz, and I found that I really responded to the whole album. Everything on it was wonderful.

I knew enough to expect that my public library would have a section of jazz recordings because I knew it was "serious." There'd be classical music and Broadway shows—and there'd be jazz. So I knew that if Ray Charles played jazz, I could go to my public library and find more Ray Charles. And I found a little more, but I discovered a lot of other things as well, and one of the first things I found was *The Playboy Jazz All-Stars*. I'm thirteen years old; it's 1960. [Today] people have a hard time relating to how buttoned down society was, but for a thirteen-year-old kid in 1960, anything with a *Playboy* logo on it was, like, *wow*! [Both laugh.] I think there were three volumes in the series, and I checked out the second volume. Ray Charles wasn't on it—but it was *Playboy*! And that's how I was introduced to Coleman Hawkins, Stan Getz, Chet Baker, Miles Davis, Louis Armstrong (whom I'd seen on TV, of course), Ella Fitzgerald . . . and that really got me going because I liked most of what I heard, and the library was a wonderful place. The librarians were not really jazz fans, but they felt an obligation to have the best of anything they were representing. They would have copies of the *Saturday Review*, and if they saw a jazz album that got a good review, they would buy the album. They had listening booths. A new recording could be taken out for fifteen cents for one week, but after six months, you could take it free of charge for two weeks. And I didn't have to spend the fifteen cents because there was so much there: [Ornette Coleman's] *The Shape of Jazz to Come*, [the Miles Davis / Gil Evans collaboration] *Porgy and Bess, Ellington at Newport*—on and on.

So I had a routine: I'd go to the library on Saturday and get my records, and on the way home I went to record departments in department stores because they had listening booths, too. I remember once when I had a Mingus album under my arm. Next to me was a guy who looked like [Bob Denver's famous Beatnik character] Maynard G. Krebs: a sweatshirt with a hole in it, scraggly beard, a beret—obviously trying to be as hip as he possibly could in 1961. He's thumbing through the Woody Herman section, and he looks at me: "Oh, *Mingus*. Pretty hip kid." I was thinking to myself, "Woody Herman . . . Come on . . ." [Both laugh.] At that point, it was just a white big band, you know? At fourteen I already had a certain attitude about this music, but I was learning as I went along.

I've often said I feel extremely fortunate to be in a situation where everything was odd. I heard the Brubeck album *Time Out* [featuring Paul Desmond] and [Coleman's] *The Shape of Jazz to Come* virtually simultaneously, and, to me, Desmond and Coleman were equally unusual in their way. It wasn't as if Paul Desmond sounded the way it was supposed to be and Ornette Coleman was an aberration. They were both different from what I was used to hearing, and I pursued each of them. That was a great way to get into the music—not to have this hierarchy in your head as you go in. Then I'd read liner notes, which might mention, for example, Roy Eldridge, so I'd find a record with Eldridge on it, read those liners notes, and they might mention Jabbo Smith, and so on. I kept digging around. Sometimes you'd find them, and sometimes you wouldn't.

Two other things in my youth were very helpful: one was a black radio station, which had what they called a daytime license. They'd have to go off the air at sundown. (In the winter, they'd go off at four thirty, but in the summer, they'd go off at eight thirty.) They had one jazz show, and it started at three in the afternoon on Sunday, so it was a ninety-minute show in the winter but about a five-hour show in the summer. I got used to calling up the DJ and asking him to play people I'd read about but couldn't find in the library. One afternoon I called and said, "You know, I've been reading about this guy Clifford Brown. Can you play something of his?" And he went off: "If Clifford Brown were alive today, nobody would be listening to Miles Davis . . ." I'd really hit a spot with the guy, but he didn't have any Clifford Brown [LPs]. He said, "Gee, if you ever find a Clifford Brown album, come down and bring it." So I ended up buying Art Blakey's *A Night in Birdland* [featuring Brown], and the next Sunday I showed up at this guy's studio. Then I got into a little routine with the guy where he would want to play certain albums, and if I had them I'd bring them in.

The second thing happened when I was about fifteen. For about six months in 1963, one of the nightclubs in the St. Louis area tried to become a serious jazz club. During that time, they brought to town—and I got to hear—[John] Coltrane, Sonny Rollins, [Rahsaan] Roland Kirk, Dizzy [Gillespie], The Jazz Messengers, Terry Gibbs (who had Alice McLeod, later Alice Coltrane, on piano). And experiencing music in a club is another order of experience than going to a concert hall, as you know. The first time I went to the club, I was brought by a friend's father (I had one friend who liked jazz) to hear Coltrane, who had opened on a Friday night and was scheduled to play ten nights. We went on Monday. Coltrane's on the stand playing "Impressions," which had been recorded but not yet released. I had the album *Coltrane Live at the Village Vanguard*, which includes "Chasin' the Trane," so I felt comfortable with what Coltrane was doing. He played this enormously long solo, then went to the men's room to practice while [his pianist, McCoy] Tyner played. He came out, finished the song, barely gave people three seconds to applaud, and then went into "It's Easy to Remember," which also hadn't been released at the time. Another long solo, into the bathroom, McCoy's playing—the whole first set goes that way. When it ends, he goes back to the bathroom and practices during the entire intermission. The second set goes the same way; he never stopped playing until the end of that second set. Then he sat down to smoke one of those little cigars and drink a beer. By that point, he'd only played his tenor, so my friend and I go up to him: "Mr. Coltrane, Mr. Coltrane—are you going to play the soprano saxophone this evening?" And he said, "Well, boys, I'd better if I want to get paid, ha ha—" You know. Then he got up and played a forty-five-minute [soprano] solo on "My Favorite Things." And I don't think I've seen this since: he got three standing ovations, two of them in the middle of his solo—in a club on a Monday night filled with people, including all the musicians in town who had gotten off their gigs. Three standing ovations in the course of one solo. It was mind-boggling.

When it was all done, my friend's father went up to the owner of the club and said, "My son and his friend love this stuff, but I don't understand it at all, so I would like to make a proposal to you: if you will let them come in here—and they're not going to try to buy alcohol; just charge them the minimum and they'll drink Cokes—I promise you I'll be here to pick them up at the end of the night." The club owner was great about it and said, "Yeah." So about three weeks later, Sonny Rollins comes to town. We get dropped off early, and there in the club is [trumpeter] Don Cherry playing Monk's solo on "Work" [from *Thelonious Monk and Sonny Rollins*] on piano.

FEINSTEIN: On *piano*?

BLUMENTHAL: Yeah. And we knew who all these guys were at that point—in our own, teenage way—and Don Cherry was just, you know, that sloppy trumpet player who played with Ornette. [Both laugh.] And he's playing Monk's solo note for *note*. He comes off the stage, and we go up to him: "Mr. Cherry, we didn't know you played the piano," and he sat down and said, "Oh, I roomed with [soprano saxophonist] Steve Lacy, and that's how we practiced: we'd transcribe all of Monk's solos." He talked to us for about twenty minutes. But the important thing about that night was this: when we'd seen Coltrane, we left thinking, "This is, without a doubt, the greatest music on Earth. There's nothing that can approach what we've just heard." And then we went back a month later and heard something that *was* as good: Sonny, Don Cherry, Henry Grimes, and Billy Higgins. To know that there was no absolute "best thing" was a very valuable lesson, particularly given where I ended up with my career, and I have tried to carry that notion with me when I write.

FEINSTEIN: Would you say, then, that liner notes acted as your first avenue connecting writing and jazz?

BLUMENTHAL: Definitely. As I said, I allowed them to lead me around. If you see Monk mentioned enough, you say, "Gee, I'd better listen to Monk."

FEINSTEIN: And did these notes ever lead you to books or magazines on jazz?

BLUMENTHAL: The library had some good reference books, though if I think back on it—if you were to ask me about the books that I would recommend to people—I'm not sure I read them at that point. But the library had [Leonard Feather's] *Encyclopedia of Jazz*. They had a book by John S. Wilson called *The Collector's Jazz: Modern [and Progressive]*; I never saw the first volume [*The Collector's Jazz: Traditional and Swing*]. Basically I used them in the same way: to lead me from one place to the next.

I started reading *Down Beat* and, for the last six months of its existence, *Metronome*, and I learned an important lesson: you couldn't always trust these people because they would say things that would be completely contrary to your own response to the music. You'd say, "That *can't* be right, even though an authority said so." LeRoi Jones, who was not yet Amiri Baraka, reviewed the Art Blakey album *A Night in Tunisia*, and he said, basically, "This is only for drum freaks." (At that time, "freak" was a completely pejorative term; there was nothing affectionate about calling someone a freak. So if you were a drum freak, it meant you had gone way beyond the line of appreciating drums.) I thought, "This guy's just wrong." And whoever it was—it may have been Bill Coss—who reviewed *Miles Davis at Carnegie Hall* and called Hank Mobley "a boppy intrusion." To me, Hank Mobley playing on top of Wynton Kelly, Paul Chambers, and Jimmy Cobb—that is what swinging is all about. He plays such great solos on that album, and I thought, "It's wrong. It's just wrong." It was a valuable lesson: just because somebody writes it, don't take it on faith. I tell that to people who read my work, too. At some point, it all comes down to subjectivity.

∼

Feinstein: At what point did you realize that writing about jazz would become a large part of your life?

Blumenthal: That completely came out of left field. Unlike some people—I know Gary [Giddins] said to you [in a previous *Brilliant Corners* interview] he knew he was going to be a writer before he was going to be in jazz—I knew that I loved jazz, and writing was the farthest thing from my mind. I went to Harvard and got involved in the radio station, primarily because I found out that they had a wonderful record library and had extra studios where you could listen to records when the studios weren't being used. This was like another library, and a great way to expand my knowledge. So I applied, and from my second semester through my entire college career, I had a radio show. But I hated writing.

Feinstein: You're serious?

Blumenthal: I never studied writing. I never took a course in writing. In fact, for most courses at Harvard, you had a midterm exam, a final exam, and a term paper, but several courses would give you the option of taking another exam in lieu of a term paper, and I always took the option of the extra exam because I hated to write.

During my junior and senior years, I had a radio show on Monday nights where I'd pick an album, play the whole album, and talk about it. One week it could be Bessie Smith, the next it could be Oliver Nelson—I mean, it jumped all over the place. In January of my senior year, I got a call during one of my shows from the assistant editor of what was then called *Boston After Dark* (now the *Boston Phoenix*), and he said to me, "I listen to your show every week and really enjoy it. The *Boston Globe* is taking out a large ad in *Boston After Dark* for their jazz festival. We have several people who can write about popular music, but we don't have anyone who can write about jazz. If you'll go and review these concerts, we'll give you free tickets to the concerts, and all your friends can read what you write the next week because we distribute the newspaper for free to college campuses."

FEINSTEIN: This is '69?

BLUMENTHAL: Sixty-nine, yeah. And I thought, "I really don't like to write, but it's jazz. I know the subject. Free tickets." So I said, "Let me try it."

At that point I also thought I had a brilliant idea of how to be the perfect jazz critic: to admit right up front what your bias was. In my first article, I said, "Look, folks. Most critics won't tell you this, but there are artists at this concert that I love, and here are the ones I don't like. Take my reaction with that in mind. So if I tell you that Nina Simone did a great set and I'm not a particularly great Nina Simone fan, or that Erroll Garner was only so-so and I love Erroll Garner, weigh my opinions with that in mind." [Smiles widely.] I thought that was brilliant, and that's how I wrote my first review.

By that point, I'd done one other music-related piece of writing. In my senior year I took Erik Erikson's course on the life cycle. The course used to be known as "Religion for Seniors." After four years of negativism, it gave people some ray of hope that life had meaning. And Erikson, who looked the part of the holy man, attracted all these great academics to be his section men and women; Stanley Hoffmann might be your section man, or in my case, Robert Coles. When it came time to do an Eriksonian, life cycle paper—and you had to do a paper; that course wasn't about exams—I chose Charlie Parker as the guy to write on.

To this day, one of my favorite books—and I know this puts me outside accepted opinion—is [Robert] Reisner's book, [the oral history] *Bird: The Legend of Charlie Parker*. The structure of it, with all these people telling stories that often conflicted, really appealed to me. (It's like the movie Bruce Weber made on Chet Baker [*Let's Get Lost*]: in a way, it's not really about jazz; it's about idolatry and mythmaking.) I figured I at least had some first-person testimony about Parker and I tried to put it in an Eriksonian context. Well, it turned out that Bob Coles was a Charlie Parker fan—*Charlie Parker with Strings* got him through his military service as an MD—so he really encouraged me, and I had never really been encouraged about anything that I had written before.

I went to law school at Harvard after I finished college, and I had no idea if I'd lose touch with jazz. (Becoming a lawyer, you get immersed and have no time for anything else.) But when I came back that fall, *Boston After Dark* called to say they'd now pay for reviews, and the combination of having some money in my pocket and knowing that they were a weekly publication (so deadlines should not be a problem) meant that I could continue to write. At that point, I suppose, I formally became a jazz critic—as a way to stay in touch with the music—and I've been doing it ever since.

I had a career as an attorney for about twenty years and would write in my spare time, and it was only in 1994, a point where I'd already been a critic for a quarter of a century, that I became dissatisfied with the job I had as a staff attorney for the State Board of Education. I'd done that for sixteen years, and at one point of maximum frustration, I gave the commissioner of education an ultimatum: "Three things have to change or I'm leaving." He said, "Well, we'll give you two of them," and I said, "Nope, I'm leaving—" without really thinking about what that meant but knowing that if I did a little more writing I could bring in a little more money to keep me going. And it took about seven years to get back to the income that I had as an attorney. By the time I delivered my ultimatum, I was working for the *Boston Globe*, and, without my realizing it, writing had become about half of my income.

Something to bear in mind: when I say, "I was a lawyer and now I'm a music critic," most people think I went from making five hundred thousand a year to five thousand, but I was a lawyer for the State, okay? I was not making even close to big money. (After twenty years as a lawyer, I was probably making less than those who go into entry-level positions at big firms.) I often say, "All it takes is an understanding spouse with a health plan." [Both laugh.]

But the eighties were good preparation for me. I had already been writing for a decade. I was still a lawyer at that point and was writing for the *Phoenix*. The *Boston Globe* was still doing their jazz festival, which had become a much bigger and more elaborate event, and they would always have a guest critic. (They felt that if they produced the festival, their own critics shouldn't review it.) And they hired great people like John Hammond, who'd come to Boston and be their guest critic for a week. So around 1982, they invited me to be their guest critic. "You can trash every concert, but you have to meet the eleven thirty deadline every night so there's a review in the next morning's paper." This was just before computers had been introduced in the newsrooms. So you'd get five hundred words, you'd have a typewriter, you'd write the review, count the words, edit, recount the words, and then either put your copy in a cab and have it driven over to the *Globe* or read it to the editor over the phone and he'd type it in. It's like riding a bicycle in the sense that it's extremely intimidating until you've done it for a while, and then it's nothing. So I did that for a couple of years, and then they introduced computers. They had this big bubble-shaped thing that was programmed to go into the copyeditor's terminal, which was then programmed to go into electronic typesetting. It bought me about forty-five minutes of time: it counted the words for me, and I didn't have to worry about getting it from where I was to the newspaper. So by the time the *Globe* recruited me from the *Phoenix*, I was well schooled in meeting deadlines and the notion that if they need five hundred words you couldn't give them six hundred, nor could you give them 450 and say, "Put a picture in the empty space." You needed to hit your marks.

FEINSTEIN: You've won two Grammy awards for your liner notes, both fairly massive projects: *Coltrane: The Classic Quartet [Complete Impulse! Studio Recordings]* and *Miles Davis & John Coltrane [The Complete Columbia Recordings, 1955–1961]*. Were these your most challenging projects?

BLUMENTHAL: I'll tell you about my most challenging project as a writer—and I did it while I was down here [in Wellfleet, Massachusetts]. About ten years ago, Warner Brothers was reissuing their Antonio Carlos Jobim recordings but they had not made up their mind whether to put them out as three single disks or a three-disk set, so they asked if I would please write three two-thousand-word essays that could either be freestanding *or* fit together, should they decide to do a box set. That, to me, was the most challenging liner note assignment I've ever had and I've often wished that, somewhere along the line, they'd put those three disks into a box so people could see that it all worked out. [Laughs.]

The Coltrane one that won the Grammy—

FEINSTEIN: The one with Miles, or—

BLUMENTHAL: No, the first one for Impulse! [*The Classic Quartet*]—that was extremely challenging because it was one of the first times where I found myself intimidated by what I was writing about. "Could I come up to the level of the music"—which, of course, was asking more than anybody could deliver. Also, I had so much to say, and here's where length gets into it: They said, "We need five thousand words," and I thought, "Boy, I've got so much to say, I'm just going to let go." I told the story about being a kid and hearing him in the club, and I'm writing about each track, and when the deadline comes in, I'm at *Crescent* [disk 3 of eight]! So I called my contact and said, "Look, I've got two problems: number one, I'm only at *Crescent*, and number two, I've already got eight thousand words." I was told, "Well, we can give you a little more time, but do something about the length. We can give you a *little* more space, but this isn't going to work." So the story of me hearing him came out, and the whole thing got retooled accordingly. And I have to admit, when I turned that in, I was thoroughly depressed. I thought I had blown a golden opportunity to do some good writing about something important. I'm a little happier with it now than I was then. (When people ask, "What's the best thing you've ever written?" I always say, "Whatever I wrote two years ago," because it's always much better with a little distance, and then you get far enough away and you've moved to another place.)

The Miles one, for whatever reason, flowed, and I knew that was good. I turned it in and said to myself, "You know, *this* is the one that deserves a Grammy, not the one that won." And I'm not sure why I found one easier than the other. I think there's a certain dynamic between Coltrane and Davis as two distinct personalities, and other people are coming in and out, so there's not only these guys but, say, what's the effect when you take Philly Joe [Jones] away and replace him with Jimmy Cobb, or what's the effect when Cannonball [Adderley] appears? It gave me something to run with. The Coltrane stuff, as it gets more abstract, can get difficult to discuss, but my reaction to it and its place in the roots of my whole aesthetic was similar.

FEINSTEIN: Were you ever surprised by a really fast and fluid response to a liner note assignment, where ideas came very quickly?

BLUMENTHAL: I'm not sure, though I can get into a routine. Down here [on Cape Cod], for example, is where I've written many of the [notes for the] RVG Blue Note reissues. I like to listen to a recording a few times without taking any notes, to let thoughts about the music congeal before I really get going. And I'm a runner, so I value the opportunity to run [with an iPod] where there are not a lot of cross streets and I can just go with the music. I've done this with a lot of the RVGs, and if I'm really inspired I tell myself that I'm just going to come home, sit down, and knock it out. And there have been a few of those, and some of the writing about stuff that I grew up with comes easily. In fact, I often have to put a brake on myself and say, "Look, the point isn't that this music changed your life when you were fourteen years old; the point is, this is a piece of music in the continuum of music, and your challenge is to decide if it's really as good as you think it is." Then I step back a bit, and it's very encouraging to me when I find that, yes, it really *is* as good as I thought it was. I'm not simply making allowances for my childhood infatuation.

FEINSTEIN: That would have to be a significant challenge. I mean, I would imagine that every CD you encounter from the Rudy Van Gelder series was initially an LP that you knew very, very well.

BLUMENTHAL: Most. I mean, I'm not a Lonnie Smith expert, and we're at the point of Lonnie Smith now. But yes, most of the stuff. Recently, I wrote the notes for *Music from "The Connection"* by Freddie Redd, which they had at the public library [when I was a teenager]. It was the first time I'd heard Jackie McLean. I went crazy. McLean's still one of my half-dozen favorite musicians. So now I had to say, "Okay, put that aside and listen to the music." I really struggled to be objective about that record because I *did* know it so well, but it was so satisfying.

There's another challenge involved with those notes [for the RVG reissues] because they print the original notes, so you want to complement them if you can. There are a few Blue Note albums where they have very impressionistic liner notes—[Herbie Hancock's] *Empyrean Isles*, or [Tony Williams's] *Life Time*—that aren't really talking about the music and you're given a clean slate to write the liner notes. But most of the time you're working in response to what's there, and that's a different kind of discipline.

As far as newly recorded music, I often find it most satisfying to write about people where there is no paper trail of previous opinion, so to speak. I mean, Bobby Previte called me to write the liner notes for his first album. I'd never heard of him. I'd never heard of three of the four guys in the band. But I responded very positively, and I still think, "Isn't it great that I was one of the first people to tell the world about Bobby Previte?"

I had the same feeling when I first heard a Dave Douglas CD. I wrote a glowing review, and Dave called me a few years later and said, "I've never asked anyone to do liner notes for me, but I'd like you to write them for my next album." That made me feel good, because I do feel as though I heard Dave at the beginning and can relate to what's been going on with his music and say something about the context that other people might find helpful. So those experiences stay with you, too.

The downside for all of it—one of the challenges, at least—is, there's so much more music available now that immersing yourself to the point where you really have that comfort level becomes more and more difficult. I learned a great lesson from one of my first editors at the time when I was being mailed albums to review and it suddenly seemed as though I was getting every jazz album on Earth! You feel as though you've found the pot of gold at the end of the rainbow, you know? And my editor said to me, "When I was a kid—and I'm sure you were the same way—you saved your money until you had enough to buy an album, you went to the store and bought the album, and you learned every note. Now, you get several a day in the mail, and your goal is to play each through once so you can file them away. You're never going to have a relationship with music today like the one you recall so fondly." And he was right. I mean, I can go into some clubs with juke boxes that contain older recordings, and I can sing along with every note because they still stay with me—and I can't do that with any music that I've heard in the last thirty years. It's a different experience. You really do feel like you've lost your innocence in a certain way, and wouldn't it be wonderful to go back to a certain point and just be a fan?

Since I stopped acting as a critic in the paper—I'm affiliated with a record company [Marsalis Music], so I'm not doing reviews—I've been taken off about three-quarters of the [reviewers] lists that I used to be on. So now, if I want to hear certain musicians I have to go into a store and put the money down. And I find that very liberating. Now I can vote, in a sense. Even some music I might not be that fond of, if I like the idea of what they're trying to do, I'll put my money down—until they lose me. I like that relationship. In a way, I think all critics should be required on a regular basis to put themselves in the position of the paying customer: go out and buy music that they're willing to pay for, and *then* say, "Gee, when I'm a critic, I'm listening to all this stuff that I don't absolutely think I'm going to love. Is that the way I'm going to treat music when I'm just a fan, or am I going to be curious enough to go outside my boundaries?"

~

FEINSTEIN: When CDs became more or less the standard format [in the mid-eighties], a new generation of people became turned on to classic jazz because the music was suddenly available, and I was frequently asked to recommend a guide book. About the only thing available was *The Rolling Stone [Jazz Record] Guide*. And I'd tell people, "There are critics in this book whose reviews you can, and should, dismiss. But look for the initials BB." [Blumenthal laughs.] "You can trust him absolutely."

This was a different type of criticism. For one, you had to give each recording a starred rating [one to five]. Also, your reviews had to be extremely brief. How difficult were those assignments?

BLUMENTHAL: I don't like ratings, and I even say in some of those listings of the truly greatest musicians—Coltrane, Monk, et cetera—that five stars in the context of these artists means *their* best, so when I give a recording of theirs three stars, that's different than a three-star recording by your average musician. As I look back, the mistakes I made reflect my personal taste. I gave *John Coltrane and Johnny Hartman* three stars. People say, "How is the greatest vocal jazz album of all time—? How can you—?" and I say, "Well, in the scheme of Coltrane's work, for me, it doesn't get up there." Over time, I appreciate it more than I did. Similarly, I've always enjoyed Pat Metheny, but I don't like the Pat Metheny Group, so I gave their first album two stars, and people went crazy. I say, "That's just my aesthetic. Live with it! I'm trying to be honest." [Both laugh.]

Originally, they put out *The Rolling Stone Record Guide* that had a section on jazz, which is where my first round of that stuff appeared. Then they decided to expand the section and turn it into a separate book, with John Swenson as the sole editor. Now, the pay was abysmally poor for those things; maybe they paid you two dollars an album.

FEINSTEIN: Oh man . . .

BLUMENTHAL: At this point, I'm working and I have a young kid, and I said, "John, I can't take the time for this money." He said, "Oh, come on. We really want you," so I said, "I'll tell you what: let's set aside an hour every Saturday. You call me up, name the artist, and I'll go to my record collection. We'll improvise; it's jazz. I'll just do them over the phone. You name the artist, we'll go through the albums, and I'll just wing it." That's how the bulk of those reviews got written.

FEINSTEIN [laughing]: You've got to be kidding!

BLUMENTHAL: I'd take them out in a stack and say, "Okay, we'll give this one five and this one four," and so on. If I'd been at the typewriter, I'm sure that I would have been agonizing over those decisions; but at that point my attitude was, "For the sake of the book—because it's a *Rolling Stone* book and people are going to see it—I'd rather write the Mingus entry than have somebody else write it!" But a lot of it got done over the phone.

FEINSTEIN: That's amazing.

BLUMENTHAL: I liked the process. I think it's foolish for people who write about jazz to equate what they do with what musicians do, but there are certain things about jazz's creative process that are good guides. I don't want to hear a musician who approaches every solo the same way, so I don't want to approach every review the same way. And sometimes I'm self-consciously saying, "Well, I tried that last time so I have to take a different approach." It's not so much steering myself into a particular area as steering myself away from a particular area. I found the spontaneity of those *Rolling Stone* reviews helped me do that.

FEINSTEIN: That book, of course, has been more or less eclipsed by the various editions of *The Penguin Guide to Jazz*. What's your response to more recent guides?

BLUMENTHAL: I haven't really looked at *The Penguin Guide* closely. I have the *All Music Guide to Jazz*, which is maybe ten years old, and I pull it out frequently because if you're writing about jazz, it's your obligation to always be listening to something that people aren't telling you to listen to—by which I mean, if you look at the jazz magazines, the covers feature someone who has a new CD coming out, or, if it's an older musician, it's something that just got reissued. And I think we have an obligation to be listening to something else.

I always have what I call my own listening project. I'll give you an example: I still love vinyl and go to used record stores, and I went to one a couple of months ago where they had the French RCA series of the complete Bennie Moten—three two-record sets. For some reason, the only Bennie Moten I had was on Bluebird CDs and a couple of Label X, ten-inch LPs. So I thought, "Boy, there's so much here that I don't know. I'm going to buy that." Whoever had sold this collection had also sold *The Complete McKinney's Cotton Pickers*, also on three two-record sets. (I had two of those but I didn't have the third one.) So I got the three Motens and the third McKinney, and this became my project—to listen to these recordings. Every day I listened to a session. And on the McKinney's final disk was Don Redman, and I just finished my Don Redman project (yesterday, actually).

So after one of these projects, I'll get out the *All Music Guide* and read the reviews, and I have to admit that I find a lot of them pretty superfluous. Of course, there are certain writers you know and certain people whose name or initials I'm happy to see at the end of the review. But you really need to know where the guys are coming from. That's what it always comes down to. If you get the *Rolling Stone Guide* and you get to my Coltrane section and you see me downgrading the Johnny Hartman session, you might think, "Oh, he just wants to hear somebody blow their brains out for twenty minutes. He doesn't like the romantic stuff."

In terms of reading things to get people into music, the two books that really inspired me—and that still inspire me—are *Jazz: Its Evolution and Essence* by [André] Hodeir, and *The Jazz Tradition* by Martin Williams. For me, they're the two best books for somebody who wants to get into the music. I find them eminently trustworthy. Not that I didn't have other favorite writers. I mean, when it comes to liner notes, the people

I think about who really brought me along were Leonard Feather, Nat Hentoff, Ira Gitler, and Ralph Gleason. They were doing the bulk of the writing in the fifties, and there was a world of information there, and I loved what I could get from them.

I don't know if you've read John Gennari's recent book, *Blowin' Hot and Cool*.

FEINSTEIN: Yes. In fact, part of that book first appeared in *Brilliant Corners*.

BLUMENTHAL: Yeah? Fantastic book. I love that book.

FEINSTEIN: Let me pull back just for a minute: Consider your list of inspiring liner-note writers and the authors you've highlighted. Why do you think jazz criticism, of all kinds, has been so dominated by white writers?

BLUMENTHAL: I think black writers had a hard time cracking white publishing back in the 1950s.

FEINSTEIN: But it's true even today.

BLUMENTHAL: Well—and I often make this point about young musicians, but it applies to writers as well—I think that there was a sudden transformation, from the point where African Americans couldn't break in to most areas of American society to the point where not only could they break in as jazz critics but they could break in many other areas. Under those circumstances, why would someone focus on becoming a jazz critic, or a jazz musician? I mean, I often say that if Fletcher Henderson were alive today, he'd be a vice president of Monsanto because he got a degree in chemistry when he went to college, but what was a black man in the 1920s going to do with a degree in chemistry? So Fletcher Henderson became a musician. Today he would be recruited by a major corporation and be very successful, I'm sure. You have many more options for people to pursue now.

You also have a situation where, I dare say, jazz music as a part of the culture of an African American family doesn't mean what it did in the 1940s and 1950s. So someone in my circumstances as a kid who's growing up and getting exposed to music (1) wouldn't necessarily gravitate toward jazz, and (2) would have all these other options if they wanted to write. And look at it from the point of view of economics. I mean, what are your prospects? So you might be less inclined to pursue it and more inclined to pursue something else. That would be my answer for what's going on.

FEINSTEIN: How would you talk about Stanley Crouch? He can be an explosive topic.

BLUMENTHAL: Stanley writes about other things as well. Yes, he's an explosive topic, and for good cause in many instances. Some of his stuff I love, and some of his stuff I completely disagree with. I think the fact that he was a drummer, regardless of how good or bad you thought he was as a drummer, gives him, to my mind, great insight about drummers. I know Stanley *slightly*, but if Stanley ever said to me, "What do you think I should be spending my time doing?" I would say, "You ought to do a history of jazz drumming. You're the perfect guy. Forget about that Charlie Parker book, forget about your novels, forget about whatever—you are the guy to write about the history of jazz drumming."

FEINSTEIN: And are you the "perfect guy" to write a book on a particular topic?

BLUMENTHAL: I'll tell you what I'd like to write on. I think what the world needs is a book that makes people comfortable listening to jazz, a book that's similar but different than *Where's the Melody?* by Martin Williams. To me, the greatest problem jazz has now is that the very word intimidates people. They think that it's over their heads. I would like to write a series of chapters that took specific pieces of music and talked about listening for certain things in them in such a way that it makes you understand how to listen generally.

 Let me give you an example. I met a chemistry tutor in college who was a jazz fan and who showed me how he introduced jazz to folks. He would play Charlie Parker's "Now's the Time," and then play the Lambert, Hendricks, and Ross version where they've added vocals. Then he would tell people that improvising is creating melodies, and to illustrate he would pass out copies of Jon Hendricks's lyrics to the Parker and Miles Davis solos and play the Parker recording again while they followed the words. Then he would play "Straight, No Chaser" from [Miles Davis's] *Milestones*, where, at the end of the piano solo, Red Garland plays Miles Davis's trumpet solo from "Now's the Time" in block chords. Again, people could follow the Jon Hendricks lyrics and see that Garland is playing the Miles Davis trumpet solo from "Now's the Time" at the end of his piano solo. I've tried this myself, and people are always amazed: "My God! This piano player played note for note a trumpet solo from thirteen years earlier."

You know, one of the pieces of writing that I recall from my youth was the liner notes to the LP where "Now's the Time" first appeared [*The Charlie Parker Story*]. The notes were by John Mehegan, the great piano instructor, who just *trashed* Miles Davis—mercilessly—and the solo that was transcribed by Lambert, Hendricks, and Ross was described by Mehegan as "lugubrious, unswinging, no ideas." [Both laugh.] As I said earlier, I learned not to trust everything in print.

When I did the box set [*Miles Davis & John Coltrane*], they had an earlier take of "Straight, No Chaser," and on the piano solo, when Garland got to the block chords, he hinted around at the trumpet solo from "Now's the Time" but didn't really have it down. As I say [more briefly] in the notes, I wonder if he went back and listened to the record between takes; or if someone took him aside and said, "Well, here's how the solo went"; or if he simply decided that he might as well quote the whole thing. But to me that's a primary example of a point I like to make to people, which is that there are layers of meaning in a performance. It's like someone who picks up a copy of *Crime and Punishment* and thinks, "Boy, that was a great story." Then they take a college course and learn about allegory, symbolism, and layers of meaning, and now it's an even better story. It doesn't mean it wasn't a good story the first time; it means that if you know more, you can appreciate more. And that's what jazz is like: if you know more, you'll appreciate more.

My first chapter would be about Charlie Parker playing "Cherokee." There's a recording somebody made in a nightclub in Harlem where he sits in with a big band in 1942. They're playing a stock arrangement of "Cherokee," and their rhythm is like oom-*pah* oom-*pah*. And he comes in, and he's Charlie Parker. Rhythmically, the band is on another planet. Then there's a recording he made with a guitar and drums in one of those home-recording booths in Kansas City, and the rhythm's a little better but they're still kind of up and down, and he's flying all over the place. And then we get to 1945, the session where he made "Ko Ko" [a tune based on the chord changes of "Cherokee"], and I wouldn't even talk about "Ko Ko" because I like the track "Warming Up a Riff," where they play "Cherokee" but the tempo's more "humane," if you will. But the rhythm section is on his wavelength now. He's playing the same song, and he hasn't changed—but the surrounding cast of characters has. And now it's a coherent ensemble experience. I think there's a great lesson there for people, and you can hear that without having to take a course in music theory. You can *hear* that everybody's feeling it the same way, and how they weren't in the earlier recordings.

FEINSTEIN: That kind of book would require a CD, no? It seems unrealistic to expect a novice to seek out and buy relatively rare recordings [such as the first two Parker sessions] because—

BLUMENTHAL:—because these things come and go. And that's a problem with all books about jazz: they're out of date before they're published in the sense that any references to recordings are always subject to change. [At the time of this interview, both of my CDs that include the first two examples of "Cherokee" were out of circulation. The 1945 session, of course, is easily obtained—SF.] But that's the book I want to write, a book where people who read it could say, "I don't know everything [about jazz], but I'm much more comfortable. I have some things to look for now."

∽

FEINSTEIN: I'm frequently asked, "Has jazz run its course?" but I'm disinterested in the question because I find the existing styles—not just the recordings—to be so unfailing. Do you have similar feelings, or do you keep listening for dynamic changes in the music?

BLUMENTHAL: Well, I have no choice, given my relationship with the record label, part of which involves A&R and listening to stuff coming in. But I know exactly what you mean. I've been working on this brief history of jazz [for the Smithsonian called *Discover Jazz*], and I was trying to think of a different way to come at this. Jazz evolved so quickly, in one sense, but we have a very distorted understanding of that evolution, so I decided to treat jazz in twenty-year segments because I wanted to drive home a couple of points: first, anyone's notion of jazz changes over time, and second, there are periods of intense activity and periods when not as much is going on. In 1920, what was jazz? In 1940, what was jazz? I've just finished the chapter on 1960, and I explain how the evolution had been so constant and so rapid. Take a guy like Miles Davis and look at his career in 1960: he was on Charlie Parker's first recording session as a leader, so he was there in the formative period of bebop; then he introduced cool jazz; then he introduced hard bop; then he introduced modal jazz. It's like there's this perpetual engine of change that's going to keep driving jazz forward—and that's the way it would have looked in 1960. When you get to 1980, there are still changes to take place stylistically (fusion was a new thing, and free jazz was something that arose and flourished after 1960), but by 1980, it's like Albert Ayler's quote on the album *The New Wave in Jazz*: "It's no longer about notes anymore, it's about feelings." By 1980, it was clear it wasn't about new waves anymore, either.

I've come to accept that, which is not a notion I would have accepted in my early years of listening because everything kept changing. And it was great to be aware enough in the sixties to hear Coltrane go through his evolution, to hear Cecil Taylor emerge, and Albert Ayler and the Art Ensemble of Chicago and Anthony Braxton and Weather Report. Tony Williams's *Life Time*. But I think it set up false expectations for people like me. So we have to rethink the issue: Perhaps jazz was the musical art form of the twentieth century. Now we're in a new century, there are new influences, new technological influences, and it becomes extremely difficult to predict what's going to happen. No one in the year 2000 would have predicted the iPod, I suspect, and yet the iPod is probably going to herald the demise of the record album, at least in many circles.

You can understand why, when Martin [Williams] put *The Smithsonian Collection* [*of Classic Jazz*] together, he did not deal with the most recent fifteen or twenty years of jazz history. It's very difficult to place something current in the context of history. I suspect that, while jazz has always been open enough to incorporate a lot of other things, there will be a point when you have to treat a certain piece of music as "jazz influenced" or "jazz inspired," but not as jazz per se. The debate goes back to Hodeir: What is the essence? And will the essence change?

In the year 2000, [producer] George Wein had a symposium at [the] Newport [Jazz Festival] to recreate panels that were held during the first years of the festival, and I talked about how the first Newport festival took place in the same year [Hodeir's] *Jazz: Its Essence and Evolution* was published in France [1954]. I wanted to see whether Hodeir's conclusions about the essence of jazz had changed. And I didn't think the essence of jazz had changed that much, whereas what's *considered* jazz has changed greatly. But I do think we're going to get into serious debates about "essence" again because as you find fewer people who had jazz in their formative experience, what comes out on the other end might not be recognizable as such.

The talk actually ended up being essence with a small "e" and Essence with a capital "E." The second part of the paper I gave was about the notion of "jazz is my religion," which is true, in my case. I found I got spiritual solace from music that I didn't get from the organized alternatives, and why I thought that, for the continued survival of the music, this idea of what I call capital E Essence might be the most important thing. As for the notion of the jazz festival—you think about bowling alone and that whole notion of the growing autonomy that we all experience. What are the collective experiences that we share now? They tend to be sporting events and concerts. Sporting events are more gladiatorial—we either win or we lose—whereas at a jazz performance, you're brought into a communal experience where everybody comes out ahead. For me, this has supplanted religion. My hope is that people will have a similar response: that jazz brings people together—it gives them a glimpse of something better, something sacred, if you will—and that, over time, we're going to see that this is the greatest value that jazz presents to us. So there's essence and there's Essence.

∼

FEINSTEIN: What advice would you give to writers of liner notes? What's essential to know?

BLUMENTHAL: The critical issue for me is always length because I find that art directors determine a lot about what goes into packaging or recordings. I find it much more difficult to write 1,500 words, turn it in, and have somebody say, "Oh, we only have room for eight hundred," and to scale it back than to know going in that they only want eight hundred words and to plan accordingly. So I always tell people to find out how long a piece is going to be and then to set their mental calipers accordingly. In terms of my personal advantages as a writer, I think I've been very good at saying, "Okay, they want eight hundred words? Fine, it's going to look like this. They want three thousand words? It's going to look like that." Like many writers, I have a very thin skin if somebody doesn't like what I've written—it gets to me—and one of the complaints that drives me the craziest is when somebody says, "These notes are inadequate." And I'll say to myself, "Well, gee—I only had 750 words and I thought that was as adequate as I could be in that space. And if the complaint is, 'He should have had more space,' it's not *my* fault. It's what I've been given to work with." This came up recently when somebody said it looked like I was writing on deadline, and that was the farthest thing from the truth. I'd been given a precise amount of space to fill, turned it in, and they decided, "Oh, you know, we really shouldn't have given you that much space, even though you hit the mark. Now you've got to go back and weed it." Given the parameters, I thought I had done an all right job, and now I'm being taken to task for it. So that's part of it.

FEINSTEIN: How about your experiences with Mosaic [Records] where you must have a much freer hand regarding length?

BLUMENTHAL: Mosaic's great because they're the one place that says, "You write as long as you want."

FEINSTEIN: Did [cofounder and producer of Mosaic] Michael [Cuscuna] come to you for these projects?

BLUMENTHAL: Michael and the other guys at Mosaic and Blue Note are very important to me. When I was writing for the *Phoenix*, Blue Note started reissuing recordings, and their first reissues were bad examples of using abstract paintings on covers. They had produced anthologies that were drawn from all over the catalog, and they were terrible. So I wrote a review of the first series: "This is horrible. People have been waiting for Blue Note to reissue stuff, and boy did they take the wrong approach to this." So the piece appears in the *Phoenix*, and then I get a call from the late Charlie Lourie, who was one of the two founders of Mosaic: "Hi, this is Charlie Lourie from Blue Note." ("Oh, God . . .") "We read your review." ("Oh my goodness, what's he going to say?") "And you were right on target. We're going to change our approach. In fact, would you like to write the liner notes for a two-LP set of outtakes from [Sonny Rollins's] *A Night at the Village Vanguard*?" Those became the second set of liner notes that I ever wrote. And it was so wonderful to get that kind of feedback. You so rarely get feedback as a writer.

FEINSTEIN: I mentioned Mosaic because I'm such a fan of their sets, and of Michael, but also because I think their open approach to notes must be liberating.

BLUMENTHAL: I don't remember whether it was Charlie or Michael, but somebody said to me, "Look, we're trying to do deluxe packages, and it's a lot cheaper to add four more pages to the booklet than it is to add another disk in the box. So you are completely unrestrained; we always have wonderful photographs we can run. Write what you need to write." That's helpful, as well as knowing that they will catch me on any musical errors that I may make (though I also catch them, sometimes). It's been a healthy relationship.

The first few I wrote for them were all my voice; I didn't feel compelled to go out to talk to people. Often they were artists who weren't around, anyway. But at a certain point, I decided that if the musicians were around and were willing to cooperate, it would be great to get their voices in. For instance, they asked me to do the Jazztet box [*The Complete Argo / Mercury Art Farmer / Benny Golson / Jazztet Sessions*], and I thought, "Boy, it would be great if Benny Golson would talk to me," and Benny invited me to his apartment in Manhattan and we spent two hours together one morning. Michael had said, "Oh, Benny's going to write his autobiography. He doesn't like to talk about this stuff." But for whatever reason—I think, for one, it became clear to him that I actually knew the recordings—he gave me great feedback.

I did the Lou Donaldson box [*The Complete Blue Note Lou Donaldson Sessions 1957–60*], but Lou is a different kind of guy; you're not going to get him to sit down forever. It was like, "Come to the Vanguard before the set starts, and I'll give you twenty minutes." But Lou is a character, and it was great to get his voice in there.

Whatever materials you have, though, I think it's helpful to keep in mind the context of how people are going to experience a recording. You always want to give them enough general information about the artist, but that means different things for different artists. If you're writing about Coltrane or Miles Davis, you assume a certain amount of knowledge and you focus in on the particular period. If you're writing about [the relatively obscure pianist] Herbie Nichols, I think you have an obligation to bring more of the life story of the individual. I also think that if you're writing about a new artist, there is certain baseline information that people want, and it's not about the particular pieces of music. I respect musicians who say, "Don't write about the music. Don't let the title lead you into assuming what the piece is about." But I do think they owe it to the listener to say, "Here is my background; here is what inspired me to be a musician; here are the experiences that I've had that have shaped me and directed me." So I encourage people to make sure that's included, particularly when we're talking about musicians who don't have as much of a reputation.

Also, don't assume that an editor is going to be at the other end of the line, improving the quality of your prose. There's a certain comfort if that is the case; when I wrote for Fantasy [Records], I knew Terri Hinte, who is no longer there, would be reading my stuff and improving it a little bit. But you can't assume that, and sometimes, when the person you're delivering to writes and you're not that fond of their writing [Feinstein laughs], you take *extra* care to make sure that everything is in place. You can't assume people will catch your mistakes the way they might at a newspaper or magazine.

Other than that, I think it's that notion of improvising. You don't come to a project with a template of what a liner note is supposed to be—this much is biography, this much is analysis, this much is cleverness, or what have you. You need to let the music lead you in a direction and see how that translates into an essay.

3

If You Can't Do Better, Might as Well Just Stay Away

Stanley Crouch

Stanley Crouch (1945–2020) was the author of several books of criticism, including *Considering Genius: Writings on Jazz*, *The Artificial White Man: Essays on Authenticity*, and *In Defense of Taboos*; his groundbreaking *Kansas City Lightning: The Rise and Times of Young Charlie Parker* was published after this interview. He was also the author of a novel, *Don't the Moon Look Lonesome: A Novel in Blues and Swing*, and a volume of poetry, *Ain't No Ambulances for No Nigguhs Tonight*. His jazz criticism appeared in such publications as the *Village Voice*, *JazzTimes*, the *New York Times*, and the *New Yorker*. At the time of the interview, he was the president of the Louis Armstrong Educational Foundation.

Unfortunately, excerpts of Stanley Crouch's writing could not be obtained for reprint in this publication. The interview took place at the Miracle Bar & Grill on Bleecker Street in Manhattan on September 29, 2007.

Interview

SASCHA FEINSTEIN: When did you realize that jazz would be at the center of your career as a writer?

STANLEY CROUCH: Well, I don't really know when I figured that out, but I knew that a number of things I'm interested in—in terms of integration; the rendition of American life; the East, West, South, and North—seemed encapsulated in jazz. And then, after a certain amount of time it just started to add up, and I was able to see many things through it. In my dad's jazz collection, I could see the Constitution; I could understand the [Harlem] Renaissance through it, in a certain kind of way. And there were many parallels in the arts to jazz that were interesting to me because they seemed to be either missed or considered too far removed from a rather single-minded body of thought about the music. So many things added up to cause me to keep returning to it.

When I wrote *Don't the Moon Look Lonesome*, I had many different jazz devices that I used in the novel, many things that I had learned both from people in literature and from people in music about theme and variation. Martin Williams, the great jazz critic, was talking about how the grammarians' term *paraphrase* could apply to the way different musicians rendered popular song. For instance, there's a section in *Don't the Moon Look Lonesome* where the character Carla is thinking; she's performing, but I have a kind of stream of consciousness in which themes that have come up in her earlier life are paraphrased through lyrics of these popular songs. Now, for somebody who doesn't know the songs, it wouldn't make any difference; I think whether one knows the songs or not, one can understand the section. But if one *does* know the songs, it adds another layer to the meaning of what's going on.

FEINSTEIN: A lot of people, even those familiar with your work, don't know about your poems.

CROUCH: Oh . . . *I* almost don't know about them.

FEINSTEIN: [Laughs.] You haven't returned to poetry in a very long time. Why is that?

CROUCH: A lot of the kinds of things that I was trying to do when I was writing poetry I've been able to insert into my prose pieces: the same concerns with meter and rhythm and different kinds of craftsmanship.

FEINSTEIN: How would you say jazz has influenced your fiction? Is it different than the way it influenced your poetry?

CROUCH: [Long pause.] Writing a poem is more like trying to write a twelve-, sixteen-, or thirty-two-bar blues, but writing a novel is more like writing a symphony. You have more space to do things in. You can address the issues from more different sides—although when I was writing *Don't the Moon Look Lonesome*, I had *The Iliad* and *The Odyssey* in mind, and I also had Auden's poem "The Shield of Achilles." I was using them to sustain certain kinds of thematic developments, and also to allude to different things that had happened in either *The Iliad* or *The Odyssey* in terms of images and events.

I was just in Sewanee [Tennessee] a couple of days ago and talking to this guy named Chris McDonough, who's a classics professor, and I was showing him how I had taken certain kinds of things that were in *The Iliad* and had dramatically changed them so that they would almost be difficult to recognize.

FEINSTEIN: Why do you think there have been so many more poets influenced by jazz than fiction writers? I'm particularly interested in your opinion on this, since you've written both.

CROUCH: I think because jazz is not a commonly recognized aesthetic source. I mean, you know: poets primarily because they have read Robert Hayden and they've read Langston Hughes and they've read other people who have been influenced [by jazz]. Even T. S. Eliot—you know, with "Shakespeherian rag" [from *The Waste Land*] and so on. You have these different elements that I think are more commonly recognized by poets. In other words, if either Hemingway or Faulkner made more use of jazz, there would be more [jazz-related fiction]—although *The Great Gatsby* is actually based on one of the stanzas of the blues. I make that point in the last essay of *The Artificial White Man*. People like Albert Murray, who are very important on issues like this—I don't even think *he* knew what Fitzgerald was doing.

In the paperback version of *Don't the Moon Look Lonesome*, I put in an afterword to actually deal with the aesthetic, technical things that I was doing. I wanted to tell people what they were and where to find them. See, there's no book, by anyone that I know of, that uses jazz on as many different levels as that book does. That's why I put that [afterword] there: If someone wants to argue, "Well, he just *said* it was a jazz novel . . . ," they can see it. It's right there: this is done on this page. It's not intended to be like *CliffsNotes* written for your own book; it just lays out and gives you a blueprint of what's going on. You might not think it worked ("A novel in blues and swing—what does that mean?") but at least you have available to you something that tells you what's happening.

Like I say in the book, some people thought I shouldn't do it; some people said I should. But, see, *I'm* the one—no one else—who figured out the relationship of F. Scott Fitzgerald and jazz. (It's in *The Artificial White Man*; it's not hidden somewhere.) In all these years, with all this stuff that's been written about Fitzgerald, nobody ever saw that. So I'm supposed to assume that I'm going to have as good a chance of being understood as he is? [Smiles.] So I put that there as a jumping-off point for someone who's interested in what I was trying to do.

I was talking with Wynton Marsalis and explaining to him that one of the reasons the guys who preceded Dizzy Gillespie and Charlie Parker didn't like them was because they tended to think like magicians, and they thought it was very, very dangerous that a guy like Dizzy Gillespie would show people the chords he was playing and all of that. They didn't believe in that. Marsalis said, "That's very unfortunate because the notes are just the notes, so somebody who's got perfect pitch can hear them, anyway. It's not like you're going to hide the music from a certain level of musician. But just think what we would have at this point if people were actually able to get Armstrong or Art Tatum or Duke Ellington or whomever into a musical discussion on how they heard a certain chord, or how they heard the use of a chord, why they would voice it this way, what they thought about rhythm, how they thought about the bass notes"—all of that. Now you have so many of the major figures gone, and their particular musical perspective on what they're doing went with them.

It's unusual in a century where, from Picasso through Ezra Pound through T. S. Eliot and on, you have such intellectual clarity about what they're doing. Cubism is essentially an intellectual assertion of a certain way of handling objects and images that Braque and Picasso were not confused about at all. If you read, as I'm sure you have, Van Gogh's . . .

FEINSTEIN: *Letters to Theo*.

CROUCH: Yeah. He wasn't confused about what he was doing. So it's interesting to have a long modernist tradition that begins, probably, with Baudelaire's *The Painter of Modern Life* [*Selected Writings on Art and Literature*], and then get to this major form [jazz] in which there's basically a bunch of babble. It's very unusual, compared to what's going on in the scene overall.

But then again, as I was saying at Andrew Hill's memorial recently, Andrew Hill was a very well read, bright guy. He wasn't like a lot of musicians because in music you can be a very good musician but you don't have to be smart. All you have to do in music is, through the language of music, render the human particulars with a certain authority and command of the form, and that's fine. You don't have to be smart. In acting, you don't have to be smart; all you have to be able to do is to make the audience believe that [character] when they see you on stage or on screen. In dance, you don't have to be smart; all you have to do is execute a requisite level of humanity through the language of dance. You can be a good or great dancer, but that's all you have to do. And that applies very much to jazz discussion. Somebody might say, "I went to talk to so and so to ask them about whatever, and he said he didn't know anything about it at all—but so what, it sounds like this—" One of the proofs of that is the rehearsal tape of Billie Holiday and Jimmy Rowles, where she says, "They asked me what key I was in. I didn't know—but I could hear it." No one will argue her superiority to ninety-nine percent of all the people who have ever sung jazz all over the world, but what becomes clear from this tape with Jimmy Rowles is that she wasn't a person who knew much about music. She could *make* music, and she could make you believe the music, and she had great time. So you can say, "Well, I just read this article about Billie Holiday. Now I'm going to have to devalue X performances of hers because I realize she made these brilliant decisions but didn't know what they were." So? She knew that they worked, or she sensed that they would fit.

When you have a performance art that engages improvisation, then you have a problem within the critical dimensions because greatness or aesthetic substance is almost inevitably based on the ability to revisit an accomplishment on the same level. "Do it again," as they say. Night after night. When Olivier was doing Oedipus, he had this blood-curdling scream that he would deliver when Oedipus plucked his eyes out, and Olivier said he had in his mind this image of seals that they'd trap in the Arctic by spreading something on the ice; the seals' tongues would get stuck to the ice, and while they were trying to pull loose, people would come and beat them to death. He would have that in mind to deliver this scream, nightly. Now, a jazz musician ain't really like that because a jazz musician is really more like a wide receiver on a football team who is running a pattern: if the ball goes in a direction that the receiver wasn't expecting, he has to twist himself in the air to catch the ball, and then fall into the end zone. No one says, "In order for those six points to stand, you have to be able to do that again." [Both laugh.] No you don't! All you have to be able to do is do it once.

I was reading an interview once with Tony Williams, and he said, "I can't play some of the stuff that I played on record when I was a kid. Can't do it." Does that mean it's invalid? No. It means when he could do it, he did it. Sometimes people wait for that moment when something comes clear to them, and then they play something they've been wanting to play. All of these kinds of things are problematic about jazz criticism because it doesn't seek to illuminate those kinds of things. If, say, for the last fifty years, people had spent a lot of time trying to clarify the improvised ensemble's theme and variations, I think jazz would be in much better shape, because theme and variation transcend style. If you actually learn that somebody is playing the variation of a theme, you can say, "Oh, that's how Armstrong does it, or how Coleman Hawkins does it, Lester Young, Charlie Parker." Then you're not stuck. When Martin Williams wrote this book called *Where's the Melody?* he was looking at that question.

FEINSTEIN: Would you consider him one of the best critics to write about jazz?

CROUCH: Absolutely. He recognized some of the central elements in music, and he also was involved in trying to clarify the question of theme and variation for the reader. And I think the enormous failure of jazz criticism is that there's been little work that actually communicates the particulars of the music short of being academic. In other words, you can get any music teacher to transcribe somebody's solo and say, "Well, that's what it was." But to actually be able to identify in prose what kinds of things someone should listen for so they actually understand the variations that take place, I think that's a bit harder, and I thought Martin Williams did an excellent job of that.

FEINSTEIN: Who else, in your opinion, has written successful jazz criticism?

CROUCH: Albert Murray's *Stompin' the Blues*—which I think Gary Giddins correctly called "the first poetics of jazz"—is very good. Whitney Balliett, extremely good. Gary Giddins, extremely good. Dan Morgenstern, extremely good. But after them, not a lot.

FEINSTEIN: Why do you think jazz criticism has become so dominantly a white field?

CROUCH: The first thing is you don't have much of an aesthetic set of concerns in black American culture. When it does take place, it's usually overly influenced by sociology and politics and stuff like that. Like I said in the introduction to *Considering Genius*, I think the enormous failure of black studies was that it basically didn't take advantage of the university system to really do great performance, oral history, and all the stuff that was available to do. And that was because the people weren't interested. So it's not, "Well, these white boys, they did this and that"—it comes down to interest. If you're interested in jazz, you start to listen to it over and over until you come up with your thoughts about what it is.

When I was teaching school from '68 to '75 in California, there was no real interest in that, because the faculties that I ran into in different situations, they didn't know anything about it. They didn't care about jazz; they liked stuff like Sly and the Family Stone, Motown, stuff like that—and whatever its bag, it's pop music. There was very little aesthetic concern, and there still *is* very little. So most of the best material is written by white guys because of their interests.

FEINSTEIN: Do you find that sad?

CROUCH: No—because if it had been left to black people, the music wouldn't even exist. It's that simple. The audience that has supported jazz as an art for the majority of time has been a white audience. First of all, you have ten times the population of white people than you have black people [chuckles], so let's say that ten percent of the white community and ten percent of the black community like jazz. That means that there are going to be ten times as many white people as there are black people.

When you get into societies where you're talking about 200, 250, 300 million people, then you begin to realize, when you look at things right, that even things that we call "popular" are not popular. Say you and I write a book that's a bestseller. That means we've sold about fifty thousand or one hundred thousand copies. Now, one hundred thousand out of 250 million? That's not a lot. If we make a pop record—say we're rappers, and we make a rap record and we sell *five million* copies, right? Okay, five million out of 250 million people? That's not popular—if you say "popular" means "more than half." Over fifty-one percent. Who's ever sold like that? Even when you talk about movies, and you begin to say, "Well, what drives the profits of movies?" Basically, the number of times teenage boys go see it. So X movie made one hundred million dollars. Did one hundred million go see it? No, more like ten million saw it—maybe. That's why so many movies are focused on adolescent concerns.

Once you look at how many people there are in the country, "popular" really doesn't mean what we think it means. It's not that many people don't know who Michael Jackson is, or have never heard of 50 Cent, or are unaware of Britney Spears—or whoever it is. But when you get right down to the numbers, you start to realize nowhere near as many people as one would think actually go and buy a CD of Britney Spears. So when you put something of real artistic complexity and value in the same arena, the numbers drop enormously.

And if you go to something like painting . . . There *may* be five thousand serious collectors—that is, people who could pay you tens of thousands for a piece of work. That means all you have to do is have your work recognized by that group of people, and they can make you a millionaire. But it's not like, if you're a big popular painter you're speaking to masses of people who are waiting for a show of yours at the Museum of Modern Art.

FEINSTEIN: This issue of popularity reminds me that I'm supposed to give a talk next week on jazz and American identity. I suspect they're expecting a Ken Burns–like approach—that, along with apple pie and baseball, this music is who we are. But in fact, very few people in America identify with jazz, and that's been true since the inception of jazz.

CROUCH: I think there's a reason for that, and it has to do with the fact that jazz musicians never made it into the same iconographic situation as the cowboy, the detective, the pioneer, the urban politician, the gangster—many of these iconographic figures that appear over and over in American film. Orson Welles was talking about doing a movie with Duke Ellington—a movie called *It's All True*—and let us say it was done and was a big success. Then you would have had extremely talented filmmakers who would have taken jazz and the jazz musicians, and the serious problem of being a musician, and would have used that figure the same way they've used the tale of the country boy who comes to the big city. Or the girl who comes and gets corrupted by the city—all of those figures that we've seen many times, right? And the jazz musician never got into that category; not enough material was made about those iconographic characters to result in the significance of the character and perhaps the idiom that's connected to the character. I don't mean you haven't had *Young Man with a Horn* and blah blah blah, but you didn't have a lot of people who were really trying to tell you what's going on—because *they* didn't know. And because so much of the discussion about jazz was inept, inane stuff.

For instance, you take an inarguable cinematic genius like Billy Wilder. Well, had somebody introduced him to jazz when he came to America, or had he become a jazz fan when he was in Europe—if he liked Duke Ellington and Count Basie and became aware of what was happening when Charlie Parker emerged, if he came to understand why Armstrong was a great artist—then you might have had something.

But the other thing is, you're talking about artists who are often closer to artisans than artists in what they have to say. What I mean is, when you read a book about Picasso, for example, compare what he's saying about what he's doing or about painting or art in general to what jazz musicians have said about their music. Or you read an interview with Stravinsky—just the difference in what kind of a guy he was and what he knew and what he understood about the arts at large—well, you have very few parallels to that in jazz. When you *do* get it in jazz, it's often pretentious. Not that there aren't these parallels, but they usually aren't understood with the kind of depth that would interest a guy of, let's say, Billy Wilder's intelligence. He would have to figure most of the stuff out himself. He wouldn't get much assistance from the musicians. Part of the reason is that jazz musicians have *tended* to be like professional magicians in that they basically don't tell you much; if you see the trick and can figure it out, good for you—but *they're* not going to tell you how they do it because there's a certain kind of competition. ("If he hears this then he might start playing it, and he might become more successful than I am," and so on.)

All of these things, when you add them up, create over a long period of time a very superficial perspective of the music. That doesn't mean that people still don't like it and listen to it, but it makes the discussion of the art something separate from the art itself. If you have a supremely talented composer and performer like Thelonious Monk—I mean, every great once in a while he would say something about the making of the music. If you happened to be in his band, he would show you a lot of stuff, but not necessarily. Take a guy like Miles Davis, who was much smarter than ninety-nine percent of the musicians. Coltrane said Miles Davis almost never talked about music. If you have a guy like Miles Davis, who is *far* more sophisticated than the average jazz musician (black or white), and you can't get much out of him, then you can imagine going down to the next level, much less going down from there to another level.

~

FEINSTEIN: The world has been waiting rather impatiently for your Charlie Parker biography. When are we going to get it?

CROUCH: You'll get volume 1 next year [*Kansas City Lightning: The Rise and Times of Young Charlie Parker*].

FEINSTEIN: No kidding? That's wonderful news! How far into Bird's life do you cover?

CROUCH: To twenty-two. It starts when they arrive from Kansas City at the Savoy, then it goes back to when he was born, and ends at the Savoy, with their coming into New York. It's one big circle.

FEINSTEIN: At what point did you realize you needed two volumes?

CROUCH: Well, I felt like, if I got one out that would encourage me to get two out.

FEINSTEIN: [Laughs.] Why do you think there have been so few reasonable (much less great) biographies on jazz musicians?

CROUCH: It's very difficult to find out how these musicians think, and the very fine writer Paul Berman said to me that since there are so few people in jazz like Armstrong, who wrote a lot of letters, that it's hard to get more than "Born at . . . Went to this band . . . Went to the hospital . . . Died."

FEINSTEIN: So how'd you overcome those issues in your biography on Bird?

CROUCH: Through extended interviews with people who were close to him, I began to get an idea of how this guy actually thought. Of course, the stories were often contradictory . . . See, he was so much smarter than the average person and the guys he was around, so he didn't really have many peers with whom he could discuss things. But there were some people: Max [Roach], and his [Parker's] wives. I talked to all of them at length. Rebecca [Ruffing], his first wife. (The second wife [Geraldine Scott] died a long time ago—I think she was interviewed only one time, by Robert Reisner, and it was a very superficial interview.) Doris [Snyder], his third wife. And I got a very long interview with Chan [Richardson, whom Parker claimed to be his fourth wife, although they were not officially married]. Then I went to Kansas City and got a lot of material; I talked to a lot of people who knew him when he was a young man. They didn't necessarily have a lot of insights, but they remembered very clearly things that he said and did. So I started to put together something.

FEINSTEIN: How much did being a musician help you with this project? Could you have written as good a book had you not been a jazz drummer?

CROUCH: I think the drama of jazz is in the success—or partial success, or failure—of the team effort. Only piano players, really, can play by themselves. Of course, flamenco guitar players can play by themselves, and some bass players. But saxophones and trumpets and all that—no. I mean, they *could* do it. The guys in [the Art Ensemble of] Chicago did have solo parts, trying to push the limits to see what was possible. But jazz is about how a rhythm section improvises within a form and creates a launching pad for the featured player, who is also improvising.

I think [Louis] Armstrong is the greatest of all. One of the most important things we have to address is that Armstrong is the only one who didn't have recordings of other people (apart from the Original Dixieland Jazz Band). [Crouch rolls his eyes and makes a contemptuous click; Feinstein laughs.] So he learned how to play from his ear and his imagination.

FEINSTEIN: And *some* inspiring musicians—

CROUCH: Yeah, but the thing is, when you really come to understand playing in a band and how to play [in general], you can get a great deal of information studying somebody's recordings.

FEINSTEIN: Sure.

CROUCH: And he didn't have any, so it all came out of him. I mean, Art Tatum had records, Lester Young had records, Charlie Parker, and so on. They're not in the same category.

FEINSTEIN: What you're saying about group effort, though, works a *little* bit in opposition to what you've been saying about Bird; so many times, particularly when he was just emerging, he did not have a rhythm section that could keep up with his ideas and energy.

CROUCH: Right.

FEINSTEIN: So it wasn't so much the group that made him great. Armstrong, too: in so many of the early recordings, nobody approaches his genius.

CROUCH: Right. But as these guys developed, the environmental relationship of the ensemble developed. So in 1945, when he [Parker] made "Ko Ko," there might have been, *maybe*, ten guys in New York who could play bebop; by the time he died in 1955, there were droves of them. And that's why he was able, after the club owners became impatient with his shenanigans and wouldn't allow him to bring a band [with him], he was able to go out as a single and play with the local rhythm sections in Boston, Chicago, Detroit, or wherever it was. So people learned it very fast, but you're right: at the start, it was very difficult.

FEINSTEIN: Since you place Armstrong at the top of this jazz pantheon, why did you decide to write your biography on Charlie Parker and not Louis Armstrong?

CROUCH: There have been and still are many more books about Armstrong, and one of the things that I discovered was that

Ross Russell's so-called biography [*Bird Lives! The High Life and Hard Times of Charlie Parker*] was so untrue, and so there was an opportunity [to repair that kind of misinformation]. Also, I had written a thing on Charlie Parker in, I think, the *New Republic*, and my agent at the time, Andrew Wiley, said, "Why don't you turn that into a book?"

FEINSTEIN: In your introduction to *Considering Genius*, you mention buying a drum set from Denardo Coleman [son of alto saxophonist Ornette Coleman and poet Jayne Cortez]. Are you still close with Jayne Cortez?

CROUCH: I talk to her every now and then.

FEINSTEIN: Do you find her work successful in terms of its marriage with jazz?

CROUCH: I think she's one of the more successful. She has a good ear.

FEINSTEIN: Who else would you put in her league?

CROUCH: [Pauses.] I don't know . . . Michael Harper—superior, actually.

FEINSTEIN: Why's that?

CROUCH: He's a real virtuoso writer. Jayne is an original. (A lot of it, it seems to me, derives from Lorca's *Poet in New York*.) But I think Michael Harper is just a master of the craft of writing. His work with inserting a number of rhythms and things inside that I think are pretty impressive.

FEINSTEIN: No one else?

CROUCH: Not that I can think of.

FEINSTEIN: How about in fiction? I think the two most famous jazz-related short stories are still Eudora Welty's "Powerhouse" and James Baldwin's "Sonny's Blues." I know how you feel about "Powerhouse."

CROUCH: Garbage.

FEINSTEIN: What's your take on "Sonny's Blues"?

CROUCH: I never really liked it. The characters in the story just didn't . . . You know, James Baldwin wrote that story a number of times, where you have a brother who's concerned with his younger brother who has problems. *Just Above My Head* is a big novel about a gospel singer that's basically the same tale as "Sonny's Blues." So there's something about familiar concerns and the problems of a sibling and how they're played out and the hope that each family has that he's not going to destroy himself. But, see, Leon Forrest's *Divine Days*—now that's somethin'. I mean, he's really got some *amazingly* inventive things in that book. [Shakes his head.] And he uses a lot of theme and variations in the way the book is formed. He also has a section in which he talks about this homosexual dancer whose mother, an ex-dancer, is very concerned about him. Well, he does that better than Baldwin. You read it and you say, "Wow . . . Yeah." *Divine Days* is an amazing book.

FEINSTEIN: Can you think of other fiction writers who really address the music in profound or moving ways?

CROUCH: I can't remember this guy's name, but he wrote a very fine novel about a blind saxophone player that was republished. [William Kelley's *A Drop of Patience*, originally published in 1965.] That was good.

FEINSTEIN: Do you think, then, that there was little of value to the Black Arts Movement of the sixties?

CROUCH: Yes.

FEINSTEIN: [Laughs.] That's the end of that?

CROUCH: Well, it's like what Leon Forrest and James McPherson say: "Where are the books?" I mean, there's all this noise that took place at the time, but where are the major books to come out of that period? That's the thing. Leon said, "You had all that talk—but a book's not talk." These people were better at changing their names than they were at creating any substantial aesthetic change.

FEINSTEIN: I'm sure if someone like Sonia Sanchez were here there'd be a lot of heat in response to that.

CROUCH: Well, could be. But to me, it's not an argument with her or anybody else. It's just that if you are making a claim that you're going to outdo or revitalize an area that has suffered from European decadence and blah blah blah, you have to do it. Here's the thing: in the end, none of these people are as good as Derek Walcott. [Crouch leaves the table.]

~

FEINSTEIN: If we consider a sweep of jazz-related writing—from early in the twentieth century to the present—you claim there's a big hole, in terms of what's really important, during the sixties.

CROUCH: Right.

FEINSTEIN: Michael Harper published his first book, *Dear John, Dear Coltrane*, in 1970. What would you say are some of the pivotal jazz-related books before then?

CROUCH: I don't know if it was pivotal, but I thought that Langston Hughes's *Ask Your Mama* [*12 Moods for Jazz* from 1961] was actually focused on jazz. But—I don't know. When I look back at it, I just see a big hole. And the other thing is, it's not to be unexpected because you have to actually be interested in jazz to make use of jazz. You can allude to it and refer to it, but it does help to actually be interested in the music and to know something about it.

During the Black Arts Movement, people were more involved in a very attenuated wing of jazz, and that's one of the reasons why a lot of people didn't convert to it, so to speak. They were promoting Albert Ayler and late Coltrane—those guys who had a kind of sound that ethnic political radicals of the time claimed was the expression of this revolution, blah blah blah. Well, most people don't like that [kind of aggressive sound], you know what I mean? This whole body of music by Miles Davis and Ahmad Jamal and all these people might have been liked had they been introduced to them, but they weren't.

Actually, I've been thinking a lot about the negative impact that I believe Black Nationalism had on black people and on black academics and intellectuals. It seems to me that at the core of it is an attempt to define yourself almost solely in opposition to white people. I've said in a number of places that I think the real issue that faces any individual within any group is to figure out how to fuse one's ethnic heritage with one's human heritage. Whatever your background is—black, Christian, Jewish, whatever—Coleman Hawkins is available to you as an aesthetic source and as a maker of aesthetic artifacts from which you can draw pleasure. There's no one who can say to you, "Well, because you weren't born in St. Louis, Missouri, like he was . . ." or "You aren't from the same ethnic group that he is . . ." But I saw that during the Black Nationalist period, and I still see a lot of it in play. That's why all of these black academics seem absolutely absurd when they give these long, involved expressions of ethnic independence from, you know, Western/European/Caucasian sources, and then, in the middle of it, cite whoever happens to be the latest person from France (usually) who's popular in the academy. "As so-and-so says . . . and we can apply that to Jay-Z." Oh, come on . . . That's so corny. [Feinstein laughs.] That is *so* corny.

It also imposed a kind of ideological self-definition that I think was unnatural. Then you began to think like, "Is this a black way to do this?" The worst extreme, of course, is Afrocentrism, a largely fraudulent body of potted history and just junk that no one takes very seriously now, but for a moment it was Afrocentric this and that. So you have a fake African history—all this stuff. I remember I went to a conference in Philadelphia ten or fifteen years ago. All these people were going through this ersatz Africanity [laughs]. They're going through this, and to back themselves up academically, so to speak, they're actually passing out Xeroxed covers of *Newsweek* magazine featuring the latest anthropological version of Adam and Eve, where Adam and Eve were definitely *not* looking white. There it was: on the one hand, "these people" are trying to deny you your place in history and deny you your contributions to civilization—and then, on the other hand, you're using copies of this popular weekly magazine to prove your point! Adam and Eve weren't white! That must prove it! See, to me, that's the kind of garbage that the country, the academy, and ethnic groups have been suffering from for almost forty years. I mean, it's slowly atrophying, but that in itself is one of the reasons why you don't have the books, the material, the aesthetic concern, the aesthetic clarity.

For example, I'm going to speak on this panel tonight at Columbia University—"Jazz from a Global Perspective." [Rolls his eyes.] Now, in *The Artificial White Man*, I point out something that I'm absolutely sure no one on that panel has ever thought, which is, that improvisation is always seen as a heroic virtue, particularly in popular culture as expressed in science fiction and monster films where, in the last fifteen minutes, the hero or the heroine has to figure out, or improvise, a way to defeat the monster. That goes all the way back to Odysseus and the Cyclops, right? And it's right in everybody's face, over and over and over, from their childhood all the way to this moment. Has anyone noticed it before? No. Is it discussed in film classes? No. But it's right *there*. "Here comes the monster. What'll we do?" "Well, we'll do this and that." He's finally gotten, almost invariably, because people have to improvise, so what they're telling you, over and over, is to think on your feet, to invent a solution to a great problem or threat on the spot. Now, the enemy is disorder to an improviser, and that's what the improviser is showing you: "We, right here together, can solve this problem and not fall into the shambles of disorder."

I was talking to a white guy about the essay "Putting the White Man in Charge" from *Considering Genius*, and he said, "I don't understand this." I said, "What do you mean?" He said,

"I don't understand what the controversy was about. You don't say, 'White musicians can't play or shouldn't play.' You have this eulogy for Martin Williams. You talk about how great Martin Williams and Whitney Balliett were, blah blah blah. And in some kind of way, because you zero in on *them*, and what they might actually want, then they decide that all that can be ignored and you can just be painted as a Louis Farrakhan, or something."

I seem to remember a book where these people were trying to paint [Wynton] Marsalis as antiwhite. So, Joe Temperly, who's a white baritone saxophone player and who was playing in the Lincoln Center Jazz Orchestra [directed by Marsalis], said, "You know, the thing I don't understand about this is they never talked to *me*. I'm in the band. They never talked to me—even off the record." And I don't know of anybody who has these racist assumptions about Marsalis who's talked to any of these [white] guys [in the band]; they just throw it out there: "I looked at it, and it's obviously racist," and that's it.

Now, interestingly, no one can get away with that anywhere else. For example, if you had a small publishing house in New York, I couldn't accuse you of having some kind of an ethnic agenda that we could see in your hiring policies, when you have people of the sort working for you who are part of the group you're victimizing. Now, I can say that about you, and never talk to anybody who works with you—I've got people who've been working around you for a decade—and I say, "He's a racist. Blah blah blah."

All of these kinds of things—on either side—are the sorts of things that have muddied the waters in jazz criticism. To me, the time that could have been spent trying to clarify to the public this theme and variation thing that I was talking about has been devoted just to some ethnic home team squabbling. Why do they have to bring that up? One thing that I know—that we all know: if you do the kinds of things that LeRoi Jones [Amiri Baraka] did, and you say the things that he said, somewhere along the line, not necessarily him but that resentment is going to come to the top. It's just like you have white people today who are in SNCC [Student Nonviolent Coordinating Committee] who, because they were white, were kicked out of the organization in 1966 when Black Power came out. They're *still* mad—at this very second, wherever they are. I went to a MacArthur reunion four or five years ago—Bob Moses was there with his wife, and so on—but there were some other SNCC people, and they were still mad about *that*. And what I contend is, if you take advantage of people, you belittle them in a certain kind of way, they're gonna get you. That's what I believe. Those people who did that are gonna pay. Now, one of the things about waiting a certain amount of time is it can then be, "Oh, how can he say that? Why does he bring that up?" No—it's not like that. There was so much hostility that came out of that period [in the sixties] . . .

I was on a panel with Cornell West and all of these people in Chicago, and I was saying that people always go for this stuff about apologies ("Let's apologize to the Japanese," "Let's apologize to the Sioux," "Let's apologize to whomever," right?) Now, black people, who were in the position to exhibit a certain kind of ethnic hostility toward whites, have never faced the fact—that's never been admitted to. I was with this guy who wrote *Black Athena* [Martin Bernal], which is like the Bible of the Afrocentric movement, even though he's Jewish, and I said, "What are we going to say about all of this rudeness, obnoxiousness?"—all the stuff that happened during the Black Power period. I said, "You don't think that affected what happened in the country? All these white students coming from places like Minnesota and who came to San Francisco and they're told, 'No, you can't come here, this is the black corridor. You can't come here—this is the black blah blah blah.' You don't think that had any impact at all on the Reagan era? You think that just went by?" Part of what has to be handled for us to unite as people once more is for people to accept what was wrong with that and be able to separate what was wrong from what was good.

But basically, I don't see, or haven't seen—again, with the exception of Leon Forrest—much real interest in appropriating some of the techniques of thematic variation as exhibited in jazz having much of an effect on people.

FEINSTEIN: So why do you write about jazz?

CROUCH: Well, the first thing is, I was never a joiner, and when you come into the arts, you're not going into car sales. You may have an effect, it may be immediate or in the long run, but you have to have integrity. As I said at Max Roach's funeral: yes, he was a genius, but genius doesn't guarantee integrity. That's self-will. Part of Max's greatness was that he was not only this great genius of drums, but he was a man of very great integrity. In a period of endorsements and so on, here's somebody who made no fusion records. There's not one Max Roach record that you can listen to and say, "Oh, he was doing that because he was trying to [follow a trend and make more money]." So I think there's a certain kind of importance to that because people who have integrity are usually disliked.

Imagine somebody like Ramsey Lewis finding himself on a subway train late at night with Monk. What do you think he's going to feel like? He knows who Monk is. And he knows who he is. So here's this guy [Lewis] who's ready to sell out at the drop of a hat, and he's on this subway car with this guy who's achieved this body of functional idealism, and he's not necessarily going to like him. If you go your own way, and you believe in what you're doing, then you'll be by yourself. That's how that goes.

4

Breaking Down the Gates

Linda Dahl

Linda Dahl is the author of three jazz-related books: *Stormy Weather: The Music and Lives of a Century of Jazzwomen*; *Morning Glory: A Biography of Mary Lou Williams* (selected by the *New York Times Book Review* as a Notable Book of the Year 2000); and *Haunted Heart: A Biography of Susannah McCorkle*. Her other books include *Loving Our Addicted Daughters Back to Life: A Guidebook for Parents*; a short story collection, *Come Back, Carmen Miranda*; a trilogy of novels—*Gringa in a Strange Land*, *Cleans Up Nicely*, and *The Bad Dream Notebook*—and a fourth that was released after this interview, *An Upside-Down Sky*. Her articles about offbeat events, characters, and the arts have appeared in *Jazz Magazine, Smithsonian, Travel and Leisure, Connoisseur*, and *MD* magazines. She lives in New York City.

The following excerpts from Dahl's writings have been reprinted with permission. The interview took place via the internet on January 14, 2022.

Stormy Weather: The Music and Lives of a Century of Jazzwomen (excerpt)

Researching many of the women's contributions to jazz is like what I imagine collecting butterflies to be—you go out with your net to many a remote, even secretive spot to track your shy and elusive quarry. Colorful, bright specimens, many of these women in jazz, far from the mainstream, and some of them downright eccentric. There are lots of them making music in small cities, pokey college towns, black neighborhoods, cheesy cocktail lounges—where record producers and jazz reviewers hardly venture. Ladies who have turned their backs on the business side of music, and who have validated themselves through their music. When I was putting together *Stormy Weather* over a period of several years, I was inspired by the personalities of the jazzwomen—the famous and the obscure, the black and the white, the young and the old. Their grit and determination and pride in their work often helped me keep going when I felt up to my ears in old newspaper dust. The struggles of these women in and out of music, their salty and witty views on life, work, men and the pursuit of happiness, lie at the heart of this book. I wanted not only to fill in the blanks of jazz history by citing their achievements, but also to capture some of the vividness of their lives. Because these are real foremothers, taboo-breakers, independent "mamas."

Morning Glory: A Biography of Mary Lou Williams (excerpt)

At times, Mary would balk when [Marian] McPartland came into The Cookery to hear her, complaining that she would steal her arrangements and style. When McPartland began what is now a long-established successful radio program called *Piano Jazz* in the fall of 1978, she invited Mary to be her first guest, and the taped encounter shows Mary's prickliness as she fairly bulldozes over her smooth hostess—but it is also a fair sampling of Mary's later brilliance, with a furiously fast "Morning Glory," a lightly seasoned "Rosa Mae" (with rare vocals by Mary), and a brilliant "I Can't Get Started." The two most famous female jazz musicians did make peace after 1978, when Mary's cancer became public knowledge. McPartland recalls that Mary softened a good deal toward her; and Mary was especially appreciative of a lovely medal of Saint Cecilia, the patron saint of music, that McPartland sent her as a gift.

The Bad Dream Notebook (excerpt)

Erica moved down the hall from the party to the sanctuary of the church, dim and almost cool that hot summer night. People sat in the pews, listening to Ken's plangent, Bill Evans-ish compositions. At the funeral the next day, he'd play a set of the beautiful jazz tunes John had selected: Billy Strayhorn, Jimmy Rowles, a New Orleans strut in "Just a Closer Walk with Thee." The loud hum from the party was a fitting counterpoint to Ken, like being in a jazz club. Her first date with John had been in a jazz club, and one of the reasons she'd liked him so much was that they had similar tastes in music. She began to shiver, though it was hot, recalled the noisy, funky club, Small's, in the Village, she thinks it was—and that charged feeling of anticipation of going to bed, later, soon, with someone brand-new who excites you. She heard a burst of laughter. The noise these people were generating with their eating and drinking and talking and, yes, laughing. And, suddenly, her mood turned dark: the noise was brutal, and she could not make sense of it, not even Ken's sensitive playing. In the wings of her mind was a different music, something savage like Stravinsky's *Rite of Spring*. As if John had been a sacrifice to give heat and light to those who mingled here.

Haunted Heart: A Biography of Susannah McCorkle (excerpt)

Susannah was also long skilled at concealing the degree to which she suffered. Psychiatrists call the planning that precedes killing oneself "suicidal ideation," and Susannah apparently plotted hers as painstakingly and well as any Oak Room performance. For her, the notion of killing oneself had been a familiar concept since childhood; it had been a fantasy with comfort in it—the relief she sought from acute, chronic psychic pain. Anyone who's been depressed knows how at such times life can feel like a prison sentence, with all the joy bleached out, replaced by a dull, feverish lack of *savor* as one plods on. . . .

Sometime before or during the evening of May 18 [2001,] Susannah wrote down Lana Cantrell's, Thea Lurie's, and Dan DiNicola's names and phone numbers on the back of one of her business cards, tucking it into the pocket of the green sweats she'd put on. She placed a copy of her will and a sealed letter with detailed instructions about disposition of her estate and belongings (including her beloved two cats) on her desk, along with a suicide letter.

"She left behind a detailed note. She would. That figures. She was always trying to be a good girl," her friend Jon Carroll was to write sadly in his May 24 obituary in the *San Francisco Chronicle*.

Interview

SASCHA FEINSTEIN: You're originally from Omaha, Nebraska, but you moved to New York City in the 1970s when you were in your twenties. That was awfully bold!

LINDA DAHL: Well, there's a lot that happened before that. I did grow up in Omaha, but then, when I was fifteen or sixteen, my dad got a job in Milwaukee so we moved there. But I lived in South America before I went to college. I told my parents, "I'm sick of going to school." [Laughs.] They were college-educated parents; it was very important to them. But we had an exchange student my senior year from Ecuador, and she and I became friendly. So I moved to the west coast of South America: working there, taking a class, really getting my Spanish honed. And the music was very Afro—Afro-Latin, all along the west coast—so I was introduced to *so* many rhythms and styles of music.

When I returned, I started going to the University of Wisconsin campus in Milwaukee and transferred after a year to Madison. This was the late sixties, when everything was happening: the Vietnam War, Black Power, black studies, women's studies, and so on. Milwaukee, both because it was near Chicago but also just for the kind of town that it was, was filled with blues and funk. And Chicago was so great to visit, in part because of the jazz. There was also a great jazz radio station in Milwaukee at night. This was what I like to call my subterranean major in college.

I had always loved music, as well as books and writing (secretively in my room), and I decided that I was going to become a travel journalist, which I did: after graduating college with my love of all things Latin American, I moved to Mexico thinking I was going to travel all the way down to South America. I basically had no money; that's what kids were doing back then. And I ended up living in the Yucatan for about a year, where the rhythms from Cuba—which is not that far away—are very important, as well as all the native Latin sounds. I had one of those portable tape recorders that I dragged along with me, so I was listening to jazz as well. And because I was writing more, I thought, "I've got to go to New York. I've got to become a writer." So I moved to Manhattan, with a small suitcase and eight hundred dollars, where I only knew one person. [Both laugh.] You're from Manhattan, so you know!

FEINSTEIN: That's astonishing! At what point did you realize you wanted to write a book about women in jazz?

DAHL: While in New York, doing travel journalism, I became more involved with the scene and even wrote for *Jazz Magazine* [1976–1980]. My friend Peter Keepnews was the editor [with Tom Stites]; he was also the jazz contributor for the *New York Post*. We were very close, so I went everywhere with him to hear all the great music. Then I had a boyfriend who was a jazz musician—the late [alto saxophonist] Richie Cole—who schooled me in bebop.

FEINSTEIN: He was an incendiary player.

DAHL: Unbelievable . . . He had a gig one night where I went along, and there was a woman playing drums: Dottie Dodgion, who passed away recently. It was the first time I'd heard a woman jazz musician, and she was really *part* of the group, part of the fraternity, if you will.

That nagged at me; it wouldn't leave me alone. Then things just worked out: I got an agent, got a contract and a wonderful editor, Joy Johannessen. And that became *Stormy Weather: The Music and Lives of a Century of Jazzwomen* [1984]. There were no computers back then, no internet. There were a *lot* of index cards! But the great thing was that I had the opportunity to meet all these women and talk to them in person.

FEINSTEIN: Yes, in fact the book closes with ten profiles of women whom you interviewed between 1979 and 1981. How did you select those particular women?

DAHL: I tried to have variety, and it was sometimes a matter of accessibility to get to them. I didn't have a lot of money, so I couldn't just fly all over the place.

FEINSTEIN: But you did fly out to California to interview [guitarist] Mary Osborne.

DAHL: Yes, I did. And I tried to track down [saxophonist] Vi Redd in LA, but I couldn't find her. [Laughs.] I just wanted to include a variety of women who were all under-sung and needed to have their stories told. [Trombonist/composer/arranger] Melba Liston . . . That was a fantastic experience for me. I love Melba Liston.

FEINSTEIN: What made it fantastic?

DAHL: There's something about her personality that was riveting to me. She was such a great arranger. She was very humble—somewhat of a mysterious person, too. For me, as a writer of fiction, what really draws me in are the characters; it's all about the people—who they are and how they present themselves and what's going on behind that. Melba had an aura about her, assured, but sad. That's part of the story, too, that we can't leave out. As hard as it is for anyone to make it in jazz, for women, it was and often still is just *phenomenal* that they stake their claim and are able to get into that world.

FEINSTEIN: Your book *Stormy Weather* is now almost forty years old. If you were to update it, who would you necessarily include?

DAHL: That's interesting because it's out-of-print now, but there's some talk about doing another edition, and if I were to do another edition, I'd have to add a couple more chapters. [Bassist] Esperanza Spalding. Oh, just a packed crew in there. [Pianist] Geri Allen would be prominently discussed.

FEINSTEIN: She'd have to be.

DAHL: I love her, and her connection to Mary Lou [Williams]. [Allen not only recorded music by Williams but, in 2019, orchestrated a three-day tribute to Williams's life and work—SF.] Renee Rosnes and Helen Sung. (I happen to love piano players.) There are *so* many, too many, I'm happy to say, to include in one go. Some standouts include [guitarist] Mary Halvorson and the saxophonists Melissa Aldana, Sharel Cassidy, and Camilla Thurman. [Trombonist] Natalie Cresman. [Cellist] Tomeka Reid.

And worldwide; I'd also want to expand it that way. Even in Burma, where my latest book, *An Upside-Down Sky*, is set. Burma, or Myanmar, was in a vice for about fifty years, before about ten years of incipient democracy and now, the recent reimposition of total power by the military dictatorship. But even there, there has been a small but hearty jazz scene, with women involved. It would be exciting for me to look at how jazz has influenced music globally in the past forty years. India. Turkey. You name it. To name but a few: [reed player] Anat Cohen is from Israel. Among pianists: Eliane Elias is from Brazil, Renee Rosnes from Canada, Patrizial Scascitelli from Italy. The drummer Yissy García from Cuba. Among vocalists: Sofia Rei is from Argentina, Malika Zarra from Morocco, and Val H. Jeanty from Haiti. Of course, I could go on. The improvisational aspect of this music in particular is so exciting to creative musicians around the world, including a lot of women.

In terms of the music today, contemporary women in jazz, such as [composer/arranger/pianist] Maria Schneider, emphasize that they have to be on top of the business side too. [Drummer] Terri Lyne Carrington is another who really takes on the business of jazz. Others who have just come out of Berklee or schools in Manhattan and elsewhere—such as trumpeter Summer Camargo, who was recently featured with the Jazz at Lincoln Center Orchestra—stress the importance of this.

∽

FEINSTEIN: *Stormy Weather* has an eight-page section on Mary Lou Williams. Is that when you realized you wanted to write a full-length biography on her [*Morning Glory*]?

DAHL: Actually, not—although it was a seed that was planted and, obviously, didn't go away. After I wrote *Stormy Weather*, I went back to my first love, fiction, and wrote a novel [*Gringa in a Strange Land*]. I got married. I had a family. Then, friends started saying to me, "When's your next book about jazz? What the heck!" And somebody mentioned Mary Lou Williams, and I thought, "Yes. Yes!" So I said, "Okay, I'm going to start doing some research."

Well, as soon as I started researching—beyond what I had already done—I simply could not believe all the aspects of her story that needed to be told. That was the start of that book. In a way, it was the most intense writing experience of my life.

FEINSTEIN: Why? What were some of the biggest challenges for you?

DAHL: At that time [mid to late nineties], so much of her music was out of print, and it was hard to get ahold of it. You could buy *some* used records at stores, and I was frequently running out to the Institute of Jazz Studies [at Rutgers University in Newark, New Jersey] and finding things there, but that was a difficulty. (At the end of writing the book, a lot of music starting finally coming out on CD.)

The second big challenge was dealing with the Keeper of the Gate, who, in this case, was Peter O'Brien. He was very protective. As you know, he was living at that time as a Jesuit priest who wasn't active: He was living in a crumbling mansion in Manhasset [Long Island] that somebody had donated to the Jesuits. It was for priests who just needed to be quietly in a room somewhere. I visited, and, in time, he became *very* candid with me about his life—to the point that I said, "Peter: I'm a writer, a biographer. You're telling me things that you may want to think about a little bit . . ." He was also difficult, and I don't mean to be disparaging when I say that.

Eventually, though, he said that in the basement of the crumbling mansion were boxes filled with all of Mary Lou's papers, music manuscripts, and tapes. "You can have them," he said, "and then eventually they'll go to the Institute of Jazz Studies." So I put them in the back of my station wagon, lugged them back to my house, and started going through them. [Feinstein's eyes widen.] Yeah. It was incredible. Shivers down my spine. Astonishing.

Like a lot of women of her generation, especially black women, she guarded very carefully a lot of her feelings and experiences. But she wrote about them all in private journals and little pieces of paper and letters—and she kept it all. So clearly, at least as I interpret it, she wanted them to be known. That's how the book really took off.

Feinstein: Amazing. I just assumed that you had been scouring the archives at the Institute of Jazz Studies, but you *were* the archives!

Dahl: [Laughs.] Well, Peter was, and then he gave me the archives.

Feinstein: Mary Lou Williams strikes me as a woman of extremes: rough and rugged on the one hand, and supremely generous and humorous on the other. Do you feel similarly about her music?

Dahl: The music? Interesting question . . . I've not really heard it phrased that way. Yeah, I think you're on to something there. The way she was schooled, as a child on up to her teens, was really rough and ready. She grew up with heavy drinkers, and that affects children profoundly, of course. She was playing before her teens in gambling dens, at parties. She had to fend for herself—just imagine—although she had protectors. Musically, she had to learn how to transpose on pianos that were out of tune, being roughly schooled by the piano men she knew in Pittsburgh and then on the road. And I didn't get into every aspect of this in the book or it would've ended up being eight hundred pages, but she first went on the road when she was twelve or thirteen. I mean, we can only imagine . . . She found protectors. *Sometimes*.

So I think she was very hurt, but she was a survivor, and she had this *beautiful*, other world inside. You're right: There were extremes, and they came out in her personality and music.

Feinstein: She had a lifelong ambition to write her autobiography but she ended up with an unfinished manuscript of about eighty pages. What do you think of her writing?

Dahl: Like a lot of people who say, "I'm going to write my autobiography," I don't think it was her métier. I don't think it was *bad*, but I don't think that's where her true strengths lay.

FEINSTEIN: I couldn't agree more. It's just interesting to me that she kept going back to the project.

DAHL: I'm extrapolating, but I think, from a psychological standpoint, she was trying to make sense of many things that had happened to her as a child and a young woman.

FEINSTEIN: There have been a few books on Mary Lou Williams that have been published since your biography. Maybe you could comment on them. I'm thinking first about Tammy Kernodle's *Soul on Soul: The Life and Music of Mary Lou Williams* [2020].

DAHL: Tammy has more of a grasp on musical aspects because I'm a nonmusician, although I did take piano lessons when I was a kid. [Laughs.] I'm not a musician. And there's a book by Deanna Witkowski, *Mary Lou Williams: Music for the Soul* [2021] that just came out. She's a piano player in Pittsburgh, and she's more into the spiritual side of Mary Lou's music. It's written for a Catholic Press—which is fine. Is there anything else on Mary Lou?

FEINSTEIN: Apart from book chapters, I know of a children's book called *The Little Piano Girl* [*The Story of Mary Lou Williams, Jazz Legend* by Ann Ingalls and Maryann Macdonald] and Sarah Bruce Kelly's *Jazz Girl: A Novel of Mary Lou Williams*.

DAHL: Yes. Great. I say, the more the merrier. And I have written a screenplay about Mary Lou! It took years: it's called *Piano Girl*. It's a three-episode biopic, as they call it in the biz, that is being looked at. This is something of an obsession for me. Mary Lou Williams's personal life was inherently dramatic and compelling and her musical journey is unique—a musician who begins with stride and ragtime and masters all of the styles that follow.

∼

FEINSTEIN: I'd like to discuss *Haunted Heart: A Biography of Susannah McCorkle*. I have various connections to her vocal albums, even her death. (Inadvertently, during a visit to Manhattan in the spring of 2001, I walked the pavement that she hit on the day of her suicide.) But I didn't know her, and you didn't, either. Of those who did, who were most illuminating for your biography?

DAHL: [Inhales.] She had a good friend, a cabaret performer named Mark Nadler, and he was very illuminating about Susannah. Her [third] ex-husband, Dan DiNicola, shared a lot of what she was going through in her later years. Her second husband—the English piano player Keith Ingham, whom she met in London early on—had a great deal to say about Susannah (not always positive, which is okay; it's all grist for the mill). And her great friend, Thea Lurie—but Thea was close to a Gate Keeper, and by that I mean protective of her friend's, shall we say, downsides. Even more so than Mary Lou, Susannah was an extremely private person.

FEINSTEIN: Like you, Susannah McCorkle wrote both fiction and nonfiction. What do you think of her writing?

DAHL: I visited her mother in San Francisco for a few days, which was amazing. She was a true eccentric, very hospitable, but you could see why Susannah had difficulties with that relationship. Her mother had kept a lot of things that she'd written early on. She was a *gifted* writer of fiction. She began as a writer, and I think the care she took with lyrics came from an exquisite awareness of language. She wrote disturbingly beautiful fiction, and part of me felt, "Oh my gosh—why didn't she continue as a writer?" But it was her decision. Her voice became that of a singer.

FEINSTEIN: What is it about Susannah McCorkle's singing that you appreciate?

DAHL: Well, as I said, her command as paired with the lyric. It can be painful to listen to her sometimes because of the feeling that she's conveying. That's certainly an accolade.

    What I had *trouble* with—and perhaps this is just personal taste—had to do with that innate quality that's often unspoken, perhaps latent, of swinging (however you want to define that): I don't think she really had that. And I think she knew that, too, which did fuel her insecurity. But she worked around it—which is great. I mean, we all have our limitations. She sculpted songs so beautifully, and she worked so hard at it.

FEINSTEIN: I think of her more as a show-tune singer than a jazz singer.

As you well know, a great wealth of her writing, including journals, has been archived in the New York Public Library. Apparently, a fair amount of material only became available after your book. Have you gone back to look at that material?

DAHL: No, I haven't, but I'm glad you mentioned that.

I was *done*, cooked, when I finished the book. Right after she died, people started calling and saying, "Please write the biography of Susannah McCorkle," and I was, like, "I'm more of a jazz person." But somebody asked me to come to the memorial at St. Peters, and I went, and, my God . . . I met all these people who were giving me fantastic anecdotes about her.

The challenge for me, literally, was coming to terms with writing as fully and honestly as I could about somebody who was suffering from a severe mental illness and who just couldn't go on and decided to end her life. That's the residue that stays with me in writing that book—which is not necessarily a bad thing. I learned a lot about manic depression—or bipolar disorder, as we call it—that I hadn't known, and I have friends, as I'm sure most of us do, with the disorder. I've seen what it can do to people. It straightjackets them in certain ways.

I felt that I was *done*. But I will go back [to the archives in the New York Public Library]. Thank you.

FEINSTEIN: I was going to ask if you thought you would have written this book had she not taken her life, but it sounds as though you wouldn't have.

DAHL: I don't think I would have. [Grimaces.] All the implications . . . No, maybe not.

You know, I always wanted to write a book on Nica [the Baroness Pannonica de Koenigswarter, who befriended and supported many legendary jazz musicians, most notably Thelonious Monk], but it was impossible. Forget even about Gate Keepers. *No way* is anybody going to get through all of that from her perspective as a Rothschild! [Laughs.] So I gave up on that.

FEINSTEIN: In your fiction, apart from a few jazz passages here and there—most notably in *The Bad Dream Notebook*—there's not much jazz as a subject. But in the novel you're working on now [working title: *Tiny Vices*], you have a character who is obsessed with finding correlatives between Charlie Parker and Mozart. Can you talk more about that?

DAHL: His name is Bernard. He's an African American man married to a white woman. He's an academic. He was raised by his father—his mother left when he was an infant—who was stymied (what a shock) in his career aspirations. But he revered music, and in the home, Bernard was constantly exposed to great jazz records. His father loved all kinds of music, though, so he was listening to classical music (Stravinsky, Chopin, all of that). Bernard becomes an academic in the music department at the University of Arizona, and he's struggling to write a book—perhaps in part it's an homage to his father—and he becomes gripped by the need to prove to the world that jazz *is* a classical music worthy of being considered with as much respect and attention as European classical music. The novel has a lot to do with race in America, too.

FEINSTEIN: This sounds wonderful! Are there authors who have written fictional jazz-related pieces whom you admire?

DAHL: Absolutely! John A. Williams. I'd never heard of him until I joined a book-reading group online at the 92nd Street Y during COVID (one of the things that helped keep me sane), and one of the books was John A. Williams's *The Man Who Cried I Am*, which is a phenomenal novel. This led me to *Clifford's Blues*, about an African American, gay, jazz pianist émigré in Europe who gets caught up in the late thirties by the Germans and sent to a camp for undesirables and is ordered to form a jazz band for the officers' entertainment. The devastation is in the details.

But if we're talking about cadences—the aesthetic language of jazz—there are so many writers . . . For me, a personal favorite: Percival Everett. Toni Morrison: the language, the rhythm. (What is it that Miles Davis said? "It's not the notes you play. It's the notes you don't play.")

FEINSTEIN: In *Stormy Weather*, you talk a lot about the disproportionate number of celebrated male musicians over female players, but the imbalance is also true for jazz scholarship. Who are some of the women jazz scholars whom you admire?

DAHL: My good friend Constance Valis Hill, whose son, Theo Hill, is a jazz pianist, has written definitively about the complex world of jazz and tap in dance, as well as a biography of the Nicholas Brothers. Another close friend, Stephanie Stein Crease, who has published books on Duke Ellington and Gil Evans, is currently finishing a biography of Chick Webb. Farah Jasmine Griffin, a longtime scholar and author, has made crucial contributions regarding Billie Holiday and others, as have Angela Davis and Sherrie Tucker in their books on women and jazz. The biographies by Lara Pellegrinelli [on Anita O'Day], Karen Chilton [on Hazel Scott], and Elaine Hayes [on Sarah Vaughan] also come to mind. There is Maxine Gordon's very personal biography on Dexter. I'm sure there are others.

FEINSTEIN: For a stretch of time, the most prominent female jazz scholar was [the late] Leslie Gourse, whose work I don't respect, even if I applaud her enthusiasm for the music.

DAHL: Leslie once said to me, "How can you spend five years working on a book about Mary Lou Williams? I get 'em done in a year. I have to support myself." My response to that was, "Well, I've had to support myself, too, but I do it in other ways to support my writing habit." I don't want to diss her, but I don't think she's going to live on as a scholar.

FEINSTEIN: Absolutely not—and you're not the only one to whom she said such things! [Both laugh.] Bottom line, Linda:

you're one of the great pioneers, and I'm grateful for your work, and for this conversation.

DAHL: You know what? Talking to you, I felt a very quick, real connection. Bless your heart.

5

Maxine Calling

Maxine Gordon

Maxine Gordon is an independent scholar with a lifetime career working with jazz musicians. She began her career in jazz as the road manager for Gil Evans and later worked in that capacity for such luminaries as Art Blakey, Johnny Griffin, Shirley Scott, Woody Shaw (with whom she had a child, Woody Louis Armstrong Shaw III), and Dexter Gordon, whom she met in 1975 and later married. In 2013, she founded The Dexter Gordon Society, a nonprofit cultural organization created to preserve, document, and present their collective life's work. Her biography *Sophisticated Giant: The Life and Legacy of Dexter Gordon* had not been released at the time of this discussion.

The following excerpts from Gordon's writings have been reprinted with permission. The interview was conducted in Dennis, Massachusetts, on August 16, 2018.

Sophisticated Giant (excerpt)

James Baldwin was one among many of our shared passions. Dexter and I owned the same Baldwin books, loved talking about *Go Tell It on the Mountain*, and would laugh about the fact that we traveled with our individual copies. Dexter knew Baldwin well enough to call him Jimmy. I only got to meet him once, at a party in Harlem, and I was stunned and wordless. Being speechless is a very rare condition for me. Dexter joked that if I pulled myself together he would introduce me to the great author. As he said that, Baldwin yelled across the room, "Hey Dex, I read in the paper that we were expatriates. I thought we were just living in Europe." Dexter roared, then strolled over and bent down and hugged Baldwin, who seemed to disappear in his embrace. *I thought we were just living in Europe*—that remark has resonated with me for years.

The years Dexter lived in Europe—1962 to 1976—are treated as "lost" years by many fans, friends, and critics. Those Europe years were when he went missing from the scene in the United States, which many believed to be not only the center of jazz at that time but also the center of the world and anything interesting that was happening in it. But Dexter was aware of everything that was happening in the States and stayed connected to his home country in many ways. Like Baldwin, he found humor in the designations that suggested he was something of an outsider.

I tried to be cool when I was introduced to Baldwin. I tried not to look nonplussed. I was New York cool—nothing, and nobody, could impress me. Baldwin was just another partygoer. But Dexter said I had tears in my eyes and looked like I was going to faint. And his ability to see past my pretensions, and make me laugh about them, was something I especially treasured. Dexter did that—he made you see yourself a little clearer and always did so with wit (sometimes a biting wit; every now and then the humor was a knife turning).

Liner Notes for *BOPland:*
The Legendary Elks Club Concert L.A. 1947 (excerpt)

What is it about that night at the Elks Auditorium . . . and Central Avenue that elicit that knowing BeBop nod of the head and insider's smile? Is it that in jazz mythology, everyone who knows about Central Avenue knows that Dexter and Wardell [Gray] recorded "The Hunt" at the Elks Ballroom? If so, isn't it strange that when you listen to the recording of the concert, it's "Cherokee" that sends the crowd into a frenzy? Of course, the playing is incredible but what did they hear that we don't hear today? In 1947, the audience was accustomed to hearing recordings of artists confined to the 3 to 4 minute durations of 78-rpm discs. On this recording, there is no complete song shorter than thirteen and a half minutes. . . .

As we lose touch with the situations that produced this music in the first place, we begin to draw distinctions between players and styles that these innovators never would have considered. It seems to make some of us a little uncomfortable to listen to these musicians as they are working out their ideas on the bandstand—mistakes and all. This is jazz composition on two feet, in the instant. Actually, a remarkable task when you think about it.

Sophisticated Giant (excerpt)

We left from Miami on the *SS Norway* . . . [that] had twelve decks and our penthouse suite came with a balcony, a sitting room, and a personal valet. When the valet came into the suite, offered to unpack our bags, and said that if I would choose what I was wearing to dinner at the captain's table that evening he would have it pressed for me, I had that "movie star wife" moment, and Dexter and I laughed out loud. He smiled and said to the valet: "Oh please don't do that. She will expect that kind of service when we get home. Just bring an iron and an ironing board to the room please." He then turned to me and said what he had been saying since *Round Midnight* created all the commotion: "Don't get used to this. We are going back to our regular life very soon." Then he would laugh. . . .

    Of course, Dexter practiced every day, as he always did. He would take his horn out on the balcony and warm up, play his way through scales, and then play whatever song came into his mind. I could always tell what kind of mood he was in and who he was thinking about by the tune he chose to play. On this trip, he kept it light and seemed to have Lester Young in mind, though that's just a guess. One day when we were in the suite, Clark Terry came by for a visit. He and Dexter sat out on the balcony and reminisced and laughed that way that jazz musicians do when one word reminds them of something or someone and they just howl. Then they say another few words and howl even louder. Then Clark said, "Hey Dex, they are saying you can't play anymore. They are talking about you."

    Dexter replied, "Oh man, I'm on vacation."

    They laughed and then Clark said: "Why don't you come down and play one tune with the band? We've got Tommy Flanagan on piano."

    There was a long silence and Dexter said, "But Clark, I'm on vacation."

    Clark looked at Dexter and after a long pause, he said, "Dex, they are saying you can't play anymore."

    Dexter stood up, looked out at the sea, turned to Clark, and said, "What time do we hit?"

Liner Notes for Dexter Gordon's *Tokyo 1975* (excerpt)

In 1973, Dexter was invited to perform in Tokyo. It was his first trip there and, according to his memory, it did not get off to a very good start. The band traveled in the cheap seats on Aeroflot, the Soviet Union's national carrier. Dexter had heard that they had a very bad safety record and he recalled that the luggage was held above the passengers' heads in open netting. There was little food, the cabin was filled with cigarette smoke, and vodka was poured freely.

He said that he drank his way to Tokyo on that flight and was worried the entire time. When they arrived, he was not in the best condition and the promoter looked very worried. At the hotel, Dexter said that he could not stand up in the bathroom as the ceiling was too low (Dexter was 6' 6" or 1.98 meters tall). His legs had to hang off the end of the bed, and his arms could touch the walls when he spread them out. Or at least that was the way he remembered things. "I am too tall for Japan," he said. . . .

When we listen to Dexter here [on the CD recorded on October 1, 1975], we are reminded of his humor, his brilliance, and the serious thought behind every one of his compositions. Dexter Gordon was always striving to be the best tenor player he could be, and he loved being a jazz musician. Even when the travel was difficult and the conditions were not the best, he would remind himself that he had been on the road with Lionel Hampton's band when he was 17 years old, riding on the bus with no heat in the winter, and was happy to be able to play this great music.

Interview

SASCHA FEINSTEIN: I know you were born in 1942. Where in New York City were you raised?

MAXINE GORDON: 102nd and West End—that's where my grandmother lived—but then we went to California. My mother had been living in California, and she was in the fashion business, a buyer for Bloomingdale's, but because of Pearl Harbor and the imminent war, my grandmother wanted me to be born in New York so my mother took a train there. After my father died when I was eight, we moved back to New York, where I was raised. Then, when we got older, my mother (with my grandmother) moved us to Kings Point, Long Island, because she'd heard that the schools in Great Neck were much better. That's where I graduated from high school, and then I went to George Washington University when I was seventeen.

FEINSTEIN: But before that, in '57 when you were only fifteen years old, you were at the Village Vanguard listening to Art Blakey! How did you end up in such a hip group?

GORDON: Well, we were already a hip group. We were like little jazz kids. We had a group, organized by a drummer, Joel O'Brien, whose father was part of Gallagher and O'Brien, the morning radio guys; everyone listened to them in the fifties. Joel's family lived in a nice house. His father had a music room, and he got free records because he was on the radio, and on Fridays we would go to his house and listen to them. We were not allowed to talk (which is really hard for me) and then have arguments about Red Garland, Wynton Kelly, whomever.

Years later, Geoffrey O'Brien, the editor of Library of America who wrote a book called *Sonata for Jukebox: Pop Music, Memory, and the Imagined Life* [2004], said that his older brother, who was a jazz fan and jazz musician, would be listening to music with friends and they wouldn't let him in the room, but he could still hear it. When I read that, I thought, "I wonder if that was that little kid bangin' on the door," so I sent him an email ("I know you don't remember me but we used to come to your house . . .") and he answered right away: "I *do* remember you, because you were nice to me. You would come out." He was seven then and we were fifteen (and they were smokin' weed in there—but they were supposed to be babysitting, watching the little brother). [Feinstein laughs.]

We could go into the city [Manhattan] and hear music at the Vanguard or Birdland. My mother was like, "Jazz. Yeah, cool." She liked the MJQ [Modern Jazz Quartet]. We had to take the last train back, but we were organized. And Max Gordon [proprietor of the Village Vanguard, no relation] got sick of us. [Feinstein laughs.] But we heard everybody. And I think what really happened with me in terms of [having a life focused on] jazz was Art Blakey and his Jazz Messengers. I was *very* fortunate to meet him and learn [about the music]. Years later, when I married Dexter, he would come to my house.

FEINSTEIN: And you were his road manager as well.

GORDON: Yeah. After Dexter died, he called me to go with him when he had a gig in Massachusetts, and that gave me flashbacks to when I was a kid listening to those records. So I thought, "How could I find a way to be around this music and these people?" (I think it was Dizzy [Gillespie] who said to someone once, "You know, she doesn't think we're weird. Other people think we're weird," and I thought, "Why would people think that?")

FEINSTEIN: In this period of the fifties and sixties, you heard Miles Davis and Sonny Rollins and Coltrane and so many others. What were one or two of the mind-blowing evenings for you?

GORDON: What are the years when John Coltrane had The [Classic] Quartet?

FEINSTEIN: Around 1962 to '65.

GORDON: I'd say it was 1963 when we would go to the Half Note to hear John Coltrane, McCoy Tyner, Jimmy Garrison, and Elvin Jones, almost every night. The club was on Hudson Street and I would take a cab there from my apartment in the East Village and meet my friend Anita Evans. Somehow we always arrived at the same time. We never missed a night of the John Coltrane Quartet if we could help it. Talk about mind-blowing! Elvin totally changed everything. And those sets when they played tunes for over an hour . . . Jimmy Garrison would play solos for I don't even know how long. That was the thing about it: They were no longer concerned with how long a set is, or how long a tune should last. It didn't have [a required] time, so that changed my concept of time.

My son [Woody Louis Armstrong Shaw III] has that. One day at seven in the morning, I asked him, "Are you getting up or are you still up?" and he said, "Mom, it's a twenty-four-hour clock.

It's not nine to five," and I was like, "I *knew* that"—[Feinstein laughs]—but I'd forgotten because I'd gone back to graduate school with classes and deadlines.

But Trane took his time with that quartet. And he said to me once, "You *know* it's Elvin's band." And it wasn't a joke. It was, of course, the four of them together, but Elvin took the lead on moving to different rhythms. I'm not a musicologist; I certainly can't talk about the genius of Elvin Jones [in technical terms], but we know that he was. Elvin was a brilliant guy, interested in theology. ("You have to read this" and "Have you read this?" I'd say, "Theology? No—don't make me read it!")

In 1973 I went to Accra [the capital of Ghana], and I had brought LPs. At customs, the guy asked what they were for and I said they were gifts for my friends. I asked, "Do you like jazz?" and he said, "Oh yes, I like jazz. Wait here, I'm calling my brother. He will drive you where you're going." (I was traveling with a friend, and she was like, "What?! We don't know these people," and I said [nonchalantly], "He likes jazz.") So the brother comes, and he asks, "Can we stop at my house? There are some people there that love jazz, and we have a turntable. Can we play some of this before you go to your friend's house?" I said, "Yeah, of course." (I remember my friend saying, "Oh my God . . .") So we went, met his mother—and it was just like me with my old jazz friends. They put on one of the John Coltrane records where Elvin had a solo, and a guy said to me, "Oh—six drummers." I said, "No, just one drummer," so they put the needle back and broke it down: foot pedal, cymbals, and so on. They broke it down to six, and I said, "No, it's not six," but of course they didn't believe me. Then a man said, "What part of Africa is he from?" and I said, "He's from Pontiac, Michigan. He's American." The man said, "No, no. That's impossible." So I left the record there, and when I returned to the States I told Elvin—and he *loved* that story. Whenever I would hear him play, he would say to people, "Tell 'em what happened when you went to Africa. Six drummers."

FEINSTEIN: Your first job as road manager was with Gil Evans, right?

GORDON: Yeah, in the early seventies when he had a band with David Sanborn and Billy Harper. I would drive him; he said I was his Harry Carney—a great compliment. We went to California and the Midwest. Frankly, I didn't know what I was doing, but, like I always say, that's how you learn.

FEINSTEIN: How did all this begin?

GORDON: I always thank or blame Louis Hayes. We were sitting in Boomers, which was a great club in New York City, and George Gruntz from the Berlin Jazz Festival was there. He said, "Does anybody know somebody who can work with the Berlin Jazz Festival? I need a road manager," and Louis said, "Oh, Max can do it." This was for, like, fifty people! George said, "Oh really? Can we have lunch tomorrow? I was hoping to have someone who spoke German, but we could have lunch." I didn't know a word of German, but I borrowed a German dictionary and learned a phrase. So when I met him for lunch, I recited my one sentence in German: "Haben Sie ein Verlàngerungskabel, bitte?" That means, "Do you have an extension cord, please?" [Feinstein laughs.] Thank you. But you need to be able to say that as a road manager because the bass amp never has the right length cord, and George said, "You're hired!" [Both laugh.] So I went to Berlin and worked with Roberta Flack and all the big artists. And Lou—Louis Hayes—will sometimes say, "You know, you wouldn't've met Dexter if I hadn't gotten you that first gig," and I'll say, "Thank you. I hear you." Now he's eighty-one, and he implored me for a year to be his tour manager when he signed with Blue Note; I'm going at the end of the month to Chicago with his band. He's like, "I need someone to travel with the band," and I said, "I'll get you someone. I retired in 1983." He said, "I don't care. I don't want someone I don't know, who doesn't know what they're doing." I couldn't say no.

~

FEINSTEIN: This is a first for me: In all the interviews that I've conducted, I've always read—with great care—the main work that's going to be discussed, but your biography [*Sophisticated*

Giant: The Life and Legacy of Dexter Gordon] won't be released for another couple of months, and, obviously, I haven't read it. But I know the project began with notes that Dexter made with the thought of writing an autobiography. He died in 1990. About how long had he been working on that?

GORDON: Not long. It was after the [1986] movie *Round Midnight* [in which he played the lead and received an Academy Award nomination]. We were living in Cuernavaca, and he'd been approached to do a book. His idea was to do it with James Baldwin, but when he called, Baldwin said, "You know, I'm not well. Just write the book." The second person he thought of was the playwright Wesley Brown. Do you know him?

FEINSTEIN: Yes, in fact he's recently appeared in *Brilliant Corners* [Winter 2011 and Summer 2015].

GORDON: He came to Mexico, and Dexter liked him. He had refused to fight in Vietnam and went to jail. But eventually Dexter said, "You know, I think I'll just do it myself."

    His idea was to write it in the third person about a character named Society Red, and he started thinking in those terms. He would write vignettes about things that happened to the character; he would handwrite them and then I would type them up on a little Olivetti. And one day I said, "I think you should have an outline." He said, "I don't want an outline. I'm not writing a book in chronological order; I don't want a timeline. I'm just writing my thoughts about what happens to the character." I said, "Trust me, it'll be easier"—not that I was right, but I was adamant, and that was something between us. I would give ten logical reasons why he should do something, and he would either say, "No, I'm not doing it," and that was over, or he'd say, "Okay, I'll *consider* it." He never would exactly agree with me. [Feinstein laughs.] He would consider or refuse, and on this he would consider, and he started making an outline, which I still have. He got to '48, and then he went to '60. He was always leaving the fifties out. He had what he wanted in the book and what he *didn't* want in the book: he didn't want anything about jail or drugs. And before he died, he said, "If I don't finish it, you finish the book," and I was like, "Yeah, sure, no problem." Who knew?

He was an avid reader, although he read what I call trash and he called thrillers.

FEINSTEIN: And J. P. Donleavy's [1955 novel] *The Ginger Man* was a favorite.

GORDON: Right, and that's not trash.

FEINSTEIN: Why do you think he liked *The Ginger Man* so much?

GORDON: That's something that's in the book. I had two people—one who knew Donleavy, and an old college friend—write about why they thought he loved *The Ginger Man*, because he knew it by heart. He had more than one copy. I think [he liked the book] because the character was so badly behaved, and to him it was so funny. The drinking culture. All that. Do you have a favorite book?

FEINSTEIN: No.

GORDON: Me neither. So for someone to have a favorite book . . . It *could* go back to him being a librarian in jail and having a limited number of books. He read some over and over. But I was trying to figure out when he would have first gotten a copy of it, because it was banned at first, right?

FEINSTEIN: Yes it was [both in the United States and Ireland].

GORDON: So I would think he got it in Europe in '62. But what I try not to do in the book is to put what *I* think over what he did.

FEINSTEIN: I understand that, but nobody knew him better. So I'm curious, for example, why you think he chose to write his autobiography from the point of view of a *character*.

GORDON: [Laughs.] Society Red. He thought of himself . . . The guy on the stage and the guy who went on the road was a separate person from the guy who read books and liked to stay home. He didn't like to socialize unless he had to. He loved baseball. He liked his poached egg a certain way. He could spend a lot of time alone and could easily take care of himself. But the public personality was someone else. He *loved* being a jazz musician, but what it takes—practice, travel, everything—is very hard work. He used to say, "I don't know why they call it 'play,' or 'playing music.' This is work; we're working at this."

He wrote the tune "Society Red" for himself, and he was going to call the book *The Saga of Society Red* because when he reflected on his life, he looked at it as a saga. How did this kid, who couldn't play that well, get a job playing with Lionel Hampton? Here was this kid hanging around Count Basie who'd talk about Lester Young and people he idolized. (When Basie did a reunion band—I think it was around 1980—Dexter asked if he could join. "Can I sit in Lester's chair? You don't have to pay me. You don't have to announce that it's me." And Count Basie said, "It's too late. There's only one bandleader in this band," and he made a joke—"You're doin' fine.") But he thought of himself as being very fortunate.

FEINSTEIN: Do you think his ability to separate his personal and public personas was one of the reasons why he really liked his acting gigs?

GORDON: Absolutely. He also said that many musicians could *easily* have worked as actors. Surely Billy Eckstine. *Many* were hilariously funny, like Harry "Sweets" [Edison]. Wayne Shorter does voices/characters. They could easily have had that career also. So when he got the opportunity, he didn't really think it was a stretch. He felt that when you go onstage you're acting.

FEINSTEIN: I know in interviews you're primarily asked about his acting roles in *Round Midnight* and, to a lesser extent, *Awakenings*, but I have to add this: one of my all-time favorite TV shows was *Crime Story* [where Dexter Gordon starred in the episode "Moulin Rouge"].

GORDON: No kidding?! You know, when people ask what I can talk about for lectures or interviews, I *always* put that in there, and they never let me talk about it!

FEINSTEIN: I loved the series even though it only lasted for two seasons [1986–1988].

GORDON: [Directed by] Michael Mann. The writing was so great!

FEINSTEIN: Were you around during the shooting?

GORDON: Oh yeah! It was in Las Vegas. So many weird things happened. But the Moulin Rouge was where Wardell Gray was working when he died [in 1955]. It was a total flashback, and they used that place in *Crime Story*. That was our set . . .

FEINSTEIN: Wow.

GORDON: I can't believe you know that series!

FEINSTEIN: Dexter was absolutely marvelous. Stole every scene.

GORDON: Thank you. You know, when he got that offer, he said, "I've been wanting to go there [to Las Vegas] and find out what happened to Wardell." This was 1987, and I said, "I don't think there will be people living who will remember 1955 and what went down there," but he was like, "Don't count it out." And when we got there, the doorman in that episode had been there. He said, "Hey, Dex!" and Dexter said, "What happened to Wardell?" and I can't repeat what he said but he named somebody who'd been with Wardell. He said that he'd OD'd but he wasn't dead. They didn't want to call the police or the hospital because then they would come and find the drugs—heroin. And they drove him into the desert and broke his neck when they dumped him out of the car. He *named* the guy, and Dexter was like, "I *knew* it was that motherfucker." (He had heard that he [Gray] had been messing with some Mafia guy's wife, but that wasn't it.) He said, "I'm glad I came and cleared that up."

    He had told [the director of *Round Midnight*] Bertrand Tavernier, "I'm not dying on the screen," but there [in *Crime Story*] he gets shot. He said, "Okay." [Gordon laughs.] Michael Mann is so wonderful, and he was a big fan of Dexter's. He had plans for him, had Dexter lived.

FEINSTEIN: Your biography has been percolating for a while and was originally going to be titled *Dexter Calling*. Why did that change?

GORDON: You'll have to ask the University of California Press. They had reasons I didn't agree with, but you can't win every battle.

FEINSTEIN: No you can't—and *Sophisticated Giant* is a great title, too. What were some of the most difficult aspects of taking his start and turning it into your biography?

GORDON: I had to go to graduate school. You know what that is. [Laughs.] I had no idea. I thought, "Oh, that'll be great. I'll go to graduate school and study African American history so I can write about Dexter Gordon. It'll be six years, and I'll just read books and take courses." I didn't know about academia—and then I realized I was better off in the music business. The people in academia were not who I thought they would be. I mean, I don't want to trash academia . . . and I was very lucky to meet brilliant scholars who love jazz.

FEINSTEIN: Robin [D. G.] Kelley, for example.

GORDON: He was my PhD advisor. And I met Farah [Jasmine] Griffin and Fred Moten and Brent Edwards. Those are people who are in academia but rise above the constraints.

FEINSTEIN: In the acknowledgments of Robin's fabulous Monk biography [*Thelonious Monk: The Life and Times of an American Original*, 2009], he thanks his research assistants and adds, "especially Maxine Gordon, whose deep ties to the jazz world proved more valuable than tracking down articles."

GORDON: Oh, did he? I never read that. [Laughs.] Thank you, Robin!

FEINSTEIN: How did you connect him to the jazz world?

GORDON: First of all, I did the research on the section [in his book] on San Juan Hill. But people wouldn't talk to him at first because he's not in the "jazz police," as I call them: an inner circle that likes to keep people out. Have you experienced that?

FEINSTEIN: I must say I've always been treated warmly.

GORDON: Really? Well, you do poetry so you're no threat. But they didn't know Robin. Dan Morgenstern [then the director of the Institute of Jazz Studies] said, "He never met Monk," and I said, "He also never met Marie Antoinette, and if he was writing about Marie Antoinette no one would have a problem with that." Dan laughed and said, "Oh . . . You might have a point." [Laughs.] I introduced Robin to Randy Weston—and then Randy opened so many doors. I just did what we do for people who are brilliant.

But the best part was to do that research on San Juan Hill and to learn how to do historical research.

FEINSTEIN: Skills that then fed your biography.

GORDON: I knew I couldn't write the book if I didn't study historical and research methods. I didn't want to write a linear book about Dexter Gordon, and Robin was very helpful with that. And his Monk book is great, isn't it?

FEINSTEIN: I think it's as good a jazz biography as any ever made.

GORDON: The best.

FEINSTEIN: What are your feelings about Stan Britt's biography [*Dexter Gordon: A Musical Biography*, 1989]?

GORDON: He's clearly a fan, and I'm happy when Dexter's music inspires writers. In fact, I'd like to talk about poems written about him, if that would be okay.

FEINSTEIN: Of course.

GORDON: I love Michael Harper [1938–2016].

FEINSTEIN: Michael was sitting right where you are now when I interviewed him for *Brilliant Corners* [Winter 2007].

GORDON: There's a second poem [in addition to Harper's "Dexter Leaps In" from *Honorable Amendments*, 1995] that he wrote for me ["Digesting Dexter Gordon at 80," later published in *Use Trouble*, 2009]. He said, "I only write one poem for a musician . . ."

FEINSTEIN: Oh, that's not true! But Michael could massage the truth.

GORDON: [Laughs.] I love the poems that he made, and I love Yusef Komunyakaa's poem, "February in Sydney." There are others that are not, you know . . . Jazz poetry is tough because they're not all that one would wish for.

FEINSTEIN: Absolutely, although that's true for any field.

GORDON: Right.

FEINSTEIN: I have Yusef's poem here:

> Dexter Gordon's tenor sax
> plays "April in Paris"
> inside my head all the way back
> on the bus from Double Bay.
> *Round Midnight*, the '50s,
> cool cobblestone streets
> resound footsteps of Bebop
> musicians with whiskey-laced voices
> from a boundless dream in French.
> Bud, Prez, Webster, & The Hawk,
> their names run together riffs.
> Painful gods jive talk through

> bloodstained reeds & shiny brass
> where music is an anesthetic.
> Unreadable faces from the human void
> float like torn pages across the bus
> windows. An old anger drips into my throat,
> & I try thinking something good,
> letting the precious bad
> settle to the salty bottom.
> Another scene keeps repeating itself:
> I emerge from the dark theatre,
> pass a woman who grabs her red purse
> & hugs it to her like a heart attack.
> Tremolo. Dexter comes back to rest
> behind my eyelids. A loneliness
> lingers like a silver needle
> under my black skin,
> as I try to feel how it is
> to scream for help through a horn.

What do you like about it?

GORDON: I love Yusef Komunyakaa's poetry. I first discovered him in *Neon Vernacular* [*New and Selected Poems*, 1993]. I can't remember where I saw the book or what made me pick it up but I was entranced with the way it was jazz on the page—not "jazz poetry" exactly but he smoothly refers to musicians and songs that I knew and it was so inside the music. Then I saw him work with Billy Bang, whom I interviewed for the Bronx African American History Project at Fordham (I am the senior interviewer and jazz researcher—don't be impressed by the title). Billy Bang's band Aftermath and Yusef Komunyakaa's work on Vietnam is so heartbreaking and so cathartic. When Billy Bang died, I went to his service at Benta's Funeral Home in Harlem. Vietnam veterans, some of whom were homeless and in trouble, spoke about how they could always go to Billy for help and he always was ready to help them. What Yusef can do with words and the way he inserts Dexter in the poem and how he uses the moment with the woman clutching her red pocketbook "like a heart attack" says so much about how the beauty of Dexter playing "April in Paris" can save us from the pain of living in a world where fear and hatred are always there.

FEINSTEIN: Amen. What do you think a lot of people get wrong about Dexter Gordon in their writing? Or, conversely, what are you trying to get *right* in your book?

GORDON: I'm trying to go beyond his career and his recordings. The joke [about Dexter's biography] used to be: he was born, his father was the first [African American] doctor in Los Angeles (which he wasn't), he went on the road with Lionel Hampton, signed with Dial Records, made the records, went to jail, and so on. What I'm trying to do is break the linear story—the story based on discography and the story based on hard times, like what happened to Charlie Parker. I mean, can we *stop* talking about Charlie Parker being a drug addict? He died in 1955. He's the most influential jazz artist after Louis Armstrong, and they're still talking about drugs.

FEINSTEIN: But I think Stanley [Crouch] did a fine job in his biography [*Kansas City Lightning: The Rise and Times of Charlie Parker*, 2013].

GORDON: Oh yeah, on the early life. Love that book. But people talk about that book instead of quoting Stanley talk about all that other stuff. So I'm trying to emphasize what Dexter said: "My life has a happy ending"—which sounds corny, in a way, but he always said that in interviews because he *really* didn't like what they did to Billie Holiday, even Coleman Hawkins . . . Not that I didn't have to insert the fifties, which he was leaving out. As I said, his outline went from '48 to '60, and I said, "You're leaving out a *decade*?" And he smiled: "It's my life." I said, "You can't leave out a decade," and he said, "If you want it in the book, write it your damn self." Those were his exact words. And that [chapter] took me a really long time to write: to get the records from prison, to interview Hadley Caliman as the main source. (They were in Chino prison together; that whole chapter is really his chapter.) I don't mean to sound as though it was "hard" to write the book because I'm grateful that I was able to live long enough to finish it. [Laughs.] But it was difficult to research, and that chapter was a bitch.

FEINSTEIN: It must be awfully difficult to explore the darker periods of his life, but to leave them out would have been a mistake.

GORDON: Of course. And I think when he said, "If you want it in the book, write it your damn self," he knew I would write about it.

FEINSTEIN: Were there observations or revelations in his writing that startled you?

GORDON: Not from his writing but from the research. He left out stuff that he never mentioned—which was something he did: if it was negative, he left it out. I knew he got arrested in Paris because he had a letter from the government giving him permission to reenter. He said something like, "Oh, I had a problem in Paris once"—but none of the details. He got arrested, put in jail. It's in the book. Letters he wrote about that. He also had a girlfriend [Lotte Nielsen] who died, which is a very sad story. I saw this picture (it's always a photograph, right?) and showed it to his best friend in Copenhagen, [the journalist Leonard] "Skip" Malone, who said, "Don't open that door. Walk away from that. Leave it alone." Then, of course, I wouldn't. I read mysteries—do you know John Harvey's writing?

FEINSTEIN: Yes. In fact I interviewed him about a year ago for *Brilliant Corners* [Summer 2017].

GORDON: Oh! Love him! Anyway, I'm not going to "walk away," and what I learned about her was very sad. I said to Skip, "He never mentioned her," and Skip said, "No, he wouldn't." (Another friend from Copenhagen said, "I don't think you should put that in the book 'cause Dexter wouldn't've wanted it," but, too late!)

FEINSTEIN: Well, it's part of who he *was*, how he lived.

GORDON: Right. But you know there are some people who only want the good to be told. "Could we all just get along?" I always hated that.

FEINSTEIN: You're now working on another book, this time on four remarkable women in jazz: Melba Liston, Velma Middleton, Maxine Sullivan, and your great friend Shirley Scott.

GORDON: Yes. And today being the day that Aretha Franklin died, I was thinking how she's part of this story of these women who dedicate their lives to making other lives better. Totally unselfish. None of them made any money, and they worked *so* hard. So hard. And, you know, Velma did buy a house in the Bronx; I don't want it to sound like they struggled for nothing. And you've heard that video where she's talking about Louis Armstrong—twenty years on the road, and she loved him—but nobody knows who she is. I don't like that. I don't.

FEINSTEIN: That's true for Velma Middleton. It's also true, frankly, for Shirley Scott. She's marginally discussed compared to [male jazz organists like] Jimmy Smith, Larry Young, Brother Jack McDuff, and so many others—but *damn* could she play!

GORDON: Right? And she could write, too. One of the things I want to do for the book is look at her album covers because her image was totally controlled by record companies. She never looked the same twice, and nobody ever recognized her in public. Remember the blond hair? And then she had, like Aretha in a way, the turban. She had the straight hair, she had the Afro, makeup, costumes. They didn't know what to do. She made an album in 1974, which is going to be reissued, *One for Me* (which she and I paid for) on Strata-East. Harold Vick, Billy Higgins, and her [and Jimmy Hopps on cowbell]. She wrote most of the material (I think she used two of Vick's tunes). We paid for the recording and everything she wanted—the mix, everything. But that was the first time ever that she did what *she* wanted to do.

FEINSTEIN: So how far along are you with the book?

GORDON: I'm on the proposal! [Both laugh.] No, I have research on all of them. I found an oral history on Maxine Sullivan at the Institute of Jazz Studies. It's seven hundred pages, and they're not digitized so it's printed out. I have it—because I want to use their own words. And with Melba it's a bit tricky because Melba didn't like to do interviews. I might write about her childhood when she came to Los Angeles. In junior high she was already better than anyone else.

FEINSTEIN: It would be wonderful to get this book out, and it seems to be the right time. We are, I think, getting better at striking a better gender balance in jazz studies.

GORDON: Slightly better. In jazz, I'm a little concerned, now that they've opened up the discussion of gender, that they isolate the women from the history, you know what I mean? To put them over *here* instead of their contributions from within.

FEINSTEIN: It's a similar issue for the women who were part of the Black Arts Movement.

GORDON: Of course. And the civil rights movement. Like my sister-in-law said, "Who did the cooking (and the organizing and the typing) and held it together?" Black Arts Movement, Panthers—it's very similar. But these young women jazz musicians, like Terri Lyne [Carrington], are standing up. It's very good.

FEINSTEIN: What was the delay in getting your Dexter bio published?

GORDON: I got the deal before the book was what I wanted it to be. Amiri Baraka was going to do a Max Roach book; I was doing the Dexter book. Amiri's idea was that we'd go on the road together. "We'll sell a lot of books. You'll interview me, I'll interview you." He had a plan. [Feinstein laughs.] Chris Calhoun was his agent—he got Chris for me—but when it was sold, I thought, "I don't like that book as described in the proposal. I have an idea." Chris was like, "Oh, great . . ." So the book I've written is not the book I set out to write. It's totally different.

Feinstein: But you're pleased?

Gordon: [Long pause.] I have stuff I would change . . . [Laughs.] But, yeah, in general I'm pleased. I think Dexter would be pleased.

Feinstein: Well, Maxine, I congratulate you, and I thank you so much for taking the time to speak with me. You know, the word on the street was that you were only accepting interviews from women or African Americans—[Gordon laughs loudly]—and I was willing to be either or both. [Gordon claps her hands. Both laugh.]

Gordon: When the press person from the University of California Press saw that in an interview, she said, "Oh my God . . . Did you really say that? What are we gonna do?" and I thought, "Oh dear." But it'll be good because the "jazz police" will be offended, and then they won't review it or . . . I know where the bad reviews are coming from already. I believe that certain people who write about jazz will have a problem with the book because it doesn't have enough about music, and because in the index I mention every name of every musician of every band. Someone has already said, "Why would she do that?" Well, because somewhere they have a relative. What is it they say on photos? "Unknown." That has always bothered me. Could we try harder? Or, at least, "Not yet identified; please come forward." That's one of the things Dexter said: Everybody in the band was just as important. Just because they didn't give up their families and go on the road doesn't mean they didn't play as well (or better). He used to say, "There's a lot of guys workin' on the railroad, and redcaps, who play much better than me. Luckily, they didn't come out here!" He never thought he played better than somebody you've never heard of. He used to say, "I'm tall. Of course I get gigs." [Both laugh.] "I look good."

So they're not going to like that. They're not going to like that it's Afrocentric. Black cultural history. I've had that before where they've said, "Oh, she went to college and studied black history and now she's 'too black.'" Okay, fine, sorry about that; it *is* black culture . . . And finally it'll be who I left out. But I say to people, "*Please* don't let this be the last book on Dexter Gordon." I said to Jimmy Heath, "Why aren't people writing about Dexter?" and he said, "They're waiting for *your* book. You've got to hurry!"

6

The Culture of Jazz

Farah Jasmine Griffin

Farah Jasmine Griffin is the author of *"Who Set You Flowin'?" The African-American Migration Narrative*; *Beloved Sisters and Loving Friends: Letters from Rebecca Primus of Royal Oak, Maryland, and Addie Brown of Hartford, Connecticut, 1854–1868*; *If You Can't Be Free, Be a Mystery: In Search of Billie Holiday*; *Harlem Nocturne: Women Artists & Progressive Politics during World War II*; and (with Salim Washington) *Clawing at the Limits of Cool: Miles Davis, John Coltrane, and the Greatest Jazz Collaboration Ever*. For theatrical productions, she has collaborated with many jazz luminaries, including Geri Allen, Dianne Reeves, and Terri Lyne Carrington. At Columbia University, she is chair of the African American and African Diaspora Studies Department, affiliate faculty of the Center for Jazz Studies, director of the Institute for Research in African American Studies, and the William B. Ransford Professor of English & Comparative Literature and African American Studies.

The following excerpts from Griffin's writings have been reprinted with permission. The interview was conducted on October 13, 2020, via the internet.

If You Can't Be Free, Be a Mystery (excerpt)

My mother named me Farah Jasmine; my father nicknamed me Jazzy. While my mother's choice was inspired by Moslem royalty, Empress Farah Diba and Princess Yasmin Khan, my father's was as much a tribute to the music he loved as a diminutive of Jasmine. Farah Jasmine was the name into which I would grow. Jazzy is the name by which I was called throughout my early life. At first, only those who knew me in an "official" capacity—teachers, doctors, classmates—called me Farah. "Jazzy" is home, South Philly, double-dutch, glamorous aunts, hip uncles and Daddy.

My father's pantheon of jazz geniuses included Charlie Parker, Miles Davis, Frank Morgan, John Coltrane and Billie Holiday. Of these, I claimed Miles and Billie as my own. Though it seems I have known about her my entire life, my fascination with her surfaced following my father's death in 1972, when I was nine years old. Along with his closets full of paperbacks, notebooks and albums, I inherited his lower lip, his political sensibilities and his passion for "the" music, "our" music—jazz.

Clawing at the Limits of Cool, Cowritten with Salim Washington (excerpt)

[Miles] Davis and [John] Coltrane were critically aware of the political environment they inhabited. And each would come to be representative of a more rebellious side of the supposedly conformist fifties. Serious, intelligent young black men: articulate, confident, refusing the antics of earlier entertainers and self-consciously affirming the complexity and unique universality of black art forms. It is in this national context that we must place the first incarnation of Miles Davis's legendary quintet. The group, including Trane, played for the first time in September 1955 in Baltimore, Maryland, a city that sat just south of the Mason-Dixon Line, but one that had an established jazz scene—after all, it is the city that produced the venerable Lady Day—and a solid African American working-class community.

"Literary Lady" (excerpt)

A number of black women writers have been inspired by [Billie] Holiday. For two of them, Gayl Jones and Ntozake Shange, Holiday is a muse/ancestor figure whose appearance sparks their protagonists to reflect upon and evaluate their own artistic commitment. Ursa Corregidora of Gayl Jones's first novel, *Corregidora*, is herself a blues woman who undergoes a hysterectomy after an act of domestic violence. Ursa's voice is often described in terms fitting

Holiday's. . . . The grain of her voice, like Holiday's, gains texture from her lived experience—the joy as well as the tragedy . . .

In Ntozake Shange's *Sassafrass, Cypress & Indigo*, Lady Day is a literal ancestor/muse appearing before the aspiring writer, Sassafrass, who has been neglecting her own work for her love, Mitch—a jazz musician. Such neglect prompts a visitation from Lady Day, who reminds the young artist that she and women like her, including Bessie Smith and Josephine Baker, may have been sad because they had the blues but they were also joyful because they had their songs. Consequently, their songs were not the embodiment of their sadness but instead a means of exorcising it.

Harlem Nocturne (excerpt)

[Mary Lou] Williams had a long-standing interest in the zodiac. At this stage in her life she hungered for spiritual meaning and guidance, but she did not have a sense of religiosity. For her, music was a spiritual medium, a conduit to something outside of herself as well as a vehicle for expressing a sense of the spiritual, if not the divine. She operated in a secular world, that of jazz and show business, yet the jazz world itself was nonetheless characterized by its own expressions of the spirit. Surprisingly, Williams found community in the context of New York night life, a world in which sex, drugs, and money were in great supply. But the scene also provided fellowship, warmth, love, and transcendence. She would later write: "Jazz is a spiritual music. It's the suffering that gives jazz its spiritual dimension." For Williams, black music offered transcendence by directly confronting and acknowledging human suffering. This was the source of its spiritual power, for suffering and our longing for transcendence from it are what join us as humans. She believed black music to be a gift to all humankind because it provided a way through pain and suffering to beauty and joy.

Interview

> Sascha Feinstein: I'm still so moved by what you wrote in *If You Can't Be Free, Be a Mystery* about becoming immersed in jazz because of your father's death in 1972 when you were only nine. Could you talk about your experience going through his LPs?

FARAH JASMINE GRIFFIN: Sure. It's interesting because I just finished a book this summer [*Read Until You Understand: The Profound Wisdom of Black Life and Literature*] that goes into all of that more deeply. I grew up [in Philadelphia] listening to the music because he was playing it all the time. I remember those album covers from Blue Note and Columbia Records—the red and black on the labels of Miles's albums, and all of that—and after he died, his music and his books were the things that were in the house. I knew he was a jazz fan, so I wanted to hear what he listened to. I tried to read his books. And I started to develop my own taste. I knew he liked certain musicians, like Billie Holiday, so I listened to them, and out of all the things I listened to, I liked Billie Holiday the most. It was a way to learn more about him and to access him in some ways.

FEINSTEIN: Is there a reason why, in the book, you don't tell the reader how he died [at forty-six]?

GRIFFIN: I tell it in this book that's coming out. It was fairly traumatic. He had a stroke—the second stroke that he had. Police were called to our home, and they thought he was drunk.

FEINSTEIN: Oh no . . .

GRIFFIN: So they took a while to take him to the hospital. But he was not drunk, and, you know, with a stroke you have to act very quickly. He lived for exactly a week after he was brought to the hospital, but he never really regained consciousness. I lived with this, but I just wasn't ready to tell the story until recently.

FEINSTEIN: I was curious largely because you say you came to realize that Billie Holiday had very much been victimized and that you felt the same way about your father.

GRIFFIN: My father struggled with addiction through part of his life, but it wasn't something that was known; he was what you might call a functional addict, going to work and all that. It wasn't something talked about, but I was curious, and I could learn about this through the musicians. He was also a very intellectually gifted man, and I felt that, had he lived in a different time, he would have been able to realize his gifts in ways that he was not during his own lifetime.

FEINSTEIN: I don't want to focus on the losses in your life, but I'd love to hear about your experiences with [pianist] Geri Allen [1957–2017]. What was it like working with her?

GRIFFIN: Geri was always trying to find a way to include people. She thrived on collaboration and community, and there were many ways that she tried to encourage me to collaborate with her. She would say, "Your writing is very musical, so I want you to read from the Billie Holiday book while I play behind you," and I'm, like, "It's not that kind of book, Geri. It's not a poem." [Both laugh.] But there I was, at one point, onstage, reading.

[In 2011,] I was often in the studio with her. She was making the Christmas album [*A Child Is Born*], which I really wanted her to do because she loved Christmas music and it's one of only three albums where she plays solo piano. [Griffin wrote the liner notes for Allen's first solo album, *Flying toward the Sound*, 2008—SF.] She said, "I want you to write a spoken word and read it over this," and I said, "No, get a spoken-word artist to do it. I'm not doing that." I go to the studio, and she says, "Okay, just say this phrase, over and over and over again." [Laughs.] So I say, about ten times, "We're gonna take this journey" [on the cut "Journey to Bethlehem"]. She was always trying to find a way to get me involved; she knew how much I loved the music.

She fooled me into the first collaboration. She said, "I have this commission from The Apollo"—they had an NEH grant or something—"and we need a historical consultant. Would you be that consultant?" So I said, "Sure. Of course." She said, "Okay. [S.] Epatha Merkerson, the actor, is going to help me stage some things, so why don't we all meet." So we met on a Wednesday afternoon in Epatha's apartment in Harlem, sitting around the kitchen table.

FEINSTEIN: How cool.

GRIFFIN: It was *so* cool. We were just talking, and Epatha would pull up the music, and we outlined a narrative for Geri's show. And at the end of that, Geri said, "I'm going to need a writer, so you [Farah] can write it," and she said to Epatha, "I'm going to need a director, so you can direct it." Epatha and I talk about this all the time: it's something that we both wanted to do—Epatha wanted to branch out into directing, and I wanted to write more creatively—but I would never have thought to do it. It was Geri who, because she was an improviser, loved throwing me out there without a net.

FEINSTEIN: That's a wonderful story. She was a remarkable artist. How did you two first meet?

GRIFFIN: I was a fan—*fan* is the word—in graduate school. I would come to New York to hear her whenever she was playing. At the time, I was dating someone who was writing an article about [the Brooklyn musical collective] M-Base for *Smithsonian* magazine, so he and I would go to all their concerts, and their individual performances, too, and Geri was just my favorite. I followed her and went to hear her all the time and bought all her albums.

Then there was a conference organized by Dwight Andrews in March 2005, at Emory University honoring [the composer] William Dawson. Geri and I were two of the speakers (she also performed). Early in the morning, I went to the room where my session was to be held to get a sense of the setup, and she was sitting there—and I had this total girl-crush moment. [Feinstein laughs.] "Oh my God, that's Geri Allen . . . Okay, I'm not going to bother her because I don't want to be one of *those* people. But, oh my God, that's Geri Allen." And then she looked at me and said, "Oh—you're the lady who wrote this book," and she pulled out the Billie Holiday book, and I said, "Yup, that's me." [Laughs.]

After that, we became close friends. She was in Montclair [New Jersey]; I was in New York. We'd go out to hear music together all the time. We spent holidays together. A friendship just unfolded.

FEINSTEIN: Since *If You Can't Be Free, Be a Mystery* came out in 2001, several books on Billie Holiday have been published, and I was hoping you might comment on a couple of them. I'm thinking first of all about Julia Blackburn's *With Billie* [2005], where you're warmly quoted.

GRIFFIN: I loved that book. She's such an incredible writer. I thought the book was very creative. She had access to an archive—Linda Kuehl, who conducted all of those marvelous interviews [with people reflecting on Billie Holiday]—and basically made first-person narratives out of them, which is something that I would not have done as a scholar. I thought it was remarkable. I can't say I "enjoy" the book because so much of it is so painful, but it's something I dip into and out of, over and over again; I really appreciate it, and I learned things about Billie Holiday that I did not know.

FEINSTEIN: Weren't the Kuehl archives the tapes that you had wanted to include in your book but couldn't afford?

GRIFFIN: Yes. I was a young assistant professor [at the University of Pennsylvania], and I think that the person who owned the rights assumed that anyone writing about Billie Holiday would have a huge advance, but I didn't. At the time, I didn't even have the research funds to pay for that kind of access. But, much later on, he did cut the fees for many of the photographs that I was able to use.

    I think many of the things that have come out since I wrote my book are much better than the ones that came out before.

FEINSTEIN: How about John Szwed's book, *Billie Holiday: The Musician and the Myth* [2015]?

GRIFFIN: John is someone I admire so much. I love his books on musicians; I think of them as his trilogy: the book on Miles [*So What*], the book on Sun Ra [*Space Is the Place*], and the book on Lady Day. He always seems to strike the right balance between the kind of context that produces the musicians and their musicianship. He raises the politics of music without being didactic or polemic. [In *Billie Holiday*,] he tells, truthfully, the story of her life without making her only a perpetual victim.

    Julia's book, his book, and *Billie Holiday: The Last Interview and Other Conversations* [2019]: those three together are a nice, solid body of work on her.

FEINSTEIN: I remember John telling me, after the Miles book was published, that he was a little disappointed—that he felt he hadn't fully captured the enormous spirit of Miles Davis.

GRIFFIN: That's interesting . . . I don't know if it's possible to capture someone like Miles Davis. He's such an elusive figure, and the closest we *think* we come is in Quincy's book [*Miles: The Autobiography*, written with Quincy Troupe] because it's told in Miles's voice, right? All autobiographies make you feel as though you've gotten it [directly from the source], but even there you've gotten only a version of it.

FEINSTEIN: A lot of people—including those we both admire, like the late Michael Harper—have been very critical of the Miles Davis autobiography because they insist that Quincy Troupe simply made up a lot of the material.

GRIFFIN: I've heard people say that, and I've heard other people say that he plagiarized material. It's funny: I still think that book is a classic in the genre, maybe because Quincy has a very good ear. I listened to the tapes of his interviews with Miles, which he generously donated to the Schomburg. Much of the time, I think so-called autobiographies are actually public performances, especially those of artists, and they're often inaccurate. [Both laugh.] And it takes a scholar, or someone who's not trying to write in the voice of the musician, to step back and give us that context and that truth.

    I'm teaching a course right now with the subtitle "The Art and Method of Writing Biography." My students and I are trying to discover that, and if it's about someone who's written an autobiography, *inevitably* the autobiography is more compelling and interesting than the biography—yet the biographer, I think, is beholden to a higher standard.

FEINSTEIN: In your Billie Holiday book, and in your notes for *Lady Day: The Complete Billie Holiday on Columbia 1933–1944*, you single out some poems about her that you admire, and I thought we could talk a bit more about them. Regarding the most famous of them—Frank O'Hara's "The Day Lady Died"—you point out that most of it is an accounting of "mundane minutiae of a city dweller." Why do you think O'Hara included all that "minutiae"?

GRIFFIN: That poem—oh my God. That poem is still one of my favorite ones. I can't say why he made that aesthetic choice, but, for me, it puts us right there. It gives us the texture of the city, and a picture of who he is. The persona is a New Yorker who's kind of cosmopolitan because he wants to know what the poets are doing in Ghana. You want to be that person, right? You want to smoke *those* kinds of cigarettes [Gauloises]. He's hip, and you're going along, inhabiting this person's life—which, for the reader, was a fantasy—and therefore, when you get to those last lines, it knocks you off your feet (just like it knocks him off his feet). There's the newspaper with her face on it. He has brought you along on that journey so you know exactly what it's like. It's absolutely brilliant. That poem and Rita Dove's "Canary" are my two favorites.

FEINSTEIN: He *is* very hip and cosmopolitan—but he's also an outsider. The bank teller always checks his balance to make sure he's good for the withdrawal; he's going to a dinner hosted by people he doesn't know. Do you think that has something to do with the importance of Billie Holiday in his life: that she sang to the people who were *not* in the fold, as it were?

GRIFFIN: Right. That's her audience. Not only does she sing *to* them but she sings *for* them. This is true of many artists: the people who are listening and rooting for them are rooting for themselves. In this case, she is representing his marginality, too.

She was someone who poets were drawn to, and maybe for that very reason that you're talking about. She's a poet herself, and poets are drawn to her as a subject, as a muse.

FEINSTEIN: You've written more than once that you admire Amiri Baraka's "The Lady." The predominant image in that very short poem is that of a whorehouse. Does that trouble you at all?

GRIFFIN: No . . . No. If we go back to the Julia Blackburn book, she talks to all the people who knew Lady Day in the brothels in Baltimore, where there's some question about what her relationship to those brothels was. (Was she working there? Cleaning? What was she doing?) And I thought about Toulouse-Lautrec—the fact that he liked being in the nightlife, and he painted and found inspiration not only in the girls who were cancan dancers but those who were, possibly, prostitutes.

If you think about New Orleans, the brothel is not only the site where there is an exchange for sex but also a site that generates creativity and artistry as well. And I believe one has to be taught to think of it in that way, and to read it in that way.

FEINSTEIN: You also praise the poet Betsy Sholl, especially her poem "Don't Explain." Betsy just completed a poem about Robert Johnson, and she said to me that she had concerns about being a white woman writing about an African American man. What are your thoughts about those concerns?

GRIFFIN: Well, I appreciate her having them, frankly, because so many people think that they can write about anything without *any* concerns, right? So the fact that she has concerns seems right—but that doesn't mean it should be off-limits, at least from my perspective. As a writer, you can write sensitively about . . . The world is really yours to make. The question is simply how do you go about doing it?

I really liked writing that chapter ["Dark Lady of the Sonnets" in *If You Can't Be Free, Be a Mystery*]. There were all those poets, who were very different in terms of race and gender and all of those things, for whom Billie Holiday had *meant* something, something deep.

~

FEINSTEIN: You cowrote *Clawing at the Limits of Cool: Miles Davis, John Coltrane, and the Greatest Jazz Collaboration Ever* with the saxophonist Salim Washington. Your voices have been completely braided. How did *your* collaboration work?

GRIFFIN: I cherished that collaboration. Someone had reached out to Salim because he had read a piece that Salim wrote and liked the idea of a musician/writer doing the book. Then Salim asked me [to join him] because he felt more comfortable with me writing. And: I loved Miles and he loved Trane, so he invited me to do it with him.

We divided the initial labor. I sketched out the narrative arc. I wrote the Miles stuff; he wrote the Trane stuff. I did the cultural history and biography, and he did the musical analyses. But even though we divided it up that way, it wasn't like, "Oh, this is my expertise and therefore you don't touch it." We'd write those sections and then exchange them, adding what we had to add. Then, finally, I went through the manuscript to smooth it all out. It really was a back-and-forth collaboration, with no such thing as, "You don't have anything to add to this part of it," just trying to make it as seamless as possible.

I learned *so* much writing that book. We had these long, wonderful interviews with people, and two of the people who were so generous and really helped shape it were Stanley Crouch and Amiri Baraka.

FEINSTEIN: Wow. How did they help you shape it?

GRIFFIN: Well, we set up interviews with all kinds of people, and I think that we knew Baraka was going to shape it because he basically taught me how to listen to Trane—reading him talking about Trane. And we had already picked the title, which comes from a Baraka poem ["AM/TRAK"].

FEINSTEIN: Right.

GRIFFIN: We interviewed Amiri—he wore an ascot, I remember—who had *known* Trane, known him and loved him. Listening to his stories really gave us a sense of who he was as a person. That helped shape the book more than any particular nugget of information.

But we wanted to interview Stanley, too, so we met at an Italian restaurant down in the Village where he was like an old-school patriarch, holding court. [Both laugh.] One of the things that he said was that you had to think about where Miles and Trane came from. They're both born in the late twenties, coming of age in the thirties and forties. You had to think about what they had in common. So we thought about their fathers, and then it made me think about their grandfathers—which is why that book opens up with the grandfathers' generation: the Reconstruction generation, the Booker T. Washington generation, the building black institutions generation. That helped me see where their sense of self came from. So Stanley was largely responsible for helping me rethink a starting point.

FEINSTEIN: And Stanley was rather brilliant at integrating cultural history. I'm thinking especially of his book on Bird [*Kansas City Lightning: The Rise and Times of Charlie Parker*].

GRIFFIN: Oh God—right? Absolutely. That's what he does so well. He knows the history, but he also knows how to create and shape the narrative. A storyteller.

FEINSTEIN: In a more recent book of yours, *Harlem Nocturne*, you have a chapter on Mary Lou Williams. In your mind, how does it expand the work by Linda Dahl [*Morning Glory: A Biography of Mary Lou Williams*]?

GRIFFIN: I discovered so much about Mary Lou because of Linda Dahl. I knew *of* her; I knew who she was. But she was not someone who was in my father's pantheon, so I hadn't pursued her.

When I was writing the Billie Holiday book and reading everything I could that was written about anybody [in jazz], I read Linda Dahl's biography. (I had already read her earlier book, *Stormy Weather: The Music and Lives of a Century of Jazzwomen*.) And I understood that she had done it—she had written the biography—and I was not going to write a biography. But I was interested in this period of time and this place [New York in the 1940s]. I had all these different women who could have been in this book [in addition to Williams, Pearl Primus, and Ann Petry]. I initially decided *not* to do Mary Lou because (1) Linda Dahl had done such a good job, and (2) I just found her so hard! [Laughs.] I remember telling Salim, "Out of all the women, I'm not going to do Mary Lou because she's just too complicated."

FEINSTEIN: Complicated and hard in what ways?

GRIFFIN: The music. I just thought, "I can't do this," and I remember him saying to me, "Then that's why you should do it." And he was right, because then you learn something.

Linda Dahl was a starting point, and she gave me a map of where to look for things. I went back through and over some of her sources, and other things were revealed. Then Tammy Kernodle's book [*Soul on Soul: The Life and Music of Mary Lou Williams*] came out shortly thereafter, and then I began a friendship with Father Peter O'Brien [director of the Mary Lou Williams Foundation], who opened up everything and made it available to me.

FEINSTEIN: Your friend and colleague, Brent Edwards, has a chapter on Mary Lou Williams—"Zoning Mary Lou Williams Zoning"—in his recent book, *Epistrophies: Jazz and the Literary Imagination*. Can you talk about that chapter, or the book in general?

GRIFFIN: I think Brent is a brilliant critic. He has a way of seeing, and a way of approaching people and things, and thinking about musicians as writers—he's unique. He's a critic, but he's also so creative. He went through the same [Williams] archives that I went through and saw things that I had never seen, and had ways of thinking about them that I simply would not have had. I think that's because I was thinking more about a narrative history. But Brent sees the world differently, and this allows us to have deeper and newer appreciation of figures we think we know.

FEINSTEIN: With Brent Edwards and Bob O'Meally, you edited *Uptown Conversation: The New Jazz Studies*, and the introduction "asserts that jazz is not only a music to define, it is a *culture*." Why do you think it's important for the world to recognize that?

GRIFFIN: I think we tend to extricate things from broader and larger contexts. If you're talking about any musical form—whether it's jazz or bebop, specifically, or hip hop—the music tends to be a part of the culture. It might be the *defining* part of the culture, might set the standards. But there's a whole culture and community (and, oftentimes, a generation) that define themselves according to that. My father and his friends were beboppers until the day they died. That was about the music, but that was also about the way they talked, and the way they thought about and saw the world. Or the way they signaled each other: My uncles would come to the house and they'd whistle to get his attention. They wouldn't knock on the door or ring the doorbell. They would whistle. And I later found out they were whistling a little phrase from a Bird tune. Like, who knew? [Both laugh.]

It's a culture and a sense of self-definition. Roy DeCarava, the photographer, is as much a part of that culture; [Romare] Bearden, a painter, part of that culture. And even within that, there are subcultures, right? Baraka's relationship to the music of the sixties is different from DeCarava's relationship to the music of the forties or fifties. The music can shape, create, and define a culture that extends, like tentacles, out beyond. Who are those people sitting in the club—not on a Saturday night but on a Tuesday night. Or Frank O'Hara! Part of that culture. That was the approach we were trying to have with jazz studies: to look at that culture, the richness of that culture.

FEINSTEIN: In *Harlem Nocturne*, you quote Mary Lou Williams as saying, "It's the suffering that gives jazz its spiritual dimension." Do you agree with her?

GRIFFIN: Yes and no. I just saw a quotation by Toni Morrison somewhere where she was talking about writers, and how we know [about their personal tragedies]—this one drank himself to death, this one died alone—and she said that made her very sad. Writers should not have to create out of that kind of sadness. So I think Mary Lou is right: Suffering does give a depth of dimension, but it is not all-defining. There's also *deep*, deep joy. Suffering and joy define each other. And it's not happiness, as in the pursuit of happiness. But the joy is also part of the spirituality—almost as intense and deeply felt *because* it fits so closely to the suffering. In both of them, we can find the spiritual source for the music and other forms of the culture. I partly agree with Mary Lou but not entirely.

FEINSTEIN: In "Lady in G-flat" [from *If You Can't Be Free, Be a Mystery*], you talk about the secretly recorded 1955 rehearsal session with Billie Holiday and [pianist] Jimmy Rowles, including that deeply painful moment when, with an ambiguous tone, he refers to her as a "goddamn bitch." Rowles said he didn't want the tapes released because Lady was plastered. The session's readily available [on *The Complete Billie Holiday on Verve 1945–1959*]. Do *you* think the tapes should have been released?

GRIFFIN: [Sighs.] That's a hard one, Sascha . . . The scholar in me wants access to *everything*, right? All of it. So I don't know if I would say it should never have been released. Perhaps: not released as a commodity. Yeah, that's it.

You know, I remember hearing the late Chuck Stewart talk on a panel with another photographer, Hugh Bell, who said he was like an investigative journalist: if he was in the room and Lady nodded from heroin, he was going to take that picture. Chuck said, "I would not. Part of the reason why I was *in* the room is because I was accepted and trusted, and they knew I wasn't going to take that shot." So I think it's that kind of tension. The tapes exist. This was her life—not her *entire* life, but it was her life. But when it is decontextualized and only feeds into a narrative that we are voyeuristically obsessed with, then I have problems with that. But I would not say that it should never have been available. It's a hard one. You gave me a question I can't really answer.

Feinstein: Well, I don't think it's a yes or no question. Apart from the edgiest aspects, I appreciate hearing them work things out, musically, and listening to her talk about her own singing, saying that she can never sing the same way twice, can never copy herself. That's right at the heart of being an astonishing artist.

Griffin: And I actually kind of enjoy their relationship.

Feinstein: There's real love there.

Griffin: There's definitely love there. Absolutely.

7

Living Archives

John Edward Hasse

John Edward Hasse is a music historian, pianist, author, and record producer. For decades he served as curator of American Music at the Smithsonian Institution's National Museum of American History, where he was founding executive director of the Smithsonian Jazz Masterworks Orchestra, an acclaimed big band, and where he founded the Jazz Appreciation Month, now celebrated in more than forty countries. He is the author of *Beyond Category: The Life and Genius of Duke Ellington*; the editor of an illustrated history, *Jazz: The First Century*; and coauthor of the textbook *Discover Jazz*, which was published after this interview. A frequent contributor to the *Wall Street Journal*, he is also the producer-author of the book and three-disk set *The Classic Hoagy Carmichael*, which was nominated for two Grammy awards, and is coauthor/coproducer of *Jazz: The Smithsonian Anthology*. He has lectured and performed in the United States, South America, Europe, Africa, Asia, and has appeared on PBS, NPR, Sirius XM, and Voice of America programs.

The following excerpts from Hasse's writings have been reprinted with permission. The interview took place on February 12, 2011, at his home in Alexandria, Virginia.

Beyond Category: The Life and Genius of Duke Ellington (excerpt)

The Bard and the Duke . . . had a number of commonalities. Shakespeare was an actor as well as a dramatist; Ellington was a performer as well as a composer. Shakespeare wrote about a range of human experiences; so did Ellington. Shakespeare had a keen understanding of human nature, led a fertile and productive artistic life, and expressed a range of emotions and values; so did Ellington. One of Shakespeare's greatest strengths was the richness of his characterizations; one of Ellington's was the richness of the musical characters he hired and the way he enhanced their individuality. Shakespeare wrote for all levels of society, from royalty to pauper; so did Ellington. Shakespeare wrote not for publication but for performance: only half of his writings were published during his lifetime, and then mostly in "corrupt" quarto editions. Likewise, Ellington never wrote for publication, but rather for performance—whether live, on record, or on film. Few of his pieces were published during his lifetime, and those that were bore poor resemblance to the originals.

As did Shakespeare, Ellington deployed his players like great actors on a stage. For nineteen years, Shakespeare was part owner of a repertory company (Lord Chamberlain's Men, which became The King's Men) and wrote *only* for that company, in fact, for particular thespians—like Richard Burbage (who played Hamlet, Richard III, Lear, and Othello), Will Kempe, and John Heminges. Likewise, Ellington had *his* own repertory company—for fifty years—and wrote almost exclusively for its players—Hodges, Nanton, and Bigard, and the others. Shakespeare's plays have outlived the actors for whom they were conceived. Ellington's music may, as the centuries pass, attain the same achievement.

"The Swing Era" from *Jazz: The First Century* (excerpt)

If novelist F. Scott Fitzgerald had it right when he called the 1920s the Jazz Age, then the 1930s through the mid-1940s could even more aptly be termed the Swing Era. That's because during that time, the swing pulse and impulse transformed jazz—and through it, much of American vernacular music.

Swing music and dancing became a huge phenomenon, almost a national obsession, taking jazz to heights of popularity never achieved before or since. More jazz musicians gained favor with the general public, more audiences turned to jazz as a backdrop for dancing and entertainment, than at any other time in history. Never before had jazz so dominated the field of popular music. At no other time was jazz such a catalyst for thousands of fans queuing up for a performance, for turn-away crowds so large and enthusiastic that the police had to be called in to keep order, for so many live radio broadcasts carrying the music to waiting listeners coast-to-coast, and for heated band battles that became the stuff of legends. . . .

What separated swing from jazz that preceded? Most of all, its rhythm. Louis Armstrong's rhythmic innovations loosened up the beat of jazz, provided a greater variety of rhythms, and made its momentum more flowing. Between 1930 and 1935, Armstrong influenced other musicians to play slightly ahead of the beat and, in so doing, transformed the rhythmic feel of jazz.

"We Saw Jazz through His Lens" (excerpt)

He journeyed to the Far East as Marlon Brando's personal photographer. He shot nudes for Hugh Hefner's *Playboy* and fashion models for *Elle* and *Marie Claire*. He photographed a den of opium smokers in Mazar-I-Sharif, Afghanistan. He roomed in Paris with Quincy Jones. But what Herman Leonard will be best remembered for is his iconic portraits of jazz masters.

Shadow, light and smoke. With these elements, Leonard, who died Aug. 14 [2010] at age 87, made indelible many of the greatest American musicians of the 20th century. He won the trust of instrumentalists and singers—even the notoriously irascible Miles Davis—and rewarded that intimacy with images luminous with truth and beauty. Leonard captured the glowing artistry and individuality of celebrated artists, and made those qualities shine through the paper and the chemicals and the books and the galleries and the decades. An eminent creative artist himself, he's been called the Charlie Parker of photography.

He improvised his life as a jazz musician would invent a long, memorable solo. Serving in the U.S. Army in Burma during World War II, he developed film in his combat helmet late at night. After apprenticing with the esteemed portrait photographer Yousuf Karsh in Ottawa, Leonard set up a portrait studio in New York. Following his passion—jazz music—into nightclubs, he persuaded club owners to let him photograph musicians in exchange for copies of the photos. Out of necessity—inadequate lighting in the clubs—came invention: He could afford only two lights, so he positioned a strobe light in the ceiling and another light behind the musicians. The result was subjects lit from front and back, fast-moving drumsticks and lazy smoke curls captured midair. That look was his trademark. And it has come to define how many think of mainstream jazz: atmospheric black-and-white images of musicians, glowing in silver light, their natural allure contrasting with the darkness of the nightclubs, accented by smoke suspended in time.

"The Team Sport of Jazz" from *Discover Jazz* (excerpt)

You can look at the performance of a jazz piece as an unusual kind of ball game. The closest analogy is basketball, where the ball is almost constantly in motion. As in basketball, where the ball is passed from player to player, in jazz the melody or solo is often passed among the soloists. In a jazz band, each player might "hold the ball," so to speak, for eight, twelve, sixteen, or more bars, but then he or she'll typically pass it to another player. In basketball, part of the thrill of a good performance is watching what each player does when the ball is his and he's in the spotlight of everyone's attention; in jazz, part of the thrill is *hearing* what each player does when it's his or her turn to take the forefront.

But in jazz, things get more complicated than in basketball. For one thing, every move is done to a rhythm—or even a series of overlapping rhythms—and the rhythms have to fit within a steady beat. (Can you imagine basketball players *having* to coordinate their every move to a steady beat?) For another, no matter who has the "ball" in a jazz performance, the other players are often interacting—the pianist is feeding chords to the band, the bassist is anchoring the beat off which everyone else plays, the drummer is urging on and reacting to the soloists. You could even imagine these ongoing interactions as being like smaller basketballs. Viewed in this way, you have a game with a main basketball and a number of smaller balls all in play at the same time—creating multiple layers of interest, suspense, and excitement, not to mention complexity.

Interview

SASCHA FEINSTEIN: How did you become involved with jazz?

JOHN EDWARD HASSE: I was in fifth grade—this was around 1960—and my father was a mathematics professor at the University of South Dakota, and he bought me a ticket to a jazz concert put on by the Phi Mu Alpha Sinfonians—a collegiate music honorary society. They had a big band and were doing a lot of Basie, Neal Hefti, music like that. I had never heard live jazz in my little town of Vermillion, South Dakota—five thousand townspeople and five thousand students at the university, hardly anyone of color, very homogeneous. But my dad bought me a ticket each year when they'd have this benefit concert.

So, while I didn't realize it at the time, this was a revelation for me.

I'd been studying piano formally since third grade, and then when I was in high school, Ramsey Lewis came out with his recording *The "In" Crowd* [1965], and, oh man—that *really* caught my ear. I'd been listening to Peter Nero and some Ferrante & Teicher—pop instrumental piano—but when *The "In" Crowd* came out, that really grabbed me. I had to get the recording *and* the sheet music. I learned it, and by the time I was a junior in high school, I'd formed a jazz trio. We played for high school dances and proms, and we got engagements at some of the college fraternities and sororities. A couple of times we even passed ourselves off as twenty-one—because you had to be twenty-one to even go into a bar, much less play at one—and played in a city thirty miles away.

In my freshman year at Carleton College in Minnesota, I met a great professor, John S. Lucas, who, as Jax Lucas, had been the research editor for *Down Beat* magazine back in the 1940s. He introduced me to [such early innovators as King] Oliver and [Louis] Armstrong and [Baby] Dodds—all the way up [to the contemporary players]. And he had known some of these musicians. He'd lived in Rome for some years and had eaten with Chet Baker; he'd met Hemingway and Picasso. He was a man of the arts. Anyway, I got into a jazz quartet [at Carleton], then a trio, and then, in the spring term of my sophomore year [1969], I had a chance to go to New York City for a quarter—[a program sponsored by] the Associated Colleges of the Midwest, with ten or twelve colleges. So I went, and we studied the arts together. We'd go to plays, and we went to artists' lofts and rehearsals; we went to [the experimental theater] Café La MaMa, the Guggenheim, the New York City Opera. And we also apprenticed with established artists in our field, so I studied piano with Roland Hanna—later Sir Roland Hanna—and Jaki Byard.

FEINSTEIN: How fabulous.

HASSE: I was a piker, but that was really something. I remember one time Roland Hanna couldn't make a gig and he offered me a chance to sub for him.

FEINSTEIN: Oh my God.

HASSE: I didn't take it, and I don't think I should have. I wasn't that good.

FEINSTEIN: Who was the better teacher?

HASSE: Roland. Roland was *much* more organized. But Jaki, I thought, was the more interesting pianist, whose style anthologized the whole history of jazz piano, from ragtime to avant-garde. And for one of my first lessons, he told me to go down to either Schirmer Bookstore or Carl Fischer Music—one of them had a retail outlet—and buy this book called *They All Played Ragtime* [*The True Story of an American Music*, edited by Rudi Blesh and Harriet Janis, 1950]. I dutifully brought it to my next lesson, and he said, "You probably want to know why I wanted you to buy this book." I said, "Yeah." He flipped to a page and said, "'Cause my picture's in here!" [Both laugh.] [The photograph only appears in later editions of the book—SF.] We had a good laugh, and then he said, "No, the real reason is because the 'Maple Leaf Rag' is in here." It was small, but the score was there, and this was the only place he knew where you could get the music. He said, "I want you to learn the 'Maple Leaf Rag.' Everybody should know some ragtime." I started working on that, and it took, I'd say, five years to master it and play in public well. That's a bear of a piece; it's really hard to play up to tempo.

At that same time, I started going to nightclubs. I heard the Thad Jones / Mel Lewis big band at the Village Vanguard. I had a conversation with Bill Evans, one of my heroes, at the Village Gate. I met Richard Davis and Billy Taylor and Dave Liebman; I somehow got backstage at Carnegie Hall and met Sonny Sharrock. Herbie Hancock and Ron Carter. It was really an eye- and ear-opening set of experiences. I followed Billy Taylor around and pestered him so much that he finally gave me some of his lead sheets. [Both laugh.] Little did I know that, years later, I'd be working with him when he was at the Kennedy Center.

The previous summer, I had worked at a public radio station in Kansas City and had a chance to meet some of my heroes.

There was a Schlitz Salute to Jazz that was touring the nation with an all-star lineup. I had a portable tape recorder because I worked at the college radio station, KARL, and I wanted to get some PSAs [public service announcements], so I went around to the various folks, and I distinctly remember Thelonious Monk trying to read this little three- or four-sentence PSA that I'd typed up. He was having problems. I don't know what was going on: "Thish iz The-lo-ni-ous Monk. Lish-en to K—" I mean, I didn't smell any alcohol, but he was having slurred speech, though he [later] played beautifully.

During the time when I was studying with Roland Hanna, I felt that he was an underappreciated pianist. Yes, he was with the Thad Jones / Mel Lewis jazz orchestra, but he was undersung. So I conducted a taped interview with him and got it published in *Down Beat*. They named it "Roland Hanna: Inside Insight" [*Down Beat* 37, no. 20 (October 15, 1970)]. I had written for small magazines before, but *Down Beat* was my first real "big" publication.

FEINSTEIN: During this time of discovery, were there any books on jazz that mattered to you?

HASSE: I don't think I read any books on jazz until I got to college. I bought sheet music . . .

FEINSTEIN: I'm asking in part because you've edited this wonderful book, *Jazz: The First Century* [2000], that's being turned into a textbook. What makes a jazz textbook really stand out? What makes it a valuable source?

HASSE: A cluster of characteristics. First, it has to be authoritative. Jazz profs tend to be *passionate* about the music; many of them have very strong opinions, and they're not going to accept anything they believe is not authoritative. Second, it has to be accessible. It can't be written down to the student level; it can't be written up. It has to hit them at the right level. Third, it has to be engaging; it can't be in stuffy academic prose. To some extent, it has to meet them where they are, and meeting students where they are today is not the same as meeting students thirty years ago. We have so many different kinds of new music, so if you, the writer, don't make direct allusions to hip hop and rap, you have to at least realize that what was musical and cultural common knowledge for someone of my generation or your generation isn't going to be there at all. If you're going to mention someone like Run-D.M.C. or 50 Cent, by the time the book comes out, that might be old hat because things change so quickly. In a couple of years, college freshmen would have been born in 1994.

Fourth, I also think you have to make the recordings [alluded to in the textbook] understandable with very carefully thought-out listening guides, and you need to hold their hands—not second by second, but with timed guiding. Fifth, a really good textbook should be pleasing to the eye, in terms of design and photo selection, layout, and the quality of printing. And, sixth, you need good content on the Web that supports the book. I think these are the keys to a really strong textbook.

FEINSTEIN: What do you think of the old argument that jazz can't be taught?

HASSE: Taught to play it or to understand it?

FEINSTEIN: Both.

HASSE: I totally disagree on both counts, and, I suppose, even more strongly with the second point. Not everyone can be taught to play jazz. You have to have some innate musical ability. You've got to have—in American jazz, at least—a sense of swing. You've got to have a good ear, a good aural memory; if you're in a band, you have to know how to interact with other people. Playing jazz requires many, many skills. But I think most people can be taught to hear jazz and learn about it. If you don't have an absolutely tin ear, there's something in jazz for everybody, and there's something to be learned about and gained from the study of jazz. I really think that jazz expresses some of the most cherished values that this country aspires to: freedom, innovation, individuality, cultural diversity, creativity, and creative collaboration. And those are *powerful* ideas. It's not usually articulated that way, but I think those values undergird the music.

~

FEINSTEIN: Do you think you would have written your biography on Duke Ellington [*Beyond Category: The Life and Genius of Duke Ellington*, 1993] had the Smithsonian not received that windfall of materials from the Ellington family?

HASSE: Probably not.

FEINSTEIN: How did that come about? Did Mercer [Ellington, Duke's son] approach you?

HASSE: Not exactly. Mercer was taping a public service announcement for the Smithsonian's Anacostia Community Museum in southeast Washington. The then-director John Kinard asked, "Whatever happened to your father's stuff?" and Mercer said, "It's stashed away in a warehouse in New York City." Just sitting there. So Kinard called Roger Kennedy, director of the National Museum of American History, where I work [as curator of American Music], who relayed the information to Gary Kulik, chairman of the Department of Social and Cultural History. Kulik called me and asked, "Would you be interested in Duke Ellington's archives?" [Hasse lunges forward in his seat, grinning almost maniacally.] "*Would* I?!" [Both laugh.] And that began a very challenging, two-and-a-half to three-year effort to acquire his archives.

FEINSTEIN: What treasures did you find in those archives?

HASSE: First of all, some of the most valuable manuscripts, like "Mood Indigo," were in a bank vault, but the bulk of it was in a room with about this footprint [in Hasse's kitchen] but twice as high, roughly ten by ten by fifteen. I had to clamber up high wooden shelves. Somewhere there's a picture of me in a raincoat, because we went there in April and it was *cold*. Unheated, un-air-conditioned. At that point, the stuff had been there eleven or twelve years, since Duke's death. Mildew had started to set in on some of the tape recordings. [Feinstein winces.] And, bless his heart, Mercer had allowed his band members to rifle through some of the music, because they, of course, were treating Duke's music as a living legacy, keeping it alive with the Duke Ellington Orchestra. So some of the parts were missing . . . It was a mess. Duke wasn't an archivist. He wasn't interested in the *last* thing he wrote; he was interested in *next* thing he wrote. And I'll praise Mercer to the skies. If it hadn't been for Mercer, we wouldn't have this—the nation wouldn't have this national treasure, the world wouldn't have this—because Duke wanted to throw everything away, but Mercer kept stashing stuff in his garage out on Long Island. Mercer had a sense of history, even if his father didn't really want to deal with it. So I have nothing but praise for Mercer.

It turns out, the [Ellington] estate owed a lot of back taxes to the IRS, so Mercer wasn't in a position to donate the archives, although he did want to donate part of it, so it was a partial-gift/partial-sale (sometimes in the museum world called a "bargain sale"). We are almost never in that position because normally Congress gives us *zero* to acquire collections; just about everything that comes to us is a gift. And it's quite a story of how we got congressional money—too long for this occasion—but we eventually got five hundred thousand dollars. As I recall, three hundred thousand went toward the acquisition of the collection, and two hundred thousand went to the storage equipment, shelving racks, acid-free folders, and hiring staff to start the process of cataloging this collection—because it's enormous: one hundred thousand pages of unpublished music.

FEINSTEIN: Wow.

HASSE: And another one hundred thousand pages of documents. A couple thousand photos. A thousand recordings. And about five hundred artifacts like trophies, medals, band music stands, his electric piano—all sorts of things. It was a huge collection, and it took ten years to catalog.

FEINSTEIN: How could all that fit into a room ten by ten by fifteen?

HASSE: Some of it was stored elsewhere. I know Mercer had some things in his apartment across from Lincoln Center. And there were a few things in a bank vault. But there was a lot of stuff packed into that room. In terms of archival collections, it's one of our biggest, and I like to think of it as one of the crown jewels of the Smithsonian—period.

FEINSTEIN: I've not seen it. Is it displayed for the public?

HASSE: We've had a number of exhibits, but currently there's not one. There is one manuscript and the corresponding published sheet music sitting side by side in an area of the museum called the Artifact Walls. But everything except the five hundred artifacts is stored in the museum's Archives Center, and researchers can make appointments to use them.

You can also go on the Web and find a pretty detailed catalog. Archives don't usually catalog down to the individual piece of paper—they usually catalog down to the folder level—but this is cataloged down to the specific piece of music. And on the Web it's cataloged down to folder level. For example, you can go to "Foreign Tours," and then "1971" (because it's chronological), and there is his tour of the USSR. Scholars will be mining the collection, particularly the music, for centuries to come, in the same way they're still mining Bach's manuscripts.

FEINSTEIN: You mined it, too, for your biography. At what point did you realize you needed to make a book? Was the project your idea or did someone propose it to you?

HASSE: My idea. I was thinking about writing a book about Hoagy Carmichael—and, ironically, Ellington and Carmichael were born in the same year: 1899. I'd done some work on Carmichael, but I mentioned Ellington to my agent, who immediately thought it was a stronger idea, which it was. My motivation, though, was born of the extreme disappointment in the last biography of Ellington: James Lincoln Collier's [*Duke Ellington*, 1987]. A dreadful book. I have respect for some of what Collier has done, including *Jazz: The American Theme Song*. But his Ellington bio is very disappointing. It was hastily written and sloppily researched. He claimed that Ellington didn't leave written music behind. There were erroneous conclusions that Ellington was writing music just to get girls and that he didn't do much of value after about 1942. It's a very poor piece of scholarship. But that was the last word on Ellington—published, of all things, by Oxford University Press, which really should have known better. So I was motivated to set the record straight, to paint a more accurate and knowing picture of Ellington, and to offer a corrective.

At that time, I was founding and overseeing the Smithsonian Jazz Masterworks Orchestra; cowriting a grant proposal that led to a seven-million-dollar grant from the Lila Wallace Reader's Digest Fund, at that point breaking three records: the largest grant they'd ever given to anybody, the largest grant the Smithsonian had ever raised, and the largest amount ever given to jazz; curating the exhibition also called *Beyond Category*, which traveled the country; commuting on weekends to see my infant daughter in Boston; and spending evenings and weekends to write this book. I look back and wonder how I got through that, but somehow I did. With all that on my plate, I had to be supermotivated to do that book, and as I got into Ellington's record, researching it before we got that collection and then after, I became more and more admiring of him, and more conscious of what a complex record he left, one that I feel still hasn't been fully appreciated. In fact, when I finished this book in the spring of '93, I was not fully aware of that magnitude. I would now assess him even more highly. I would like to say he was the greatest all-around musician the United States has produced. By that I mean: composer, bandleader/conductor, orchestrator/arranger, soloist, and accompanist. This country, of course, has produced many brilliant musicians: Ives, Gershwin, Copland, Armstrong, Charlie Parker, et cetera. But I can't think of one who's done *all* those things so brilliantly and so enduringly. To me, Ellington is a giant of American culture, a pillar of American music, and I wish I had said that in the book.

FEINSTEIN: There are books on Ellington that I like even less than Collier's. I'm thinking of Don George's *Sweet Man* [1981].

HASSE: Yeah, that's an odd one. And then there's one by Austin Lawrence [*Duke Ellington and His World*, 2001] where he quotes one conversation after another, verbatim—but I don't believe he taped a single one. How can you rely on a conversation that's been reconstructed from decades ago, where the subject is no longer around to correct, refute, or confirm it? The book's so full of errors that a number of Ellington scholars wrote to the publisher asking them to retract the book.

FEINSTEIN: Was there any scholarship that you found magnificent—that really helped your book?

HASSE: Mark Tucker's magisterial *The Ellington Reader* came out at about the same time as my book, so I wasn't privy to that, but his earlier *Ellington: The Early Years* [1991] was a model of scholarship on a period that was largely unknown, neglected, and very difficult to research. But Mark did it; he did his doctoral dissertation on that subject at the suggestion of [critic and scholar] Martin Williams, who took him under his wing and gave him a lot of encouragement. And that's a magnificent book in terms of bringing to light and reconstructing the formative years of Ellington. I think that was the best source at that time.

We now have Harvey Cohen's book, *Duke Ellington's America* [2010], and he heavily researched that from the Smithsonian's Duke Ellington Collection. It's written by a cultural historian—he's not a musicologist—and it's an important book.

FEINSTEIN: In what crucial ways does Cohen's book differ from your biography?

HASSE: Harvey gives a lot more context. For example, he went to Arkansas and looked into the State Department's records of Ellington's tours abroad. He looked extensively at Ellington's business records. It's not a cradle-to-grave biography—mine's a cradle-to-grave biography, and beyond—but Harvey offers a lot of new insights, and I think it's a really valuable book.

Had my book been written later, I would have treated [Billy] Strayhorn differently—more fully. In *Beyond Category*,

Strayhorn doesn't loom as large as he could have and should have. But the fact is, at the time I wrote this, there was no biography on Strayhorn. There was no musicological study; the scores hadn't been available—they'd been locked away. So that was a province for others, and, thankfully, David Hajdu [with *Lush Life: A Biography of Billy Strayhorn*, 1997] and Walter van de Leur [with *Something to Live For: The Music of Billy Strayhorn*, 2002] stepped to the plate. They're both important works. Strayhorn is getting his due, and that's really gratifying.

∼

FEINSTEIN: Tell me about your other projects, like the book you edited on ragtime [*Ragtime: Its History, Composers, and Music*, 1986].

HASSE: It started with Jaki Byard.

FEINSTEIN: [Smiles.] You know, when you were talking about Byard and "Maple Leaf Rag," I wanted to ask this question but didn't want to interrupt you so early in our conversation. But it's the first thing that came to mind.

HASSE: Yeah, it did start with Byard. I mean, I'd heard *some* ragtime, but I was playing "Watermelon Man" and "Satin Doll" and things like that. He got me learning the "Maple Leaf Rag," and then in 1970, Joshua Rifkin came out with his recording of Scott Joplin's piano rags. I glommed onto that—although I also thought he treated those rags too classically. (Joplin wasn't Chopin.) But Rifkin did a lot to hasten the revival of ragtime—a *lot*. He and [producer] Teresa Sterne at Nonesuch Records, as did Vera Brodsky Lawrence, who edited the *Complete Piano Works* of Scott Joplin, published by the New York Public Library. That was *big*, because it suddenly brought all Joplin's works into the domain where they were available to pianists like me, and when I bought that, I started learning some of the rags that I'd heard Rifkin play.

I got to Indiana University [for graduate school] in 1973 and started studying with David Baker, but within a year or two

I started playing in the Tudor Room, an elegant dining facility for parents and alumni.

Feinstein: I remember that room. [In 1986, I also attended graduate school at Indiana University.]

Hasse: Oh you do? In the [Student] Union Building?

Feinstein: Yeah.

Hasse: They would have elegant lunches there, and I would play piano. Then I started getting gigs where I would give lecture/concerts. I made slides of the sheet music covers, so when I was talking about Joplin, there'd be a picture of Joplin on the screen; when I was playing the "Maple Leaf Rag," there'd be a picture of the sheet music cover in full color. I went all around Indiana doing that, and then, in 1975, I landed a job playing two nights a week in Nashville, Indiana, at a colonial-themed tavern called The Ordinary. They had a wonderful, old upright piano. The whole place was wood inside, so the wood actually acted as an adjunct to the wood of the piano and carried the vibrations throughout the establishment. You could feel it through your feet. I played six hundred nights—just about every weekend for six years. I specialized in ragtime and got much more comfortable playing in public. While I was there, some regulars became fans and put up some money, and I recorded an album of ragtime piano solos: *ExtraOrdinary Ragtime: Choice Piano Rags by Scott Joplin, James Scott, Irving Berlin, &c.* [Sunflower Records, 1980]. I'll show it to you if you want.

Feinstein: I'd love to see it. [Hasse leaves the room and returns with albums and books.]

Hasse: I wrote my doctoral dissertation on ragtime piano composers from Indianapolis, which turned out to be a hotbed of ragtime publishing—the third or fourth most prolific center. Then I got a grant from the Lilly Endowment and coproduced [with Frank J. Gillis] this album [*Indiana Ragtime: A Documentary Album*, 1981].

FEINSTEIN: This booklet is amazing.

HASSE: Thank you. It won an ASCAP / Deems Taylor Award for excellence in writing about music. So then I started working on Hoagy Carmichael. [Hasse picks up a four-LP set called *The Classic Hoagy Carmichael*; The Indiana Historical Society and the Smithsonian Collection of Readings, 1989.] The research spanned ten years.

FEINSTEIN: The essays [in this expansive, sixty-four-page booklet] are yours?

HASSE: Yes they are . . .

FEINSTEIN: [Spots a photo in the booklet of pianist Dave McKenna.] There's Dave! I miss Dave.

HASSE: A friend of yours? I used to go hear him play at the Copley Plaza in Boston.

FEINSTEIN: Yes indeed! I sat in with Dave once at the Copley Plaza.

HASSE: Really?

FEINSTEIN: Yeah. I had *no business* doing that . . . [Hasse laughs.] No business at all. But I was seventeen and had my alto with me, and he was *so* kind to me.

HASSE: Oh, he was a sweetheart. Shy. Really shy. You know, [tuba genius] Harvey Phillips started a Hoagy Carmichael Jazz Society in Bloomington [Indiana] and brought McKenna in to do an inaugural concert [in May 1983, some of which appears on *A Celebration of Hoagy Carmichael*]. There were two concerts, actually: a private concert at Harvey's house [The Tuba Ranch] and a public one [at The Second Story Club]. Unfortunately, during the best number at the private concert—a tour de force, thirteen-minute version of "Lazy River"—a piece of sheet music fell on the strings in the piano and started buzzing. Ruined the recording.

FEINSTEIN: Oh no . . .

HASSE: [Points to the Carmichael boxed set.] This was nominated for two Grammys—Best Historical Album and Best Album Notes—and in both categories it lost out to a reissue of Eric Clapton. How could the name Carmichael compete with Clapton? Which is why the jazz producer Bob Porter said to me, "John, the real honor in these categories is being nominated. The nominations are made by a committee of experts, but *anybody* in the Academy can vote for the final decision." Partly he was trying to make me feel better, but I think it was partly the truth, too.

FEINSTEIN: What do you think the world badly needs in terms of literature on jazz?

HASSE: I don't know if there's something that the world badly needs on jazz—in terms of literature—but I'm quite confident in saying that there's something the world of jazz badly needs, and that's more audience. We have *so* many gifted musicians; the music schools are cranking them out. We have people from Joe Wilder's age (he's in his nineties) all the way down. But a lot of them just can't get work. They can't find an audience. Nightclubs are disappearing. Radio stations are playing less jazz than they used to. You can hardly ever find jazz on network television.

FEINSTEIN: And how do you think the Smithsonian can help with that?

HASSE: I think we need to continue to do what we're doing. [Points to the forthcoming six-CD set, *Jazz: The Smithsonian Anthology*.] To the degree that this jazz anthology is accepted/adopted; acquired by libraries; put on display in libraries; publicized on public radio and mainstream publications; and people think, "Oh, yeah—Smithsonian." Either they remember the previous album [boxed set, *The Smithsonian Collection of Jazz*, compiled by Martin Williams] and want something up to date, or they don't know the previous album but are looking for an authoritative guide. This will help *some*.

I think Jazz Appreciation Month [April] is an important part of what the Smithsonian can do, which is to help create an annual occasion and platform for all sorts of public celebrations in schools, colleges, libraries, museums, concert halls, and public broadcasting schedules. The amount of activity that goes on in schools during April is largely invisible to the national media. You don't see it discussed even in *Down Beat* or *JazzTimes*, much less the *New York Times* or NPR, but it's out there.

This is what's key: reaching the next generation of adults, giving them some exposure to jazz. I find wherever I go—throughout the United States and around the world—hardly anybody says, "I hate jazz." But a lot of people will tell me, "I don't *know* jazz," which is entirely different. If you expose people to jazz, most will find things to like. There's something in jazz for just about everybody. Maybe you don't like bebop but you like hip hop–infused jazz; maybe you don't like Herbie [Hancock]'s acoustic stuff but you like his electric [piano recordings]—or vice versa. Maybe you like the traditional sound of collective improvisation in New Orleans jazz. There's just *so* much.

It's like classical music. Most people don't equally like all the music from plainchant to Stockhausen and Boulez; they're more likely going to love some part of the spectrum of classical music. And I think the same is true for jazz. There are parts of music that speak especially to certain people and parts that speak especially to others. There's really something for everyone.

But the Smithsonian, as much as it's a national platform that's highly respected with a ninety-two percent household recognition rate in this country, cannot by any stretch of the imagination do it all, or even carry the bulk of the burden. It's going to take lots of folks and lots of institutions to do their part to insure that this music survives as a living art form, and that future generations understand and value it as a great part of America's cultural patrimony, just as are the work of Twain, Hemingway, Faulkner, Sandburg, Frost, Ralph Ellison, Winslow

Homer, Frank Lloyd Wright—all the great creative artists this country has produced.

I've spoken with people who've grown up in Germany, and they say, "It's unthinkable that anyone completing high school in Germany would not have been exposed to the names Bach, Mozart, Beethoven, Brahms." But here [in the States], not only can someone graduate from high school, they can graduate from college—they can get a master's degree in education—and never have heard the names Ellington, Armstrong, Gershwin, Porter. It's appalling that Americans don't know who some of their greatest cultural figures are. They haven't even heard the names.

There's so much work to be done. And I think it's centered in education, particularly precollege. That's the key. We've got to get to people before they get to be juniors and seniors in high school, when their tastes are really formed by what's on their boom boxes or, these days, iTunes and what their peers are listening to. We've got to get to them *before* that age. We've *got* to get them.

8

Taking It Back

Willard Jenkins

Willard Jenkins is a journalist, arts consultant and presenter, coauthor of *African Rhythms: The Autobiography of Randy Weston*, and artistic director of the DC Jazz Festival. His writing has appeared in scores of publications, including *JazzTimes*, *Down Beat*, *Jazz Forum*, and *Jazzwise*; he has also written liner notes for such jazz luminaries as Dizzy Gillespie, Clifford Jordan, Joe Lovano, and Cannonball Adderley. In 1983, he conducted research that spearheaded the nation's first regional jazz service program at Arts Midwest (Minneapolis, Minnesota); working there from 1984 to 1989, he developed the first regional jazz database and wrote a series of how-to technical assistance booklets for musicians, presenters, educators, and organizations. A radio broadcaster for WPFW, he acted as executive director of the National Jazz Service Organization (NJSO) in Washington, DC, from 1989 to 1994. He writes and edits a blog, *The Independent Ear*, on his website OpenSkyJazz.com, which includes the series Ain't But a Few of Us. Since this interview, he has edited *Ain't But a Few of Us: Black Music Writers Tell Their Story* and received the 2024 A. B. Spellman NEA Jazz Masters Fellowship for Jazz Advocacy.

The following excerpts from Jenkins's writings have been reprinted with permission. The interview took place near his home in Montgomery County, Maryland, on May 1, 2015.

Arranger's Preface to *African Rhythms* (excerpt)

Early on, it became clear that this would not be your conventional jazz book in many respects. Randy and I have each observed that there are relatively few true jazz *autobiographies*, which makes this book all the more unique. It is not a particularly linear book. Randy doesn't dwell on the technical aspects of his craft, unlike the authors of more typical jazz books. And his apprenticeship as a sideman was not extensive. What is central to the book is Randy's stress on what defines his musical expression—what he has referred to on record, in composition, and numerous times in conversation as *the spirits of our ancestors*. Though not a churchgoing man in the traditional sense or an adherent of any one religion, Randy Weston is a deeply spiritual man who believes fervently in the Creator, the ancestral spirits up above, and their ultimate guidance over his life's experiences.

Our interviews were inspired by ongoing research and augmented by the prodigious wealth of materials that Randy has accumulated throughout his journey. He has saved every significant scrap of paper, taped every performance, and kept every article, letter, and memo, and assorted ephemera, from his career. I transcribed all our conversations and provided Randy with the transcripts. He painstakingly made additions, corrections, and suggestions throughout the process, which would often lead us down new streams of discovery and remembrance, and his comments were subsequently edited into the transcriptions. One of the hallmarks of our interviews is that without fail Randy would offhandedly make some new revelation or take us down another path. The freshness of each conversation was a marvel, even when we were covering ground that I thought we had sufficiently traversed.

Liner Notes for the CD Reissue of *Dizzy's Big 4* (excerpt)

At 57, not yet the lion in winter and at just about the tail end of his largely small group domination middle period, Dizzy Gillespie was afforded this precipitous opportunity to encounter three fellow travelers in the studio, per producer Norman Granz. Blessed with arguably the keenest eye for all-star musician collaborations in the annals of jazz, Granz had been a favored presence in Dizzy's storied life for about twenty years. Their relationship dated back to one of the impresario's first recording dates for his Norgran label (circa 1953), an encounter between Dizzy and Stan Getz (in typical Granz simplicity, a date titled "Diz and Getz"); the producer had long favored Gillespie's artistry. . . .

Befitting a Pablo session, the four musicians comprising "Dizzy Gillespie's Big 4" have an obvious simpatico with each other's artistry. Dizzy and Ray Brown went back to the mid-40s and Gillespie's pioneering big band period. The bass master recalled their being introduced on 52nd Street by the pianist Hank Jones. Almost immediately after shaking hands, Diz, ever the talent scout, inquired about Brown's bass prowess. With Hank Jones's amen, Gillespie quickly invited the younger bassist to his home for an afternoon rehearsal. When Brown arrived he was stunned to encounter Charlie Parker, Max Roach, and Bud Powell on the set, realizing immediately that he was in high cotton! Even more astonishing was the music set before Brown; clearly these men were busy at work on the "new thing," which the critics dubbed bebop, or modern jazz, and which the musicians referred to as "our music."

"What's Your Take: Is Racism Still an Issue in Jazz?" (excerpt)

The recent [2003] hullabaloo over Stanley Crouch's dismissal from his *JazzTimes* column raised some prickly issues that continue to haunt us, despite naive contrary protestations and observations. Yes, racism remains an issue in jazz. The hysteria and vitriol pitched in Crouch's direction throughout his tenure at *JazzTimes*, and particularly in response to his dismissal, was quite visceral and somewhat disturbing in the aggregate.

But this is not a Stanley Crouch apologia, just an observation of some essential questions that continue to dog this art form and which his 15 minutes of *JazzTimes* controversy once again brought to the surface. Lost in the firestorm subsequent to Crouch's sacking were several points he made about the general jazz condition, points in which even African American jazz practitioners and observers who had long ago dismissed Crouch's various pronouncements as those of a perpetually "frustrated" musician, found a certain agreement.

Chief among them was an element which African American observers of this art form have always found irritating: the sudden premature elevation of white jazz artists, most often while they are still quite green. . . . Such cogent observations from Crouch unfortunately got lost in the foggy glasses of many in the jazz community's patent dismissal of Stanley as Wynton Marsalis' erstwhile Boswell. Writers such as Stuart Nicholson and Terry Teachout are among the publicists of this flavor-of-the-month club. Does anybody recall Nicholson's overheated elevation a few seasons back of a few Nordic jazzers as the only real happening thing in jazz? Have any African American jazz writers ever been given such a platform to postulate on the next big thing? Nicholson's predictions not only graced the pages of *JazzTimes*, but also the *New York Times*. The dearth of African American staff jazz writers at daily newspapers and monthly jazz specialty magazines is yet another crying issue. Of course nowadays when black folks raise these issues, we're accused of "playing the race card," which has become an all too convenient dismissal of these and other very real considerations of racial conditions in jazz. Yes, Jim Crow lives, he has a thirst for jazz, and no blizzard of ignorance or avoidance is going to bury his miserable ass.

Introduction to *Ain't But a Few of Us: Black Music Writers Tell Their Story* (excerpt)

Reading about jazz became an expanded pursuit, revealing important archival contributions from African Americans: Amiri Baraka (née LeRoi Jones), A. B. Spellman, Ralph Ellison, Albert Murray, and the contemporary writings of Stanley Crouch, Ron Welburn, and next-gen peers like Don Palmer, Nelson George, Vernon Gibbs, my homeboy Robert Fleming, and later Greg Tate, brothers of my approximate generation versed in jazz, whose prose encompassed other branches of the black music tree. . . .

Opportunities for black writers on jazz expanded a bit with the 1979 launch of the *Jazz Spotlite News*, published by the jazz enthusiast and gig presenter Jim Harrison. *Jazz Spotlite News* was one of what has been a minuscule number of jazz-oriented publications that actively sought the black perspective on jazz. Preceding the *Jazz Spotlite News*'s black slant on jazz had been such other worthy and lamentably short-lived efforts as Amiri Baraka's *Cricket* and Ron Welburn's *The Grackle*. Succeeding the *Jazz Spotlite News*, with a similar Afrocentric orientation, were the California-based *Jazz Now* and, later, the Brooklyn-based *Pure Jazz*; both provided vehicles for black jazz writers. Recognizing the disparity of black pens chronicling jazz, I contributed enthusiastically to each of these publications, continuing to write about jazz as a freelancer.

Interview

SASCHA FEINSTEIN: I know you started seriously writing about music when you were at Kent State, but I don't know much about your youth. You were born in '49; were you born and raised in Cleveland?

WILLARD JENKINS: No, I was born in Pittsburgh, and we left Pittsburgh when I was twelve years old because my dad was a newspaper man—a typographer—and at the time, he was a member of an excellent union. He was working for the *Pittsburgh Sun Telegraph*, which was sold and merged with the *Pittsburgh Post Gazette*. All of the men at his union were offered job opportunities at other newspapers; if they weren't going to work for the *Post Gazette*, they were going to work for newspapers around the country automatically. So he chose the *Cleveland Plain Dealer* as his opportunity. For several months, he worked in Cleveland Monday through Friday, came home every weekend, and left again on Sunday night. It was tough on us all, but especially my mom. Then he got a place and moved us to Cleveland, where I grew up thereafter.

    I always enjoyed writing, and in college [Kent State, 1969–1973], I enjoyed those courses where we had essay tests—I always could sell the notes—so I knew I had some ability to write. My interest in the music, which started with my dad's record collection, was developing rapidly; when I got to college, I got a real thirst for new records. I would often drive thirty-five miles to Cleveland because in those days records were released regionally instead of nationally; records would come to Cleveland before they came to stores in Kent. So I had this interest in records, and the black student newspaper, the *Black Watch*, was developing, and I saw an opportunity to write about music. Then, lo and behold, I found if I wrote about music, they would send me records. It was like a drug. (Thirty or so years later, it became, "Oh my God, here come some more records . . ." [Both laugh.]) But back then, as a college student, you didn't have any money, it was great. So I began writing record reviews.

    Then there was this place in Cleveland called the Smiling Dog Saloon on West Twenty-Fifth. (When I grew up, Cleveland was like two cities: you had the West Side and the East Side. Going to the West Side was an adventure in and of itself.) But this club brought everybody, and it became the place where I had my first opportunities to hear a lot of people I hadn't heard before; musicians weren't traveling through Cleveland for concerts, and back then, the whole idea of a "jazz concert" was confined to the Ellingtons or the Basies or big singers or whatnot. Wasn't what it is today. So it was the club or nothing. But all these great people were coming [to the Smiling Dog Saloon]. I had the opportunity to hear the original Weather Report; the original Return to Forever with Flora [Purim] and Airto [Moreira]; Mingus; the Keith Jarrett quartet with Dewey Redman, Charlie Haden, and Paul Motian—all these kinds of musicians were coming through on a weekly basis, and we would travel the thirty-five miles on the weekends. I started writing little observations about what I experienced at the Smiling Dog. That's how it began.

FEINSTEIN: You began college at the height of the Black Arts Movement. Did that influence you as a writer?

JENKINS: It did, though not as directly as you might imagine. It did in terms of establishing the need, desire, and philosophy of this black student newspaper. We had a strong black student movement on campus; we developed an organization called BUS (Black United Students).

It's always interesting: when people find out I went to Kent State, automatically May 4, 1970, comes up. "Were you there?" "Yeah, I was there"—but that day, I was on the bus going to class, and they told us to get back on the bus and go home. I saw it all develop: they burned the ROTC building on a Thursday night; by the weekend, the [Ohio] National Guard was on campus, and we were like an army base. Monday is when the incident happened.

Now, the black students had had an insurrection of our own the year prior. The Oakland Police Department was going around to different campuses recruiting, and we knew their reputation for suppressing the Black Panther Party in Oakland, so we organized a protest of them coming on our campus. That protest escalated to us taking over one of the campus buildings, and at a certain point, the sheriff's department and campus police and others gathered in great force; they were about to bust us all. So we decided that discretion was the better part of valor: we would march around campus and demonstrate after we exited this building. But some students got loud with us, and fights broke out and it became a big incident. It escalated over the weekend. Then someone in the Black United Students discovered some kind of statute in terms of universities receiving funding that mandated they had to have a certain percentage of so-called minority student population or they'd be defunded. So we decided that we, en masse, would march off campus—leave—and threaten the university with being defunded unless they met certain demands. Among those demands was the development of what is now the Pan African Studies Department and building—the whole thing. We went off campus for a week, during which time we made a manifesto; then they met our demands and we came back.

So we had had an action the year prior. What happened culminating on May 4, 1970, was basically an SDS [Students for a Democratic Society] action. We had colleagues and friends in SDS, but that was an SDS action.

FEINSTEIN: After college, when you started writing for the same newspaper as your father [the *Cleveland Plain Dealer*], were you also writing music reviews?

JENKINS: Well, here's the thing: I wasn't working for the newspaper.

FEINSTEIN: You weren't writing for them?

JENKINS: I was writing for it, yes, but as a stringer. My dad got me a meeting with a man named Robert (Bob) Roach, the editor of the Friday magazine. (Most major daily newspapers have a Friday Arts and Entertainment supplement.) Believe it or not, they actually had two jazz writers at the same time. Chris Colombi, whom I'd grown up listening to on the radio and reading his stuff in the *Plain Dealer*, wrote the regular record review column. What Bob Roach had me do was write previews: who was playing that week in town, who was playing the following week—that kind of thing. I did that for about twelve years, and that developed into other writing opportunities. I started writing for several alternative weeklies. That's how I got started. But I never made a living writing. Never—it's been a base, a core, a foundation.

FEINSTEIN: You've written a great many liner notes, which I've appreciated for decades.

JENKINS: Thank you. The first one I wrote was for a Rodney Jones album, *Articulation* [1978], for a Joe Fields label [Timeless Muse].

FEINSTEIN: You've been writing for Joe Lovano since 1991.

JENKINS: Growing up in Cleveland, there were two tenor players who were my peers: one a little bit younger, one a bit older. The older one was Ernie Krivda; the younger one was Joe Lovano. I've seen them in practically every stage of their development. Joe's father was highly respected among a lot of musicians. I can remember being in the Smiling Dog when Elvin Jones was playing. Joe walks in, and Elvin says, "Where's your dad?" Everybody knew Big T—Tony Lovano. He was very much a union guy, so he played with everybody.

FEINSTEIN: I'd like to hear you talk about your really expansive notes for the Mosaic Records release *The Complete Clifford Jordan Strata-East Sessions*. I'm a huge fan of [producer] Michael Cuscuna and Mosaic. Apart from the music itself, their LP-sized booklets give a writer a lot of room to introduce the artists, establish the historical context, discuss the music tune by tune, and so on. What was your process in creating those notes?

JENKINS: I've known Michael Cuscuna for years, and he contacted me about this opportunity to reissue what was in essence the Clifford Jordan series on Strata-East. I thought it would be great; I knew a lot of those records when they'd been released as LPs. I also had been friends with [pianist] Stanley Cowell [who recorded on Strata-East] when he was living here in the [DC] area, so it seemed like a natural opportunity, a no-brainer. Those were records that I was very warm to, and I was happy that they were finally being reissued digitally. And, like you, I'm a great appreciator of Mosaic and what that label has been about.

FEINSTEIN: In your notes—as with your book created with Randy Weston [*African Rhythms*]—you lean on interviews. That seems to be one of your primary moves.

JENKINS: In any notes that I do, I always want to have the artist's voice. I don't feel that I as the liner note writer should be the final arbiter of the recording's benefits. In this case, Clifford wasn't around anymore, but I knew I could get Stanley Cowell, [Clifford's wife] Sandy Jordan, and others.

FEINSTEIN: In your notes for the Mosaic set, you quote Randy Weston on why he hired Clifford Jordan, and he said, "I like the music to sound like the way black people talk." Is that true for you, too, and what does that mean?

JENKINS: You know, you'd have to ask him about that. I understand what he was saying.

FEINSTEIN: How do you interpret the line?

JENKINS: Well, the instrument is the extension of the human voice, and in his experience with musicians, he can hear the black vernacular coming through their instrument the same as he can in speech. That's what he meant. And that was an extremely interesting point. It was not something he had said during the course of writing the book [*African Rhythms*]. Again, with him it's a constant revelation and evolution of thought. But I'm glad you picked that out; it was a very interesting point, and it started me thinking about a lot of things. I can't own that. That was his original thought. But I know where he was coming from, and it's something I began to contemplate more closely once he said that.

FEINSTEIN: When you write notes for albums that first appeared as LPs or CDs with different liners—Benny Green's notes for *Dizzy's Big Four*, say, or Orrin Keepnews's notes for Cannonball Adderley's *Things Are Getting Better*—do you try to respond to the earlier texts?

JENKINS: No, I actually avoid reading the original before I get started. At some point I read them, but I want to avoid that because I don't want them to be overly influential on what I say. I want mine to be original thoughts. Also, I realize that what they wrote was locked in a certain time frame. What I'm writing is often based upon a reexamination of that particular artist or session based on the passage of time and, perhaps, influenced by what that artist has come to mean since the time of those recordings. For example, with Cannonball: a lot transpired in Cannonball's career, even though he lived a short life [1928–1975], between the time that session was made [1958] and the time that he passed, particularly in terms of his popularity. You want to take those kinds of things into account. It's not as though I want to avoid what Orrin wrote because I have a lot of respect for Orrin—in fact I interviewed him for Randy's book. I just wanted to keep it as fresh as I could.

FEINSTEIN: Speaking of your book with Randy Weston: ordinarily, I would ask the author about the process of making such a work—concept, approach, and so on—but your introduction to *African Rhythms* explains things so clearly that I'll simply encourage people to read the book. Wonderful stories about being invited on trips to Africa. What would you say were some of the greatest surprises for you during the process?

JENKINS: Well, I'm not sure you would call them surprises—more like revelations, I guess. The whole aspect of Morocco being revealed was important. That first trip was an eye-opener for me because my perception of North Africa was based on it being entirely Arab. At its core, that's the case, but I didn't realize how many black Moroccans there were, nor did I know much about Berber culture. Having those kinds of things revealed to me, and experiencing the country through his experiences there, was wonderful. We went in May of 2001, and I've been back six or seven times—mainly for the Gnawa [World Music] Festival. And that's a funny thing, too, because some of Randy's Gnawa friends early on disparaged the festival; one of his collaborators in Marrakech, who, my sense was, had not been invited down to play at the Gnawa Festival, referred to the festival as Gnawa A-Go-Go—a festivalization of sacred music. But I did not find that to be the case, and I subsequently became friendly with the woman who produces the Gnawa Festival, Neila Tazi. I recognized the purity in what they were trying to do there. So [I found] Morocco in particular, and much of Africa, revealed through working with Randy. I had never been to Africa before he and I started working, and now, in addition to the trips to Morocco, I've been several times to Ghana and South Africa. I've just scratched the surface, but I hadn't even had that experience before working with him.

FEINSTEIN: You say in the book that you gave him full authorization to excise anything he didn't want, and that some of his edits were a little heartbreaking to cut. I'm *not* asking you to reveal those—

JENKINS: There're no deep revelations.

FEINSTEIN: I'm just wondering about the process: Did you try to coax him to leave things in? It must be difficult when you're working collaboratively.

JENKINS: Well, first off, he didn't take out a lot, and what he took out was, in essence, not in any way harmful to the draft that I had given him, so there was no controversy. It was never, "Oh man, he really emasculated what I said! We need to go back and rethink this." But he didn't want any kiss-and-tell aspects, and he didn't want a whole lot about his love life (except for the chapter on Fatoumata, his current wife). So there's very little in the book on his first wife, the mother of his children, and I didn't press him on that because he was so forthcoming about so much and has such great recall. Why press him on this because I'm getting so much, you know what I'm saying?

FEINSTEIN: Right. What he recalled seemed fresh as a spring. Weston was quite close to Langston Hughes. What are your feelings about Hughes's contributions to the album *Uhuru Afrika* [1960]?

JENKINS: They were very important. His contributions to that session were like a seal of approval from the classic African American literature side. The fact that he would *eagerly* agree to write lyrics to one of the pieces, the liner notes, as well as the freedom poem (as Randy refers to it) that opens the piece—it was all very important. I think that they've been undervalued historically because not a lot of people realize that until it's told to them. It's an eye-opener for a lot of people. "Oh . . . Langston Hughes contributed to that album. He didn't do that for anyone else." Langston was a jazz fan—we know that—but he didn't necessarily go that far for other artists, so Randy must have been special to him.

One of the more humorous anecdotes in the book took place at Langston Hughes's funeral. Langston's assistant revealed that Langston wanted Randy to play at it. Randy didn't know that, and he was so touched and honored. They played a set of blues, and Randy said all these great friends of Langston's were there, like Lena Horne, and she said [Feinstein and Jenkins speak in unison]: "I didn't know whether to pat my foot or not." [Both laugh.]

FEINSTEIN: And also the note written by Hughes to Weston saying to make sure the musicians were paid scale. [Both laugh.] So great.

Do you have other book projects in mind?

JENKINS: Yeah, I do. I've been wrestling with a couple of ideas. As I said, I've never written for a living—I've always done other things—and it's difficult to carve out time to properly nurture a book project. But I did a series of interviews on my site [Open-SkyJazz.com]. It started innocently enough with looking around and realizing, "Hmm, it's curious to me why there have been so few African American writers on the subject of jazz music." So I started interviewing a few that I knew, and it grew into a series called Ain't But a Few of Us.

FEINSTEIN: Did you get that title from the Bags album [Milt Jackson's *Ain't But a Few of Us Left*]?

JENKINS: No. That just came to mind—because there ain't but a few of us. So that's one project, and the other is on the history of jazz radio because there's not been a book done on that. That's a larger project and will require a lot of research.

FEINSTEIN: One of my favorite photos of you is the picture with Amiri Baraka [from 2013]. You look *so* happy. How well did you know him?

JENKINS: I didn't know him that well. I knew him because, for one, Tom Porter—a guy who used to be program director at WPFW and who invited me to come on the air when we first moved to DC in '89—was a great friend of Baraka's and would talk about him all the time. He also brought him to town, and Baraka performed most recently at Bohemian Caverns. So I would go to hear him. (Actually, going to hear him was more like *experiencing* him.) We had a nodding acquaintance and would speak.

He was the recipient of the Lifetime Achievement Award from the Jazz Journalists Association in 2012, the year before I received it, so he was elected to give the award to me. He got up for his introductory remarks and, in typical Baraka fashion he said, "Yeah, you know, I have to say I have some issues with that Ain't But a Few of Us series because, you know, some of us were doing that when we were doing *The Cricket* publication [1968–1969]," et cetera. "But this is the man who wrote the Randy Weston book . . ." So then he introduced me. I went up and accepted the award, and I told the audience, "This is great: to get an award *and* get a backhand at the same time from Amiri Baraka." [Both laugh.] Everybody cracked up. Then the photographers came up to take shots of the two of us standing there, so as a gag I reached over and grabbed him by the neck like I was choking him. The picture you saw was the aftermath of that, when we were both laughing.

FEINSTEIN: That's wonderful.

JENKINS: I had my Baraka moment.

FEINSTEIN: Did his writing influence you?

JENKINS: Oh, yeah. Clearly—because of *who* he was writing about in the music. He wasn't so much concerned with the

Taking It Back | 157

aspects of the science of music as he was the deeper meanings of music in terms of the musicians and what they were trying to express and what they were contributing culturally. He wrote from a uniquely black perspective on jazz, and I always respected that. I can't say that he was a writing model, but I appreciated a lot of metaphorical things he would write and the humor in a lot of what he wrote. He never seemed to be someone who took himself too seriously, but the music was as serious as a heart attack to him, and that came through. He didn't have a holier-than-thou attitude in his writing; he came through as being humane.

FEINSTEIN: Who *were* some of your models?

JENKINS: The usual suspects. Coming up, you're reading Nat Hentoff, [Dan] Morgenstern, Leonard Feather—who was very kind to me, I have to say. When I was working at Arts Midwest running their regional jazz program, I had a quarterly news publication. He got a couple of copies and sent me a nice letter saying he appreciated what we were trying to do. I would see him at George Wein's festivals in New York. He was kind, and I always appreciated what he wrote as well. There was another guy I was reading early on named Alan Heineman. He was someone who was as much versed in Frank Zappa as he was in John Coltrane, and, at the time, I too was involved with rock music as well. I appreciated his approach; he was obviously from my generation. Ron Welburn is another person I was reading quite a bit. Various people. I was at a point in my development as a reader and writer where certain names would be marks of quality. If I saw a certain person's byline, I knew, whether I agreed with the opinion or not, it would be worth reading.

FEINSTEIN: You've spent a lot of time with A. B. Spellman. What do you think of his creative work?

JENKINS: A. B. Spellman has always been first class. I first knew him not as a poet or jazz writer (although I read *Four Lives* [*in the Bebop Business*] coming up); I knew him as the director of the Expansion Arts program at the National Endowment for the Arts. At the time, he was one of the few African Americans running a program at the NEA. I was working at Arts Midwest and got invited to serve on various panels as "a jazz guy," and eventually that created opportunities to be a panelist for the NEA. I got to know him through his sterling reputation with Expansion Arts; it was later, when I moved here in '89, when I became more closely acquainted to him as a person. He's someone I greatly appreciate.

FEINSTEIN: You wrote a powerful piece about racism and jazz that was inspired, in part, by Stanley Crouch being let go by *JazzTimes*. Crouch himself has been a little more one-sided on this topic (perhaps ironically, in this context): he places the blame for not having more black writers on African Americans. He says it's this way simply because more white people have expressed interest in the music.

JENKINS: And there's some truth to that, for certain. There's an interesting yin and yang to that whole aspect. I've heard African American people express thoughts to the effect that, "Oh, they're taking our music away from us," and my response has always been, "Nothing's being taken; you've *given* it away, and you've given it away through neglect." You need to look no further than the [predominantly white] jazz audience.

On the other hand, we wrestle with the African American sector of the jazz audience, and how often you see very few African Americans at jazz presentations. That's a little different here in DC because of the populace. But, you know, when you also look at free festivals or free presentations in urban areas, such as the Chicago Jazz Festival, you will always see a robust African American audience at that festival. I suppose a lot of it breaks down to economics and whatnot. But I feel that a lot of folks have abdicated the throne when it comes to this music and the whole idea of where this music originally came from, and how important this music is to the African experience in America. Certain people have either (a) lost sight of that, (b) never had sight of it, or (c) simply have neglected that aspect. I've thought about this a lot, and I blame my own generation to a certain respect. I know this is an oversimplification, but I don't see where my generation—the baby boom generation—experienced the same evolution through music as, for example, our parents' generation. I think back on my father's record collection, and to his friends: My parents' generation seemed to start with the popular music of the day, but then their musical tastes evolved and further developed. Whereas, I see a lot of my peers continue throughout their lives to be consumers of pop music. They got seduced by pop music. During my development—the baby boomers' development, and yours, too, I'm sure—rock and pop and R & B became what they are today and began to truly overwhelm the marketplace. Many in my generation did not take the next step to more creative forms of music. So there are a lot of reasons why we have this disparity of African American audiences for jazz—a lot of reasons far beyond what I've theorized on—but it does exist, and it's been part of a puzzle for me. The only thing I can do is continue to push the envelope in whatever I do: my writing, presenting, radio work.

FEINSTEIN: In your contribution to the biography *David Baker: A Legacy in Music*, you mention the writer Sam Greenlee.

JENKINS: *The Spook Who Sat by the Door* [Greenlee's novel from 1969].

FEINSTEIN: Greenlee once wrote that he thought of himself as a jazz musician with a typewriter as his instrument. Do you feel similarly?

JENKINS: I guess there is some validity to that because I've never been a musician. (My grandmother gave me a trumpet as a middle school kid, and I didn't want to practice, so I fell by the wayside in terms of my music aspirations.) Once I became more immersed in the music and became part of the so-called community, my means of expressing my love for the music as well as my listener's sense of the music was through the written word and broadcasting.

FEINSTEIN: You alluded to Greenlee with Dave [Baker] as a way of asking him if he felt racism had played a part regarding being quieted in panel discussions. He chuckles—he hears you—but he doesn't bite.

Jenkins: Maybe that's politic. Dave is very forthright about a lot of things, but Dave has never been a finger-pointer. That's not his attitude, not who he is. He's not one to call people or things out. He recognizes systemic disparities and issues, but he's not a hanging judge, like Stanley [Crouch] wants to be.

Feinstein: That holds true for John Coltrane, too, in interviews like the famous one with Frank Kofsky, who keeps trying to push the conversation to black politics influencing jazz but Trane will only talk about music.

Jenkins: That's because Trane was on a path. Trane had a vision, and that wasn't part of his vision; that wasn't what he was trying to address musically. So I guess he didn't want to be drawn into that. With some people, you recognize that they know what time it is, but they don't necessarily want to be controversial in how they express that.

Feinstein: Has that been frustrating for you as an interviewer—when people don't want to address topics of race?

Jenkins: I won't say it's been frustrating because you recognize where people are coming from philosophically pretty early in the game and so you work with them from that perspective.

~

Feinstein: I want to congratulate you on being the new artistic director of the DC Jazz Festival.

Jenkins: Thank you.

Feinstein: It's a huge honor, and a daunting task, I would think.

Jenkins: It is.

FEINSTEIN: I'm really sorry that I won't be able to attend the events. I would especially love to hear the sets by Jack DeJohnette, The Cookers, and Nicholas Payton. What is the process for selecting the festival artists?

JENKINS: It's a process that's based on a lot of different variables. Number one, of course, is fundraising, but number two is this community and the capacity of this community and the venues that you're trying to serve within this community, as well as the desire to be festive. In other words, the desire to do things that are not available throughout the year. That's a more daunting task than it was in Cleveland because here there's so much happening throughout the year. People would be surprised at the level of jazz activity here in this community. We also have a high level of resident jazz musicians.

The DC Jazz Festival has a lot of moving parts. It has been striving—and has achieved—a "big tent" kind of effect. It has marshaled a lot of the forces that work with or present jazz throughout the year to come under the big tent during festival time. You've got these different venues to work with in terms of what they're going to contribute to the festival and what we're going to contribute to them. We also have this philosophy of serving the entire city, and there are parts of this city that rarely (if ever) have jazz performances—particularly east of the Anacostia River—but which do during the festival. So there's a component called East River Jazz Festival, which was developed by a man named Vernard Gray (he's the curator of that), so they're bringing jazz east of the river where it's rarely performed. We're in all four quadrants, and that's a big task to marshal all those different forces, but bringing a diverse sense of the music is an important part of the juggling act.

With festivals, in order to achieve a lasting success, you have to diversify; you have to bring a diverse perspective of music. You have to try to represent a lot of different branches of this tree we call jazz. Jazz is not one style of music; it's more like an aesthetic umbrella under which all these different forms exist, 'cause if you put a hundred people in a room and ask them, "What is jazz?" you might get seventy-five different definitions.

FEINSTEIN: Maybe one hundred.

JENKINS: Yeah. So you look at what we're doing, and you see someone like [hip hop artist] Common on the lineup, and you say, "Common's not a jazz artist." Well, Common has had relations with jazz artists. He has had jazz artists as his musical director (like Derrick Hodge and Robert Glasper). He has great respect for the form. And what he does as a wordist has a relationship, historically, to jazz. So I think it fits. In addition, he's part of an evening that's in a big park on the river front, so there's a lot of capacity to fill that park, and we have a responsibility of filling that park. And, unfortunately, if we had a lineup of jazz musicians like people you just mentioned—Jack DeJohnette, Nicholas Payton, and The Cookers—it would not fill that park. But we have a responsibility to do that, both to sustain the festival and to try to bring as broad a constituency as we can. We know that if you've got a younger person who is attracted to the fact that they want to come to Yards Park to hear Common and Esperanza Spalding and Femi Kuti on that Saturday night, hopefully they're going to have a really good experience, and that really good experience is going to translate to, "Oh, the DC Jazz Festival—that's about quality. Let's go experience some of these other things that we may not know. Let's go to Bohemian Caverns and hear Lionel Loueke and Gretchen Parlato, or the Bohemian Caverns Jazz Orchestra with Oliver Lake. Let's go to CapitalBop and experience their AACM [Association for the Advancement of Creative Musicians] fiftieth anniversary tribute." Meeting the needs of this diverse community has been refreshing, challenging, and enjoyable.

We also have opportunities to make this event unique from a District of Columbia perspective because we have some resources that other cities don't. For example, we have the Fishman Young Artist [Embassy] series, named for DC Jazz Festival founder Charlie Fishman, that's held at embassies, so we've cultivated various relationships with different embassies. Most of them want the young artists to be nationals from their country, so we have a lot of people from different countries playing here in town. We also have a relationship with Berklee

[College of Music], and they have top-flight students from over 140 countries, so we can bring some of those young people to perform at these events. There's no other festival that can claim this kind of relationship with foreign embassies, and, hopefully, the upshot will also enable us to bring some of their professionals to the festival. We're working now with the French Embassy to bring one of their French jazz composers for next year, and we're working with the Embassy of South Africa to bring artists here because South Africa has a rich and deep jazz tradition with great musicians. We're working an international angle because, for one, it's a mark of distinction for our community.

FEINSTEIN: How much of a free hand do you have, personally, in selecting the artists?

JENKINS: I have a free hand in selecting artists for a lot of different elements. For events curated by other venues, we have a working relationship where we discuss certain ideas. With Bohemian Caverns, for example, we discuss certain ideas they have just to make sure that they mesh with the overall themes with what we're doing.

FEINSTEIN: If a journalist came to you and said, "I've been sent to cover the DC Jazz Festival," given how spread out everything is, what would your advice be? It's literally impossible to cover everything.

JENKINS: Oh, it *is* impossible. Absolutely. There's so much overlap. I would suggest they take a good look at the schedule, be cognizant of the times, and consider distances/geography. You need to map out a plan 'cause, like you say, you're not going to be able to go to everything. This will be my first experience trying to go to as much as I can, and I know that's going to be difficult. In fact, I'm going to be staying in a hotel downtown just to try and do as much as I can. But you have to map out a strategy—just like you do, for example with [the festivals at] Montreal and Monterey. At Monterey, although everything is right there on the fairgrounds, you need to have a strategy for what you really want to see and how much of it you really want to see because there's going to be some overlap. So-and-so may be over at the Garden Stage, but you're over at Dizzy's, and you want to see somebody at the Arena Stage. You have to map these things out. And here, the challenge is even greater because there are transportation issues going from place to place.

FEINSTEIN: Exactly. That's partly why I asked. I remember Dan Morgenstern telling me that the most difficult assignments for him were covering festivals. It seems all the more challenging here in DC.

JENKINS: Hustling around from place to place. I guess that's a good question to ask somebody like Mike West, who writes for the *Washington Post* and for *JazzTimes*, and for the alternative weekly, *City Paper*.

FEINSTEIN: You've taught classes on the history of jazz.

JENKINS: I've taught at two places. I taught, briefly when we were in Minneapolis, at one of those adult education schools without walls called Open University, but the main two places were Cleveland State and Kent State, my alma mater. At Kent State, I taught online courses. At Cleveland State, I taught a jazz survey course and the history of jazz course.

FEINSTEIN: What do you think is the most difficult thing for you (or anybody) in terms of trying to teach jazz?

JENKINS: As I said, I don't have practical experience performing; I teach from the perspective of an enthusiast. And you need to recognize who you're teaching. Early on, it became clear that I was teaching to people for whom this was their first jazz experience, whether it was the survey course or the history course. I can't tell you how many students have said things to the effect of, "This really opened up a new world of music to me. I didn't know this music existed." I gave up being astounded by that, and just recognized what that was about.

  The fact that I was not a practitioner didn't matter after a while. I had to develop myself as a historian to go beyond the enthusiast level. One of the hardest things to get people to understand is what it means to improvise. A lot of people think that improvising means just playing whatever you want, and that's not the case in this music. There is a blueprint at work (in most cases), and people are improvising off of that blueprint.

My friend Howie Smith, a saxophonist and composer who taught for years at Cleveland State, would do an interesting thing that would make it crystal clear to these students what it meant to improvise. He would come in with one or two of his horns—he played all the reed instruments—and he'd have one of those Jamey Aebersold music-minus-one recordings. Then he would demonstrate the different means of improvising on the same piece of music. He would start out by just playing it straight, and then he would do different variations. And it was real clear to them, after they heard that, what the whole aspect of improvisation meant. So that was a big hurdle that he would help clear.

When I taught at Kent State, it was an online course, so clearly I did not have that kind of resource. This was a very specific course related to my work on that book [with Randy Weston]. It was something that came to me as I was writing and dealing with different aspects of the music. I called the course Jazz Imagines Africa. If you think about the origins of the music, part of the origins come from Africa, and you have this African sensibility and this marriage with other elements of music. So there's that root source. But then you have musicians in the second half of the twentieth century who, through their compositions and music, are imagining their African roots and their African origins, like Randy with *Uhuru Afrika*, et cetera. Robin Kelley talked a lot about this in his book, *Africa Speaks, America Answers*. (Those were the two texts: *African Rhythms* and Robin's book.) We would explore things like Yusef Lateef's residency in Nigeria, some of the things Archie Shepp wrote, a number of different things—including the Danish guitar player Pierre Dørge: his interactions with South African musicians like Johnny Dyani, and how he crafted the Jungle Orchestra based partly on Duke [Ellington] but based primarily on the African root. And, like I said, there's that same reaction: "Wow . . . a new world of music. I didn't know this music existed." [Both laugh.] I began to recognize and appreciate what these students had been exposed to, what they'd *not* been exposed to (obviously), and that, okay, this was my responsibility to be a door opener.

FEINSTEIN: You conclude your contribution to the Dave Baker bio by quoting the NEA master: "My life's lesson to kids now is to go to wisdom sources whenever you can, take advantage of these jazz masters that we're going to be losing at some point. We're trying to expose people to as much truth as we can by going back to these sources." Is that largely your mission as well?

JENKINS: Everything I do is really based upon further exposure for the music. You know this, too: you kind of feel like a loner sometimes when you're among your peers. "Yeah, he's the *jazz* guy," you know what I'm saying? [Both laugh.] "Ask him about it. He knows about it. I don't know anything about it, but he knows about that jazz." [Both laugh.] Any time a jazz reference comes up, they want to refer to you, or hip you to it (like you don't know about it). "You know, I was readin' about this *jazz* musician . . ." You become sort of a disciple of the music, and you feel a certain responsibility to do whatever you can to expose as many people as you can to the music and broaden the audience. We've got all these great musicians, and the biggest issue for me is always audience development. That's the core of what this work I'm doing here in DC and what I did in Cleveland: the biggest hurdle is trying to develop the audience.

You hear these things from students: "You opened up a world of music to me." Or you take a friend [to a jazz performance]: "Wow! That was great. I really enjoyed that. I didn't know I liked jazz." Or this common response: "Wow, I didn't know *that* was jazz." That's what I mean by that whole aesthetic umbrella. "I thought I didn't like jazz." I've heard that so many times. So you write, you broadcast, you present—all these different things to try to broaden the audience.

I got into presenting concerts back in Cleveland. The Smiling Dog Saloon was forced to close down [in 1975] based on racism. As I said earlier, the Smiling Dog was located on West Twenty-Fifth—west of the river. East of the river was where the great majority of the African American population lived; west of the river was the exact opposite (at least then—it's different now). You had this jazz club located on the West Side, and, unfortunately, people in the neighborhood of the club began to complain to their city councilmen 'bout all these people coming over—not that there was this overwhelming black audience, but there were enough black people coming to the Smiling Dog that certain people in the neighborhood began to complain. And the city councilmen found a way to drive them away. The guy who ran the place, Roger Bohn, began presenting jazz concerts downtown at the Allen theater: Miles [Davis] several times, a double bill once with Keith Jarrett and Gato Barbieri, Sun Ra. But that dried up. And around the same time, an article in *Down Beat* appeared ["How to Step Out into Jazz Society" by Dr. William L. Fowler, November 1977], and it included interviews with two guys: one was Monk Montgomery—Wes's brother, who was in Vegas at the time—and Danny Skea, a keyboard player who worked a lot of the Vegas shows. They were talking about the development of the Las Vegas Jazz Society and how they put it together—their reasons and philosophy behind it—and what they had been able to achieve at the time. I found this article to be very interesting because we were in a jazz deficit at that time; no touring artists were coming through town at the time.

  I got together with a couple of friends and said, "Read this article. Think we can do that here in this community?" So we founded an organization called the Northeast Ohio Jazz Society. The whole thing was about creating a higher profile for jazz music and developing the audience. We started presenting concerts, and that's how my interest in curating and presenting concerts began. That, to me, is the most exciting and continually interesting work that I have done in this music—not to say that the writing or broadcasting or teaching hasn't been very stimulating, but the whole idea of trying to figure out a community, an audience, a venue; trying to figure out what people are interested in hearing . . . It's a real hit or miss thing. Always is. But it was a *real* hit or miss thing when I first started. Certain musicians I thought people wanted to hear: we would lose our shirts. But we just kept doing it, kept developing. It's a juggling act, a gambling act, but it's something I really love doing: Bringing the music to audiences.

9

But I Know What Time It Is Now

Hettie Jones

Hettie Jones (1934–2024) was the author of a memoir, *How I Became Hettie Jones*, and three poetry collections: *Drive*, *All Told*, and *Doing 70*. She also published many books for children and young adults, including *Big Star Fallin' Mama: Five Women in Black Music*. Having worked at the *Partisan Review*, she later cofounded the magazine *Yugen* (1957–1963). She was the chair of the PEN Prison Writing Committee, and, from 1989 to 2002, ran a writing workshop at the New York State Correctional Facility for Women at Bedford Hills. She lectured widely and teaches at The New School and the 92nd Street Y Poetry Center.

Unfortunately, excerpts of Hettie Jones's writing could not be obtained for reprint in this publication. The interview took place at her home in Manhattan's East Village on November 23, 2013.

Interview

SASCHA FEINSTEIN: At how many different places are you teaching right now?

HETTIE JONES: Oh! Well, I teach memoir for the 92nd Street Y, and I teach at The New School, which recently gave me a grant to teach at the Lower East Side Girls Club. Years ago I taught, say, sixty students at four different places, but I'm a little older than I used to be! [Laughs.]

FEINSTEIN: How long have you been at The New School?

JONES: Since the eighties.

FEINSTEIN: Were you friends with Sekou Sundiata?

JONES: [Wistfully:] Yeah.

FEINSTEIN: That was such a loss. [Sundiata died in 2007 at the age of fifty-eight.]

JONES: I know . . . I remember when I gave a reading in a little bookstore in Brooklyn, a place I hadn't even heard of myself, and he just showed right up, you know? Someplace you wouldn't expect. But he was like that.

FEINSTEIN: What did you think of his projects uniting poetry and jazz?

JONES: I just thought that anything he did was fine! [Laughs.] Whatever you want to do, honey, that's okay with me. I'm so used to people doing whatever they want to do, and it usually works out into something unique and not replaceable.

FEINSTEIN: He's the only poet I've ever known who had a tenured professorship without a book—everything was on CD.

JONES: That's the way he wanted to do it. And spoken word is lovely. There's an organization in New York called Urban Word, for kids, and I judged their final contest at the Apollo [Theater] last spring. And the kids were so good. Mostly they were writing—not poetry, really, but memoir, basically. Talking about their lives; that's what kids like to talk about. The personal essay. And I think that's just fine.

FEINSTEIN: This apartment is astonishing. Tell me a little about it.

JONES: This was the attic. These were the maids' rooms. The house was built in 1844/'45 by a cartman with the name of Pinckney, and I thought, "Oh! He was a black person." But my daughter Kellie, who's very knowledgeable about everything, said, "Don't get all excited, Mom." [Both laugh.] She said, "It's an English name."

FEINSTEIN: And you've been here half a century.

JONES: Yes. It'll be fifty-one years in January.

FEINSTEIN: What's kept you here?

JONES: There's a lot of room, although it didn't seem so roomy when there were all those people here [in the 1960s when she was married to the late LeRoi Jones, later known as Amiri Baraka]: me, the former LeRoi (that's what I call him), the kids [two daughters, Kellie and Lisa], and anyone else who happened to drop by and needed a place to stay. Now it's very roomy; it's all mine.

    As you get older, everyone gets more worried. "Mom . . . You have to worry about being *safe*." And it was pretty funky around here for a little while. But it's a safe neighborhood. I've known all my neighbors for years and years. The owner had an auto supply store, and they were here almost as long as I have. They always looked after us, especially when I was raising the kids by myself. It's a very private house. [Tenor saxophonist] Archie Shepp used to live downstairs. Below, a guy named Marzette Watts, who made some recordings [on saxophones and bass clarinet].

FEINSTEIN: How long did the Shepps live below you?

JONES: Quite some time. They arrived with two children and left with four. [Laughs.] That's the way I can measure it. Around ten years. They left when Archie got a job at the University of Massachusetts. Of us all, Archie was the one who had serious experience: he had a degree from Goddard, but he was also doing home schooling for kids with disabilities. He worked hard.

FEINSTEIN: Did you ever talk with him about any crossovers between literature and jazz?

JONES: No, because Archie was always moving around. Of course, he wrote plays as well.

FEINSTEIN: That's partly why I asked.

JONES: I think there were so many people doing whatever they wanted to do back then. Nothing was really called "crossover." It was just, "Oh, that's what he does"—and, I have to admit, very little of "That's what *she* does," because "she" was in the kitchen. But I wasn't in the kitchen because I was working. And I don't have any regrets about when I started to write or anything like that, and I try to encourage young women not to be concerned if everyone around them already has a book out. Just keep going because you never can tell.

FEINSTEIN: Nor is publication the ball game.

JONES: That's right. Really.

FEINSTEIN: In your memoir, you write, "Music was my first written language—I read notes before words—and it had also come coded."

JONES: I think I'm a writer because I'm a musician manqué. As I said, I read music before I could read words. I lived at the edge of Queens, and I passed the test for Music and Art High School (one of the three competitive high schools in New York), but I didn't go because it would've meant a *long* walk to the bus, and then two trains. Also, I come from a family where there were no artists, where my exceptionalism was viewed with a little suspicion. And when you're a thirteen-year-old girl, what you want is acceptance. I have an older sister who's very pretty, blond with a waist like this [Jones closes her hand to create a circle about the size of a fifty-cent piece]. She was the pretty one and I was the smart one. Those distinctions were very clearly made. So, I played a little piano, took some lessons, but nothing satisfied me. Then, when I got to college [at Mary Washington College, then the women's college of the University of Virginia in 1951], I was allowed to do *anything*, so I wrote musical comedies, and played piano—but I found I just didn't have enough training in music, apart from my ear.

One of my sons-in-law is Guthrie Ramsey who [has written widely about music and] teaches at the University of Pennsylvania. When I showed him that I could play major, minor, augmented, diminished chords, he said, "Well, you can do that all by ear. Now you need to study," and I thought, "Uh . . . I think it's a little late." [Laughs.]

When I first heard [Thelonious] Monk, I thought, "Oh! *That*'s what I've always wanted to do: to play something that wasn't familiar, something that would startle. [Growing up,] I hadn't heard jazz. I think my father once said Mahalia Jackson was the best singer in the world, but what did I know? There was nothing to encourage me; I had to find my own way.

Many people say to me, "You have so much music when you recite," but it's natural. I didn't adopt it from anywhere. But when I learned from the Black Mountain people about the breath and finding your own rhythm—that's how you measure your own line—that made such sense to me, and I kept going forward.

FEINSTEIN: In your memoir, you mention Monk—hearing him in 1957—and you said he pulled out a sword.

JONES: Yes! He had a cane. We were standing on the sidewalk, probably outside the Five Spot. We were admiring his cane, and out of the cane came this sword! [Both laugh.] What?!

FEINSTEIN: Were there any questions asked?

JONES: No, you didn't ask Monk any questions. [Both laugh.]

FEINSTEIN: So he just resheathed it and left?

JONES: Yes, leaving everyone open-mouthed. He could always surprise you. My favorite memory of Monk is of him standing over the keyboard as though fixing his fingers, and then he would go, "Pah!" [Jones thrusts her splayed hands down as though pounding out a huge, dissonant chord.]

When I was four, a piano appeared [in our house]. It cost fifty cents for a piano lesson, and I had the change clutched in my hand. But I wanted to play; I was fooling around on the piano, and I dropped a quarter in between the keys. I burst out crying. Inconsolable. My parents came running: "What's the matter?" And I told them, and they said, "But look—it still works." But they didn't hear. *I* heard the money jingling, but they didn't hear the off-tone, and I couldn't understand why they couldn't hear it. I just kept crying.

FEINSTEIN: Has your ear been invaluable to you as a writer?

JONES: Oh, sure. Nothing really works until you read it aloud. I keep telling that to my students: Read to the mirror, lock yourself in the bathroom, do whatever you want—but read it aloud. Then you'll get it.

FEINSTEIN: At what point did you decide you needed to write your memoir?

JONES: I had a lot of trouble because people were after me to do that for a long time.

FEINSTEIN: I bet. It's such a wonderful book.

JONES: Thank you. Maybe I waited until I could write a wonderful book. I just thought that everybody wanted to get between the sheets. That was their whole idea: "What's it like—interracial sex?" Prurient interests. And I wanted to do other things. I wanted to talk not about who I was attached to but what I was doing on my own. So before I did any of this [Jones points to the table where I had stacked her memoir and three poetry collections], I wrote thirteen kids' books. Nobody knows anything about them. It's also a drag being ahead of your time: I wrote a teen novel about an interracial girl, and there was something called the Council on Interracial Books for Children, believe it or not, and [after its publication in 1980] they said it was terrible that I showed how the child had a few problems with her identity. You weren't supposed to do that.

FEINSTEIN: In other words, you weren't allowed to speak the truth.

JONES: That's right. This wasn't even based on my own kids or anything; it was completely fictional. But the publisher shredded it; they didn't want to pay warehouse fees. It was gone. I had probably the one copy in the world. (I didn't know then that you have to buy some of your books in order to have them.) If you wrote that book now, it would be published in half a second.

FEINSTEIN: I'm embarrassed to say I've not read it.

JONES: No one has! It was shredded. It disappeared in the eighties.

FEINSTEIN: What was it called?

JONES: *I Hate to Talk about Your Mother.*

FEINSTEIN: Great title!

JONES: There were maybe two dirty words in it. But, you know, I teach YA [Young Adult] and kids' literature—writing workshops—and you hear this all the time. They talk about sex, no holds barred. So, again, doing something ahead of its time can get you in trouble, but after that experience, I had nothing left to do. I had no means of earning a living. I used to alternate my time between writing and editing at home, and I agreed to focus on this memoir. I wrote a few chapters, and my agent sold it to Little, Brown [and Company]. [Photographer] Gordon Parks's wife bought it, but a few weeks later, she left the company. And then, when I sent the first draft to my assigned editor, he said, "This is not the book we expected."

FEINSTEIN: Oh, no . . .

JONES: I know. So then my agent resold it to Dutton, and as soon as Dutton got it, *that* editor got fired, so it was an orphaned book. Then Viking had it and sold out of the hardback quickly, so they published a teeny-weeny paperback. Then that went out of print, and they said, "Oh, sorry. We can't continue it because we have to have more Beat women and publish them all at once; it can't stand on its own." [Feinstein shakes his head, and Jones laughs.] I had made friends with people at Grove Press—I used to do freelance work for them—and they've kept it in print since 1995.

FEINSTEIN: Apart from the publishing traumas, what were some of the surprises for you once you became involved in the memoir?

JONES: Because enough time had passed, I wasn't angry. Whenever I've given readings from it, people expect me to be angry. They want you to be angry because your husband has left you. They want you to be angry because you made a bargain, and then you got screwed. But they didn't have black children, and that was my understanding of it: Who was I to stand in LeRoi's way? The kids were little then, but we experienced plenty of prejudice. People would make comments—whatever. I just wanted a future where my children would be more secure, and whatever had to be done had to be done. At that time [in the sixties], my family had disowned me, and my only family was his family—and I didn't want anything to happen to those people. As I wrote in the book, my favorite line: "Anger has its own kind of string. Unless you let it go, it ties you down," and that's true. I am *not* angry. I have *no* regrets. None at all. And people don't understand that. Or maybe they do now—I don't know.

FEINSTEIN: Before we met, you said you didn't want to talk about Baraka, and I want to respect that, so please feel free to pass on this question if you like: You edited his manuscript *Blues People*.

JONES: That's true. [Laughs.]

FEINSTEIN: What kinds of fingerprints did you leave in that book?

JONES: Oh, no—I just fixed his sentences. And whenever I'd talk to [the writer] Joyce Johnson—I'm not sure if she was the main editor for it but she was the one who made the connection for him—she'd say it needed further editing. But I don't know if it really needed any more editing. He set it up; he knew what he wanted to say. I haven't read it in a long time.

∽

FEINSTEIN: In your memoir, you keep returning to Billie Holiday. Do you feel a spiritual connection with her, a sisterhood?

JONES: Well, my God . . . It's her incredible musicianship, and her command of notes. I could listen to her and listen to her. People say you get tired . . . LeRoi's line in *Black Music*: "Sometimes you are afraid to listen to this lady." It's not the subject matter; you can disregard the subject matter. But you can just listen to her voice, and she always said that: "I consider my voice an instrument." That's fascinating to me. Yeah, she had a hard, hard, hard life—harder than anything—but she had guts.

It was just that awful dope; it's a scourge. And now . . . They make one illegal, and another one pops up. Prescription drugs. Do you know how many people I've seen go under? The musicians. The painters Bob Thompson and William White both died in their *twenties*. Oh wow . . .

FEINSTEIN: A related but lighter note: Frank O'Hara used to hang in this apartment. Did you ever talk to him about Billie Holiday or his justly famous poem ["The Day Lady Died"]?

JONES: No. [Both laugh.] No, but Frank was . . . Maybe because he was gay—I don't know—but maybe that made him so open to accepting women. As you know, he had many women friends. I wrote about him [in the memoir] calling me "Hettie Cohen" and LeRoi saying, "Her name is Jones now." But he always saw me as the woman who was running the *Partisan Review*; he didn't see me as simply the wife and the mother—you know, the Madonna. He always credited that. He should still be alive . . .

FEINSTEIN: Maybe the most bizarre death of any American poet. [O'Hara died at the age of forty in 1966 after being hit by a dune buggy.]

JONES: I know, and in the time we're living now, they would have airlifted him to the best hospital and saved his life. But *everybody* tries to imitate him. I was recently reading from [O'Hara's] *Meditations in an Emergency* [1957], and I thought, "That's Frank. Nobody else can say it [like that]. Nobody else can pull it off." I have a few poems that I called my Frank O'Hara poems (and I have a poem with long lines that I call my Allen Ginsberg poem), but you don't want to imitate people.

FEINSTEIN: In your own poetry, I think the only musician whom you mention more than once is [saxophonist] Albert Ayler.

JONES: Yeah, and I didn't even know him very well. But it was also his tragic death: found in the East River. Everybody thought he was murdered, some weird drug deal gone bad. What a chancy life, you know? What a chancy life.

    I had a forty-year correspondence with [poet] Ed Dorn's first wife, Helene, who became a sculptor. Our letters are very interesting; *some*day someone will publish them. (I have a book all ready to go. People say they can't sell it—though the University of New Mexico Press just published the correspondence between Ed and LeRoi. I'm still fighting the second-class thing.) But in these letters, we justify being married and being on this scene, and everyone said, "Well, it was still a traditional time, and you didn't get treated any better than—" blah blah blah. But at least we didn't have to live "straight"—in the middle-class world.

    In one of my poems, and in my memoir (obviously this was important to me), I see this sign for Mamaroneck [in Westchester County, New York], and this guy says, "When you grow up, you'll go to the suburbs, like Marjorie Morningstar [from Herman Wouk's novel]." But I had absolutely no vision of that—at all. Helene and I used to write about this: No matter how hard the life was, at least we didn't have to do *that*. And that made all the difference. It didn't matter that it was hard;

we had some kind of freedom, and we were married to guys who we were interested in and who we didn't think we were smarter than, in one way or another. Do you know how many of those suburban women from the sixties were popping pills out of sheer boredom? It was really weird.

Sometime this year, there was this question posed to Ann Charters: "Do you consider the Beat women protofeminists?" And Ann said that Joyce Johnson and I weren't feminists. [Feinstein shakes his head and Jones laughs.] Well, what is the name for us, then? I don't know. Yeah: you can be a feminist and have kids and be married. But it's not like I didn't have a job and pay the rent.

FEINSTEIN: When you started working at the *Record Changer* around 1956, you got to know [jazz critic] Martin Williams. What was he like?

JONES: He was a complicated guy. He was certain about what he knew about music. It's possible he felt unsure about his sexuality, but he was certain about the music. He and Nat Hentoff were the first people I knew who were the scholars of jazz, and it was fascinating to hear them talking. The *Record Changer* was not as wide as this room; it was one of those narrow little storefronts, and it had a room in the back where [owner and critic] Dick Hadlock slept. He had stacked milk crates with old 78s. Those guys were the first to call jazz an American music, and I thought that made perfect sense. It *was*. Why did it seem to be in everyone's heart in a certain way? Why did it capture our imagination? Why was it something that people like Jack Kerouac and LeRoi Jones could like in the same way? Because it was an American music.

Martin was always wonderful to me, a good friend. By the time he got to the Smithsonian [Institution, where, among other things, he compiled and annotated *The Smithsonian Collection of Classic Jazz*], I was writing *Big Star Fallin' Mama* [*Five Women in Black Music*]. Actually, he read the manuscript for the publisher, and he wrote back, "Everything here is fine, but there's one grammatical error." [Both laugh.] He was a terrific guy.

FEINSTEIN: Do you consider Williams and Hentoff to be among the strongest writers about jazz? Are there others?

JONES: I didn't find most of the other people as interesting. Who was that fellow who, for the longest time, had a program on KCR, or BGO . . .

FEINSTEIN: Phil Schaap? [Jones looks nauseated, and Feinstein laughs loudly.]

JONES: No. Phil Schaap bores me silly. [Both laugh.] Sorry! Did I make a terrible face?

FEINSTEIN: Priceless.

JONES: It was the guy who used to run the Rutgers Institute [of Jazz Studies].

FEINSTEIN: Dan Morgenstern.

JONES: Maybe he hadn't started writing yet, or maybe he was writing for *Down Beat* and *Metronome*, and I didn't see so much of his writing because, you know, I didn't have any money to buy magazines at that time. God, we lived on *nothing*. I wrote about this: we used to get a salad together and split it.

FEINSTEIN: What about the poets? Do you think that Kerouac's jazz-related poetry works well?

JONES: No. I don't think very much of him as a poet. (His little haikus . . . I'd rather read Bashō!) But as a prose stylist—you can always hear it. He just wasn't a poet, not like Allen [Ginsberg], who understood the line.

FEINSTEIN: Who are some of the poets you admire who have been strongly influenced by jazz?

JONES: Maybe [Robert] Creeley and his short lines. The younger poets . . . You know, in *Brilliant Corners*, you published Lyrae

Van Clief-Stefanon, who was my student when I taught a memoir class at Penn State for one semester. (I used to drive from here, 250 miles!) Cornelius Eady, who's a dear friend; I've known Cornelius for about thirty years, and he has that kind of an ear. All the young people who have come out of Cave Canem are influenced because they're allowed and encouraged to.

    Back then, there really wasn't anybody . . . even Ted Joans [whose books included *Black Pow-Wow: Jazz Poems* from 1969]. I mean, Ted Joans was Ted Joans. He was an anomaly, a certain person.

FEINSTEIN: Talk about him. What was it like being around Ted Joans?

JONES: He was just such a weirdo, but totally likeable. There were several guys, one named Jack Micheline, who would walk around with their body of work under their arm, and you would think, "Oh! They're going to lose it one day, or they'll fall asleep or get drunk and it'll vanish from the face of the earth." But Ted, he was just so dear, and he always managed to get along. I never knew how he earned his living; I think women always took care of him, but that's just my personal opinion. [Smiles widely.]
    Bob Kaufman.

FEINSTEIN: Did you ever hang with Bob Kaufman?

JONES: No, he was on the West Coast. I never knew him. But somebody who had an ear, so I know she must have listened, was Denise Levertov. I never saw her in the clubs, but she must have listened to jazz.

FEINSTEIN: Who were some of the writers who'd hang with you at the jazz clubs?

JONES: It was mostly musicians, although maybe I didn't know that many writers at that time. Of course Allen [Ginsberg] was always there, and Frank [O'Hara]. But Kenneth Koch and, later on, Ron Padgett, and John Ashbery—those people . . . I'm going to call them "the white guys." [Laughs.] Sorry. I don't mean it like that, but that's where that came from.

FEINSTEIN: That's where what came from?

JONES: I made judgments like that. Their background was more academic, and they hadn't broken from it as much as somebody like Allen or Frank. It's not as though Frank O'Hara hadn't been to college, and Allen went to Columbia (in a manner of speaking). [Both laugh.] But I've got to say that Kenneth Koch really stretched out; as he got older, he got much looser, probably because of readings.

I'm giving a lecture soon at SUNY Purchase, where I used to teach, on how this new American poetry gave birth to spoken word. Because it did. People began to hear each other. And this goes back to [Charles] Olson and the breath: What you hear, not what you're reading, your own self and making your own aural judgments in your head. When you're actually hearing people and their emphases, then you understand it better and absorb it better.

The only poet I ever heard as a kid—maybe I was in college—was T. S. Eliot. [Groans:] "I grow old, I grow old . . ." [Laughs.] It was so monotonous.

FEINSTEIN: In your own poetry, when you invoke jazz musicians, they tend to be more avant-garde players: [Albert] Ayler, [drummer] Rashid Ali. It's farther out. Would you say that their music, from, say, the mid to late sixties, has most of your heart?

JONES: Well, I'm so much older now. [Laughs.] I had a professor once who said that art is about change, and maybe that's why I liked Albert and Archie [Shepp] and those people: I felt they were pushing it forward. I admired them for stepping out—Rashid with his drums, and Albert with his screeching. Cecil Taylor *rolling* over the piano. (I've heard people say, "Oh, Cecil can't really play. That's why he—" What?! Do you want him to play nursery rhymes?) But those people had the chutzpah to play what they felt they had to and to add that in. There are times, now, when I listen to old recordings of Archie and Albert—no one plays Albert Ayler on the radio anymore; they just don't; it's too bad—and I think, "Oh! How could I have listened to all that screeching?" But maybe that's what I was feeling then: that I was screeching, or that they were screeching for me. They interested me because they took it to another level, and why not? You could always come back from that; you could always tone it down.

I've been very fortunate. Archie's studio used to be right under my bedroom. He would compose on the piano, and I used to fall asleep listening to him. (I know this from my letters.) It was a time when I was mourning, I suppose, and I thought maybe I couldn't have the domestic life that I had wanted, but I had this house. (It was threatened all the time: "Why do you want to keep this old house?" You know how New York is with its real estate.) But there was still that life that was here. I thought, "At least I can go to sleep in peace. I know that I'm among friends, and I know that people respect me here and will let me be as I am." I didn't have to go where people looked askance at you—because people still looked askance.

But those people [Ayler and Ali] came along with what they played. [Alto saxophonist] Marion Brown has a piece called "27 Cooper Square" [named after her address and recorded in 1965]. They remind me of a time in my life that was wonderful but also really difficult, and I lived through it. But I can't say they took my whole heart because I also remember the day [John Coltrane's] *My Favorite Things* came. I put it on the box and stood there in my house on Fourteenth Street—like the most giant loft you can think of—and I thought, "Look at that! He's taken the corniest song, and it's so beautiful." Trane, you know?

Also bebop. Who doesn't like bebop? Those beginning notes to "I Didn't Know What Time It Was," when you hear Bird going—[Jones scats Charlie Parker's intro from his 1949 session with strings, and then sings the opening lyrics.] I can get all whacked out on that, too!

The other day, I happened to catch part of *Sketches of Spain* on the radio, and I thought, "No wonder people gave Miles [Davis] such a hard time." Because it's so totally beautiful, and so different in its impetus. [In a mocking, square tone:] "Why isn't he playing what he used to play?" That's partly the nature of criticism: a lot of times, you only have references that have been there already, and you can't judge something because it's new.

And there are young people like [pianist] Jason Moran and [bassist] Christian McBride: those young people just knock me out. (Christian McBride played at my daughter Lisa's wedding.) These *kids* (they're kids to me) are wonderful. The way Jason plays with time, and with history . . .

FEINSTEIN: And his marvelous interplay with [saxophonist] Charles Lloyd. Magical.

JONES: Yeah. And Charles Lloyd is somebody who goes *way* back. It's nice because I listen to all of them, and I have no objection to younger people being as good as older people. [Both laugh.] No objection; none at all.

FEINSTEIN: In a previous issue of *Brilliant Corners*, I asked several musicians if they thought jazz was a language, and you said you really liked that question. Why?

JONES: That story I told you about dropping the quarter in that piano, when I finally wrote about it a thousand years later, I said that the piano had come "as a language." That's what music is: a language. I noticed when I read through your interviews that people went from jazz to music itself. It's a language of the spirit.

The first music that I probably heard and loved was Hebrew music. At the hotel next door, one of the bellmen is a little Jewish boy from Detroit, and he was talking to me about his bar mitzvah. I began to sing the whole bar mitzvah prayer, and his eyes widened. He said, "You remember it better than I do." [Laughs.] That's because they wouldn't let me sing it . . .

In the memoir, I write about a scene at the Five Spot when someone, I don't know who, played "Greensleeves," and everyone got real, real quiet. It was the first time I felt that I was in church. So music is a language. It's nonverbal, but it's from the source, from feelings, and if you can learn to write with words like that, then you've achieved something.

10

Evidence

Robin D. G. Kelley

Robin D. G. Kelley's books include *Race Rebels: Culture, Politics, and the Black Working Class*; *Freedom Dreams: The Black Radical Imagination*; *Yo' Mama's DisFunktional! Fighting the Culture Wars in Urban America*, which was selected as one of the top ten books of 1998 by the *Village Voice*; and *Thelonious Monk: The Life and Times of an American Original*, the focus of this interview. (*Africa Speaks, America Answers: Modern Jazz in Revolution* was published after this conversation.) His coedited collections include *Imagining Home: Class, Culture, and Nationalism in the African Diaspora* (with Sidney J. Lemelle), and (with Earl Lewis) *To Make Our World Anew: A History of African Americans*, a Choice Outstanding Academic Title and a History Book Club Selection. Kelley has written on music for the *New York Times*, the *Village Voice*, *JazzTimes*, *Lenox Avenue*, the *Nation*, and other publications. He is Professor of History and American Studies at the University of Southern California.

The following excerpts from Kelley's writings have been reprinted with permission. The interview took place on the Upper West Side of Manhattan on October 9, 2009.

Thelonious Monk: The Life and Times of an American Original (excerpt)

The bookings were few and far between. He might have inherited a little bit of money from his mother, who may have stashed away some of her settlement from the bus accident. Nellie probably made just enough to cover most of the basic expenses, which included a reasonable rent of about $30 or $35 a month. And when money was really tight, he could always depend on Nica. In fact, following Barbara's death, Nica offered Thelonious the most generous gift he had ever received from anyone: She bought him a car. Monk wasn't the first musician upon whom she bestowed such a gift. A year or two earlier, she bought Art Blakey a Cadillac, which stunned some in the jazz world and elicited some lighthearted teasing from Thelonious. But now it was his turn, and like a boy in a toy store he picked his favorite: a brand-new black and white 1956 Buick Special. . . . Monk took great pleasure in driving and often recruited family and friends to ride with him. His niece Judith Smith ("Muffin") remembered how he "used to come up to the Bronx and he'd have leather driving gloves in the summertime. He would whistle up to the window and say 'Who's going south?'" The kids found driving with Uncle Thelonious to be a thrilling experience. Evelyn Smith: "He was reckless! He had that Buick Special and he would take us for a ride down Third Avenue, and he would drive around each pole. Once, on the Grand Central Parkway, he crossed the island and there was oncoming traffic."

Thelonious Monk: The Life and Times of an American Original (excerpt)

Indeed, "Eronel" is not even Monk's song, despite the initial credit he received as co-composer. It is significant for the stories behind it—stories of love and theft. Pianist Sadik Hakim, a recent convert to Islam, co-wrote it with Idrees Sulieman. But it was Hakim who named it "Eronel"—Lenore spelled backwards—after an old flame of his. . . .

The story of "Eronel" reveals the depths of Hakim's personal investment in the song. He and Sulieman believed they had something special, and tried to interest Miles Davis in recording it. He did add it to his repertoire briefly, though he disliked the bridge. So Sulieman took it to Monk, who kept changing one note—the last note of the second bar. "I said, 'That's the wrong note but play it again. Leave that note in. We'll do the writers' credits three ways.'" Monk did a little more than contribute one note. The chord voicings are his, as are little embellishments in both the A-section and the bridge, but the melody clearly belongs to Sulieman and Hakim. Unfortunately, when the record was released and the song copyrighted, only Monk's name appeared. Both Sulieman and Hakim were hurt, and Sulieman spent a better part of his life giving Thelonious grief about the error. Years later, while they were all in Copenhagen, he appealed to Monk: "Why don't you make a statement and tell them how it really happened?" But Thelonious would just smile and say, "They forgot it, ha ha."

Unpublished Manuscript from *Thelonious Monk: The Life and Times of an American Original* (excerpt)

We get to hear more of Thelonious on the two jump tunes, "On the Bean," based on the chord changes of "Whispering," and "Flying Hawk." Monk opens "On the Bean" with a distinctively "Monkish" introduction (though less adventurous than his renowned intros at Minton's), followed by some creative comping behind [Coleman] Hawkins with accents slightly off the beat. He then takes a sixteen-bar solo that begins with two bars of syncopated eighth notes exploring Ab to G intervals landing consistently on the down beat, which probably sounded corny to committed modernists but prepared the way for the next measure consisting of an offbeat phrasing of the G octave—a slight reference to Gillespie's "Salt Peanuts." The remaining measures are chock-full of Monkisms: whole-tone scales, minor second clusters, and even a hint of his composition "I Mean You" in measures 5–6. Monk also takes an economical solo on "Flying Hawk," a swinging jump tune harmonically enriched by Monk's substitute descending chord progressions. When he was not filling his solo space with whole tone runs, he stuck close to the tonic (F major).

Thelonious Monk: The Life and Times of an American Original (excerpt)

For over four decades, Nellie had been his rock, his foundation, his sounding board. She picked up after him, dressed him, nursed him, and created the kind of environment that allowed him to work whenever he felt like it. Nica was there for him, but she was no substitute for Nellie. One day, about 1980 or '81, perhaps feeling a little romantic or nostalgic, he emerged from his room and sat down at the piano with Barry Harris. "He said, 'Let's play "My Ideal."' So he started playing 'My Ideal.' He played a chorus; I played a chorus . . . I wish somebody had had a tape recorder because he made me play maybe a hundred choruses of 'My Ideal' and he played a hundred back and forth—nonstop. . . . Well it could have been—I know it was over an hour but he made me just play that." Monk knew the lyrics to every song he played, thus the simple words of hopeful, elusive love rang through his mind as he explored every dimension of J. Newell Chase's lovely ballad. And I bet Nellie was on his mind, too. After the final chorus, he got up from the piano and quietly retired to his room.

Interview

SASCHA FEINSTEIN: You are very humble in your introduction [to *Thelonious Monk*] about your own musical abilities, but it's very evident that you *really* know music. Tell me a little about your musical background.

ROBIN D. G. KELLEY: Sure. As far as piano goes, I'm basically self-taught. My interest in this music goes back to my childhood. My mother loved jazz. In fact, there's a footnote in the book where my mom and my dad, when they were dating, were actually at one of Monk's performances in Boston when he didn't show up until much later. She set me up to have trumpet lessons with Jimmy Owens. Of course, as a kid—I was seven years old—I didn't know anything about Jimmy Owens; all I knew was that he charged five dollars, and I used to spend my Saturdays at his house. (I just saw Jimmy, and I interviewed him for the book, which is a nice coming around.) I played some French horn in junior high school, but I had no models. I didn't know anything about Julius Watkins or David Amram; I knew nothing about a jazz French horn player and figured the French horn had to be in orchestras. But in my high school years, my mother remarried; her husband, Paul Morehouse, was a jazz musician—a fine saxophone player, mainly an educator. He knew people like [bassist] Buell Neidlinger—he knew all those people, grew up with them. So he was teaching me bits and pieces, and he introduced me, on record, to Monk, Bud Powell, Charlie Parker. I simply listened and tried to reproduce what I heard. And he began teaching me, on and off, about chord progressions. So even now, if you give me some piano music that has left and right hand, I struggle with bass clef; I can't do that kind of stuff [with the left hand]. But I could read chord progressions. I could voice them and play well enough to make them make sense.

And I loved Monk's music. At first, it took a while to understand it—and I'm still trying to understand it. I'd be lying if I said [just because] I spent fourteen years of my life focusing on this book that I understand everything, because I really don't. I'm still working on that. But playing his music was like a vista for me in terms of harmonic and rhythmic possibility, and it was my exercise: my way of understanding the dynamics and mechanics of the piano. No one sat down and taught me anything—I sort of figured stuff out—and to this day, I rarely play in public. I probably know more than I can execute, and I've learned, after all these years, that I don't have to sound like Monk to play his music. I'm still trying to sound like me. [Smiles.]

FEINSTEIN: One of the many wonderful qualities of this biography has to do with your sense of cadence, chapter after chapter. Do you credit that to your musical sensibility?

KELLEY: I never thought of it that way. I probably should, huh? [Laughs.] It's funny because I'm better at closing a chapter than I am ending a song. It's like that famous moment when Coltrane says, "I don't know how to stop," and Miles says, "Well, take the horn out of your mouth." [Laughs.] I'm always saying that.

The cadence [to each chapter] really grows out of Monk's life. In many cases, a death, or a transition, marked not so much the end of a period as a transition to the next moment of his life. I mean, death was *so* important to him; he took it *hard*.

FEINSTEIN: That comes up repeatedly in the book—[his son] Toot saying, "My father couldn't handle death."

KELLEY: Exactly, and I don't know actually how that happened, but closing each chapter, with some exceptions, seemed natural—although I do admit that there were a couple of places where I combined some chapters that had originally been split.

I come out of an academic background—an academic historian—and historians are trained to collect the evidence: make a big sweeping statement, and then support that statement with a lot of evidence. For so many history books, you tell your students, "You don't have to read the whole thing; just know the thesis." [Both laugh.] But I couldn't do this with Monk. Every moment was kind of electric. It was like walking through a life that required narrative and storytelling, and it required understanding the barriers and challenges and openings each step of the way. So one thing I did learn from Monk, which really shaped the way I wrote this narrative, was in a couple of places where he says, "It's a lot easier to play fast than it is to play slow and swing and make something out of that." There's another moment when he's telling the band in 1959, rehearsing for [the famous big band concert at New York's] Town Hall, where he says, "Some bands run the whole book [of concert charts] down in one night and don't learn shit. I need you to go one bar at a time and learn one song a day. One song." That struck me; I learned something from that. Unfortunately, we're living in a culture of the sound bite, a culture of fast information. That's why people can't read poetry. They can't slow down to stop and feel and think and relish. I do readings [from the biography] and I'm always warning people, "Walk through Monk's life and the lives of those around him. Know them; take your time. It will be well worth the trip." I get people who look at the [size of the] book and say, "Oh my God—I don't know . . ." or they go straight to the index. That's like skipping to the twentieth bar of something and deciding to flounder in that. No—it's the whole song, the whole piece, and that was my challenge.

FEINSTEIN: You had remarkable access to private archives. What were some of your most exciting moments as a historian?

KELLEY: Let me just say one thing off the bat: despite what I say in the book, I wish the archives were deeper. The family actually didn't have a whole lot.

FEINSTEIN: Because of the apartment fires?

KELLEY: Yeah. Also, neither Monk nor Nellie was into saving a lot of documentation. And Monk didn't write letters; he didn't write postcards. There's no correspondence. There was him and his music. And he *did* write music, of course, and had manuscripts, although a lot of those burned in the fires. In terms of the private tapes [recorded by Nellie], there really wasn't that much; I don't think there were more than five or six hours of material. Now, Nica, the Baroness, has a lot of audio tapes, which I did not have access to.

FEINSTEIN: Why not?

KELLEY: I don't know. It has to do with the [Rothschild] family; they're protective. At one point, there was talk of releasing some of those jam sessions [recorded in the Baroness's apartment] on CD, and I believe [the late] Joel Dorn was producing it—and then they pulled it. I don't know the details, but there's still more material and more conversations to learn about.

A lot of the material that I was able to find I found the old-fashioned way. All those tax returns—that didn't come from Monk's estate; that came from dusty municipal archives in New York City because there was an estate challenge after Thelonious died. I found material all over the globe. I found interviews in different languages; I was dealing with nearly a dozen different languages and hired people to translate them. I found snippets of information the old-fashioned way. Also, the black press was a great, great resource. So there was a lot of material that was new to the Monk family, stuff that they didn't know.

And you have so many myths that I was contending with, some small, some big. With the question of money, it's true we did know that he struggled, but the story on Monk for so long in all the published work was that once he signed with Columbia Records, his fortunes increased. But when you actually look and follow the money—I mean, I had access to the correspondence, artist contracts, and things through [Columbia Records producer] Teo Macero, who left his papers to the New York Public Library. It's a rich, rich archive. And that's where you begin to see the money trail and begin to realize that, even at its height, even at the moment in the mid-sixties when Monk's supposed to be making a lot, he's *still* struggling. Better than some, but not nearly as well as we thought. So, if there is a subplot [to the biography], it is the almost-common story of even great musicians who never earn their value.

FEINSTEIN: Inevitably—even in an expansive publication such as your book—there's some material that gets cut. What was the heartbreaker for you? What was toughest to leave out?

KELLEY: One of my favorite stories that I cut tremendously, which is not so much about Monk, is the story of the song "Eronel," written for Lenore Gordon. I had a great interview with her, and I framed my discussion with an interlude; this was as a love story between Lenore Gordon and Sadik Hakim. There was a lot going on in their relationship that brought life to the song for me. But it really was a segue away from Monk, and so I cut that down substantially. In general, I had to give up stories that I couldn't quite confirm and condense some stories, and I did lose the voices of people; I had substantial quotes, and I like when other people tell their stories, but for the sake of space I often had to summarize their stories.

The biggest passages that I lost were my discussions of the music. I would say two-thirds or more of what was dropped were descriptions and some analyses of Monk's music, but my editor insisted that it was too technical. [An example of the extracted musical analysis appears in the prose excerpts that precede this interview—SF.] In fact, the little appendix was literally part of the text in the Minton's chapter, but he pulled it and said either delete or put it in an appendix (and make it shorter, which I did). I'm not dissatisfied with what I lost. I think the book was probably too long then. Obviously, if I had another year, it would be much better—but after that year, I would want another year.

∼

FEINSTEIN: You mention in your acknowledgments that Orrin Keepnews [Monk's record producer at Riverside] refused to be interviewed. I'm assuming he was trying to protect his son's project. [Peter Keepnews has been working on a Monk biography for decades.]

KELLEY: I think that's part of it, although he didn't say that to me. [Pause.] I got the impression that he just didn't particularly care for me—not personally (we've never met), but he's protective not only of his son's project but his own relationship to Thelonious. He has a particular narrative that he's put out in his book [*The View from Within*, 1988] and in his liner notes, and there's a concern that his narrative might be derailed in some ways. I guess everyone has a concern like that, so I don't take it personally. But when I sent him my proposal and told him what I was going to do, he just had really disparaging words: "You, like everybody else, wants to write this book. You think you know about song titles, and half those titles he didn't come up with himself." There was a real defensiveness on his part. And I found it really unfortunate. I said, "Look, no matter what you think about me, I think it's important for your voice to be heard to get the record straight."

FEINSTEIN: What would you have asked him?

KELLEY: I would have followed up on a lot of the unanswered questions in *The View from Within* about exactly how he went about producing these records. Who made what decisions? Orrin Keepnews tends to present himself as the ultimate decision maker, even though Thelonious does have an opinion. His comment about Monk not really knowing Ellington's music [prior to Monk's first recording for Riverside, *Monk Plays Ellington*] and not being terribly enthusiastic even though it worked out really well—I'm a little skeptical of that. I'm interested in learning how Thelonious absorbed the music, even old music, like the way he absorbed "I'm Getting Sentimental over You." When you listen to those [private] tapes [of Monk practicing that tune], it sounds as though he really doesn't know the song, but what he's trying to do is figure it out, very slowly, one phrase at a time.

FEINSTEIN: Deep exploration.

KELLEY: Very deep. And these are things that Keepnews has seen, but he interprets them differently. So I wanted to get more detail about what he was seeing and hearing, and who the decision maker was. Compare, for example, Keepnews's story about what happens in the recording booth at Riverside versus what I heard in those tapes from the Twenty-Eighth Street loft when Monk was rehearsing the band with Hall Overton. Hall Overton is a brilliant arranger whom Monk really respects, but it's Monk who's in control. It's Monk saying, "This is what I want. This is how I want it." He's telling his musicians, "Don't do that, do this." That level of command in 1959, just as his period with Riverside is about to end—how could he go from having that kind of command with a big band and not having that level of command in the studio? So I question those relationships [reported by Keepnews].

What I really wanted to talk to him about were the things that I learned from Chris Albertson, who worked for Riverside Records and who had a completely different take on Monk's relationship to Keepnews. Here's Chris Albertson bursting the bubble in some ways, and I wanted Keepnews to have the opportunity to respond, but it never happened. And I'm sure he *will* respond. I'm sure there will be both letters and publications and lectures about the problems with my book, but I had to go with the evidence. I tried to be fair. I thought he wrote a really fine, fine piece on Monk in 1948. Keepnews, Paul Bacon, and, of course, Herbie Nichols were among the very few who really took Monk's music seriously at that time. Keepnews respected Monk and he had a good ear, and that's why I give him credit throughout the book for the role that he plays. But I also acknowledge those places of tension and struggle.

FEINSTEIN: It often hinges on financial issues.

KELLEY: Absolutely.

FEINSTEIN: That's where he comes off the worst, and one of the reasons I really wish he had agreed to an interview with you was that it's been my understanding that the books were cooked by [Keepnews's partner, Bill] Grauer.

Kelley: Yes, and I basically say that—that Grauer was behind that, and I don't think Keepnews knew of this, or if he knew, it was too late. I also try to explain exactly what it is that Riverside did because it's different than stealing from an artist; I don't think they stole from the artists. What happened was they used all manner of methods to get investors to keep giving them money, and it was stretched too thin. So they'd print too many LPs to say, "Look at our record sales," but the records would end up in discount bins.

Keepnews certainly wasn't getting rich off of Monk. That's a fact. I don't think Grauer got rich, either. It was just bad business. Very bad business. And yet, I don't think it was all that unusual. I mean, think about it: What record label in those periods had really good business practices, you know? [Both laugh.] I think it was typical, and they just got caught.

Feinstein: Do you feel comfortable talking openly about the previous Monk biographies?

Kelley: Oh, sure.

Feinstein: In your seven pages of acknowledgments, you don't mention the [English-language] biographies on Monk.

Kelley: Well, the one I mention, and the one I cite the most, is the [Jacques] Ponzio and [François] Postif book [*Blue Monk: Portrait de Thelonious*, 1995]. For me, that book, which is still not translated in English, was the best Monk biography. I think Leslie Gourse's book [*Straight, No Chaser: The Life and Genius of Thelonious Monk*, 1997] is, in many ways, *very* problematic.

Feinstein: I think all her biographies are problematic.

Kelley: Yes. [Laughs.]

Feinstein: I think they're slapped together with the magpie sensibility of a clever undergraduate.

Kelley: Exactly. It *was* slapped together. In fact, I know exactly what she did: she went to the Institute of Jazz Studies [at Rutgers

University] and went through the vertical file. (You can tell this from certain footnotes in the book.) Then she got on the phone and called certain people. Some things actually never happened. For instance, she claims to have interviewed Nellie Monk, but that's not true. I think she caught her backstage at some event and asked her one question, which Nellie might have answered in passing. Nellie wasn't talking to *anyone*. I was the first person since Frank London Brown [in 1958] and Nat Hentoff [in 1960] to interview Nellie. And Nellie wasn't giving me everything; I'll certainly admit that, and I respect her for it. There are certain things she wanted to take with her.

The Laurent de Wilde book [*Monk*, 1996], for me, is a really quirky and interesting read. I didn't learn anything [historical] from it, although I enjoyed it as his idiosyncratic romp through Monk, so I really couldn't cite it. Thomas Fitterling published a German biography [*Thelonious Monk: sein Leben, seine Musik, seine Schallplaten*, translated as *Thelonious Monk: His Life and Music*, 1997]. It's so interesting that the Europeans were more on the mark; Leslie Gourse wrote the first English-language bio of Monk, and it was terrible.

I once met Leslie Gourse. We were both receiving awards from the New York Public Library. I introduced myself—and this is before her book came out, so I didn't know she had just finished a book on Monk—and said, "I'm writing a book on Monk." And she said, "You don't need to. I already did it. There's no need to waste your time."

FEINSTEIN: Wow . . .

KELLEY: It was pretty interesting . . .

But I can't stress enough: Jacques Ponzio is a very fine scholar and someone who's really generous. If I had a question, he was there. If I couldn't find something, he'd help me find it. Another person who was really generous was Chris Sheridan [author of *Brilliant Corners: A Bio-Discography of Thelonious Monk*, 2001].

FEINSTEIN: What an amazing source *that* is.

KELLEY: It *is* an amazing source. Although I found dozens of errors, I don't blame him for those errors because they're errors that I would have made had I been doing the discography [at that time], and hopefully, if another edition can come out, he can correct those. Just small things. And, again: he's another European.

∼

FEINSTEIN: Among the people you acknowledge in your dedication—those who have, as you put it, joined the ancestors—you include the wonderful poet Sekou Sundiata [1948–2007]. He was such a beautiful spirit, and I was wondering if you would talk a bit about his gifts for music and language.

KELLEY: Yes, yes. I am such a fan of Sekou's work—his poetry, his performance, his rich musical sensibilities, that voice, his love of humanity. We were supposed to meet first at Dartmouth College, where I was giving a lecture, but he got in a terrible car accident. We eventually met later at Dartmouth when he spoke to my class, and I recognized immediately that, besides all of his other great talents, he was a wonderful teacher who cared about people irrespective of their race, gender, or age. He cared about all people.

His one-man show [*Blessing the Boats*] about his kidney transplant struggled with the question of death. He's one of these amazing poets who can be rooted in his own culture, tradition, time, and place, yet speak with a universal voice. No matter what your generation, you could understand the pain, humor, and possibilities in the story that he tells. One thing I really feel sad about: When Sekou was working on *The Fifty-First (Dream) State*, he had asked me to be the historical consultant. We talked a lot about the project; he was very moved by 9/11, and I got to know Sekou very well. (I mention him in my book *Freedom Dreams*. For me, he is one of the unsung surrealists, even if he did not identify himself in that way.) And then I moved to California and we didn't follow up on the project. He ended up doing it, and it was absolutely stunning. But to lose Sekou . . . In my mind, he was one of the readers of this book—he and Ted Joans. There were a number of poets who really shaped my approach to this project and whom I interviewed, poets who either knew Monk or wrote about Monk: Jayne Cortez, Ted Joans.

FEINSTEIN: [Amiri] Baraka's prominently mentioned.

KELLEY: Exactly. These are folks who are also inspired by Monk.

It's interesting—I don't know if I ever told you this—but when I first started this project, it took about five years before the Monk family, especially Thelonious Monk Jr., gave me the green light. And in those five years, I had come up with a different project altogether about Monk. This is why I was reading all your work: I was going to write a book about Monk's meaning in American culture—and not just American culture but cultures around the world. I wanted to know about the poets, the painters. And, yes, the other musicians, but not primarily the musicians. Writers like Julio Cortázar. All these people who are writing about, from, and in a space of Monk. I was collecting all this material. What does Monk mean to postwar culture? I was actually halfway done with that book, and then once I connected with the [Monk] family, I scrapped it. I thought I'd be able to slip that into the book [*Thelonious Monk*], but all that material started to take away from the central story.

FEINSTEIN: But it's not lost; it's just a separate book.

KELLEY: It's a separate book, yeah. And that's one of the things I love about [the journal] *Brilliant Corners*: Monk is not just a CD. He's not just in the live music. He is in art and literature; there's so much you can talk about in terms of the influence of Monk. It's wide open.

FEINSTEIN: In the book, you mention your first encounter with the Monk family, how you left feeling that you didn't know Monk at all. What did you mean by that?

KELLEY: Well, I sat there and listened to Thelonious Jr.—Toot—tell stories that I had never heard before: stories of his own childhood, stories that had been passed on to him. And that's when it struck me: I'm working on a book about the constructions of Monk, the inventions of Monk, Monk in the cultural ether, and yet, the real man and his world were so much more fascinating than all the anecdotes. In some ways, it was much more complicated; in others, there was a certain simplicity, which begged to be heard. With a lot of iconic figures, we demand something more extraordinary. Whether you call this eccentricity or something larger than life, it's something we're looking for. Things that make them special. But for me, what was striking was Monk and the mundane: Monk changing his daughter's diapers; Monk getting up in the morning and drinking his concoction of raw egg and milk; Monk putting on his driving gloves and driving like a maniac on the wrong side of the street. These are the things that for me make him more human and provide the ground for his own writing. What was his writing about? His writing is about trying to capture those close to him. So many of his songs are written for people who are related to him by blood, or who are friends. I mean, this is a man who, as far as I know—and I did *so* much research—only dated three women in his life, and they all lived within about a two-block radius! [Both laugh.] He's like, "This is my world," and I had to sort of get inside that world—inside the mundane and the everyday—to understand how he and the people around him operated. So the larger-than-life extraordinary aspects, which people often look for, ceased to be as interesting as the everyday and mundane.

FEINSTEIN: You spoke to his wife, Nellie, and so many other family members and friends. You spoke to his son, Toot. What would you have asked Barbara [Boo Boo, Monk's other child, who died in 1983]?

KELLEY: Well, she was always a mystery to me, but I would have asked her basically the same questions I asked Toot: "I want to know your story from the beginning. What are your earliest memories of your father?" I would have asked her about the piano lessons that he gave her, because she played a little bit of piano. (Her cousin, Jackie, a wonderful pianist for whom "Jackie-ing" was written, also gave her some musical support.) I would have asked about her love of dance and if she remembered the days when she was at the Village Vanguard; she was four years old, dancing onstage to her father's music. I would have asked her what it meant to go away to boarding school for the first time and what it felt to be one of the very few African American children—and a girl at that. I would have asked how did she feel when her brother, in some ways, became the anointed one. I don't want to make too much of that, but he was the one they were pushing to play with their father, to be Monk's drummer, to be the next Thelonious Monk—when at the very same time, Boo Boo is dancing with [pianist] Randy Weston. She's dancing with Chuck Davis's dance troupe. She's making a name and a life for herself as a significant cultural figure. I would also ask her about her decision to try to preserve the history of San Juan Hill and her father's legacy, and how she felt when it fell upon her to do so. She was the catalyst more than anyone else. But I would have a million questions. I did everything I could to take her out of the ether, but she was probably the biggest mystery in terms of the immediate family.

FEINSTEIN: There are plenty of mysteries just within Thelonious Monk himself.

KELLEY: Absolutely.

FEINSTEIN: One of the moving aspects of your biography has to do with the feeling of constant repair: how Monk's life kept becoming fractured by various kinds of adversity—his physical and mental health, the fires that ravaged his apartment, the financial struggles, prison, and so on. During the fourteen years that you took to make this biography, you went through a great deal, too: new job, new coast [Kelley moved from Columbia University to the University of Southern California]. A divorce and a new marriage. You got hit by a car. Did these tumultuous experiences create a greater empathy for Monk's struggles?

KELLEY: Oh, yeah. In fact, there are times when I think I was supposed to deal with all that—although not because it paralleled Monk's experience. For me, each moment of adversity produced great things for the book. Literally.

I've got to tell you a really good story about getting hit by that car. I wish I had put it in the book. I was writing the foreword to *Freedom Dreams*—the very last part of the book—when 9/11 happened. I was living downtown and looking out my window at the World Trade Center when *bang*. So that was September, and it was really traumatic. Then on November 9th, I put the final touches on the manuscript and sent it off that morning. I said, "My God, I can't believe it—I'm actually going to get back to Monk again," because I had been away from the project for a while. So I went to the Institute of Jazz Studies at Rutgers, my first day working with Mary Lou Williams's papers—a wonderful collection.

FEINSTEIN: Yes indeed.

KELLEY: Oh my God. So I'm there all day long. It's the first time getting my fingers dirty again in an archive, and one of the things I find are receipts that she had from Nellie for seamstress work that she did for Mary Lou. Outside, it's a beautiful day. I pull out my cell phone and call Nellie, because I used to call her and check in. So I tell her I've found the receipts and I say, "This is just so exciting!" And she says, "Oh . . . I can't stand that Mary Lou Williams." I say, "What? Say that again?" "I can't *stand* that Mary Lou Williams. She is such a witch. She *stole* from me, and she complaining about the dresses not fitting her right and she not wanting to pay me. I can't stand that Mary Lou Williams." [Feinstein laughs.] She's going on and on—and this is Nellie, right? Nellie, whom we imagine to be, like, the help maid, but she's cursing her out! [Feinstein laughs.] She's gone! And this is exciting for me because this is the most animated that Nellie's ever been with me. I hang up the phone, put it in my pocket, step off the curb, walk two steps, and, *boom!* get hit by a car. I'm flying in the air of downtown Newark. I felt like I was floating as high as this ceiling, and I hear from the streets a collective, "Oh, shit . . ." Then, *boom*! I'm knocked out; I wake up; cops are there. I'm taken to the hospital. I'm pretty roughed up, but I'm okay.

I get home, and the next day I get a call from Nellie. Somehow she'd heard about the accident, and Nellie is a healer.

She devoted the second half of her life to healing others through natural juices. She says, "Oh, Robin. I heard you got hit by a car. Are you okay?" She's really concerned. I go, "Yeah, yeah." (I'm on Vicodin, so I'm a little hazy.) She asks what happened, and I explain that this woman was making a left-hand turn, trying to beat the traffic, and she didn't see me in the crosswalk. Nellie asks, "What kind of woman was this?" I said, "Young, black woman." She says, "Well, did she get out of the car to help you?" I said, "No, she just stayed in the car. I had cops there." And she said, "Just like Mary Lou Williams! Mary Lou Williams will run you over and leave you in the gutter!" [Feinstein laughs loudly.] "Just like that Mary Lou Williams!" Meanwhile, I'm laughing like crazy, though I'm in so much pain, but she's dead serious: "The only person who could've done that was someone like Mary Lou Williams." [Both laugh.]

But you know, *because* I was down—because I lost a year of work with two surgeries—Nellie began sending me stuff: little concoctions, stuff to put on my knee postsurgery. She had a certain kind of sympathy for me, and that sympathy translated into a deeper trust. It's almost as though she got to know me better as a result of my getting hit. That's when I got access to the storage facility and literally dug through piles and piles of trash to pull out a lot of stuff that I was able to find—stuff they didn't know they had. So that was a blessing in disguise.

Knowing Monk's adversity had a greater impact on me than dealing with my own. It's hard to explain, but all my adversities were linked to great things. Sure, I got divorced—but I married this most amazing, incredibly talented, beautiful woman. Throughout all this stuff, I was able to get the book done. In working on Monk, I felt I was able to discover my self, so I don't feel as though I've dealt with any adversity. I had certain challenges, but to read Monk's story, and to *write* Monk's story, was hard because I thought he never got a break, you know? You keep asking yourself, "What if psychiatry had been in a better place and had given him the proper diagnosis and support? What if record companies were fair places, and it wasn't about capitalism and exploitation but about making good music? What if all the sidemen and musicians that he wanted to play with had actually been available to him? What if his nephew hadn't overdosed, and what if heroin hadn't been flooding the Bronx and Harlem? If all these things had been different, what would he have produced?"

I'm not one who believes that the lower you are and the more troubled you are somehow equates to someone who produces genius. I'm like, "You makin' it in *spite* of that," you know? So that was hard for me to take, and my wife, LisaGay Hamilton, when she read the manuscript, she kept writing, "Ugh! Ugh!" Every time he was on the verge of something good: Ugh. He's got a gig in 1948 at the Royal Roost; life is finally working and—[Kelley slaps his hands]—he's arrested for marijuana possession. Gets his cabaret card back, coming off this *great* long gig with Coltrane, moving into 1958 with a new quartet with Charlie Rouse—[Kelley slaps his hands again]—beaten by police in Delaware and loses his cabaret card again. These are the kinds of things that make you think, "Dang, when will it change?" That was harder for me than whatever I had to deal with.

∼

FEINSTEIN: Your book keeps pushing toward the racial politics of the time, even though Monk himself seemed to push against political conversations. If that hadn't been the case with Monk—if, for example, he described [his composition] "Brilliant Corners" as representing oppression for the slow half and liberation during the double-time feel—would you hear his music differently?

KELLEY: That's an *excellent* question . . . I think it's possible that I would hear it differently. You know, it's interesting—you've hit on a key theme in what I was trying to struggle with, and that is, sometimes what you hear is Monk's music filtered through the background noise. In some respects, I think Monk's resistance to talk about race had much to do with the fact that it was so ever-present. In other words, at the height of the civil rights movement, at the moment when the whole future of America *rested* on what was then called "The Negro Question," every artist—every entertainer and intellectual who was black—was always asked the question, "What about the racial issue?" So I think the fact that he's always asked the question led him, in some ways, to push back. And his position was pretty clear. He said, "Look, my vocation is a musician, and as a musician I make music." That's not to say he doesn't care about the world, but he kept saying that if you wanted to know the answer to those questions, you ask someone whose *vocation* is racial politics. And that's something that's relevant today. When you're going to have a big debate about race in American and you've got Spike Lee as your spokesperson, then you've got to ask the question, "What about the people whose job it is, as social movement activists or scholars, to raise these issues?" I think Monk pushed back against it precisely because it was so visible, and yet he was the first one to appear at those benefits for CORE and SNCC [Congress of Racial Equality and Student Nonviolent Coordinating Committee]. He had a *very* clear sense of racial politics not "for the race" but racial politics as justice for all. His whole thing was about fairness: if the black man is going to use hatred or exploit a situation, that's just as bad as anybody else. He was against anyone who lived on injustice.

There's a moment in the book when I quote at length his interview with Val Wilmer, who was so generous to share that original tape. In that conversation, he pushes back not just about talking about race and racial politics, but against the idea that somehow he ought to be obligated to the needs and struggles of other people. He says over and over again, "Look, I've got a family to feed. I've got a wife and two kids. Why should I be worrying about what's going on around the corner?" And then there's kind of an abrupt switch where he says, "Well, these are things I don't like about America: the police beat you for no reason." He's saying this at a time when the cities of America are burning over questions about police brutality; police brutality becomes the catalyst for all these uprisings that he's very much aware of. So in some ways, he's aware and concerned, but his concern is not what people expected it should be. Even the statements that were attributed to him he was ambivalent about, like the fact that he backpedaled from the statement he made to Frank London Brown [for *Down Beat* where Monk was quoted as saying he "would have written the same way even if I had not been a Negro"]: "I would never say anything like that. That's crazy." But I really do believe he said that. Everything is situational. Time and place. There are moments when these things are so palpable for him. When he's sitting there and watching the march on Washington, and he turns to his longtime manager, Harry Colomby, and says, "You know, I think I contributed enough. I don't have to be there to march." He's thinking, "Well, what did I do?" He really *wants* to participate, and that's why he would do these benefits. On the other hand, it's striking that he would watch the march on Washington and, a week later, suffer the loss of his nephew to another struggle: the presence of heroin. So when he says, "I can't worry about what's going on around the corner because I've got my own problems," he *does* have his own problems. They're problems that are social, problems that are political, problems that are tied to bigger things, but they affect him *directly*, and in his heart, because he's always been a family guy. So what I tried to do is understand that these are his politics. It's not an accident that he's going to do a benefit for the Morningside Community Center, or the very local community centers, because these are centers that help local folks, yet he's not going down to Alabama. It's still politics. It's still liberatory.

FEINSTEIN: I have to ask the question that you'll be asked ad infinitum: Do you feel drawn to write another astonishing biography?

KELLEY: I don't think I'll ever write another biography. Otherwise, I may not make it. But if I did have the energy, I'll tell you the person whom I just adore and find so interesting: Eric Dolphy. He's a very different person, and there's some stuff on Dolphy but no great biography. I've always been a little sad that Dolphy and Monk never got together [to record], as much as Dolphy loved Monk. But this is my first and last biography. It really wore me out. There are so many challenges. One, as I said, is getting material. Another is trying to sum up a life. People always ask me, "What is the big significance?" I'll do radio shows and such, and they don't really care about the big picture; they only care about the summary.

One of my challenges was to stay in the story and keep Monk centered, and yet bring everyone else into the story who is shaping his life. I had to accept the fact that by the end of it, except for his injunction that everyone needs to be original, I couldn't make the one-sentence summary. I don't have the sound bite that says, "This is how you sum up Monk." He resisted that, and he resisted that in the music. You know this better than anyone: Every time you read something where people say, "He always played in between the beats." Well, no! [Feinstein laughs.] Or, "He always played angular lines." Well, sometimes they were and sometimes they weren't. Every time you *think* you've figured it out, he's going to do something else. Every possibility is there. It's when you take the whole that you can feel it. That's why I love poetry. Sometimes you just can't find the sentence, the prose, that can express what this music means. It's visceral. It's emotional. Sometimes it's completely ineffable. And that's why it's music.

11

The Artist's Way

Laurie Pepper

Laurie Pepper is the coauthor of *Straight Life: The Story of Art Pepper* and the author of *Art: Why I Stuck with a Junkie Jazzman*. A former staff photographer for the *Los Angeles Free Press*, she managed Art Pepper's career and bands; after his death in 1982, she continued to manage his publishing company, Arthur Pepper Music Corporation, and she has continued to produce and promote his music. Since 2006, her small record label, Widow's Taste, has released invaluable, previously unreleased Art Pepper performances (lauriepepper.net).

The following excerpts from Pepper's writings have been reprinted with permission. The interview was conducted via the internet on February 27, 2023.

Liner Notes for *Atlanta: Unreleased Art Pepper, Volume 11* (excerpt)

When I interviewed him for our book, *Straight Life*, Art referred to this song ["Patricia"], offhandedly, as "probably the prettiest thing I've written to this day." To me this performance of it [May 1980] is the best, and I believe I've heard them all.

Art was telling me, then, about how he started writing his own original tunes in the 1950s, after the army, after leaving Kenton's band. (He wrote the tune "Straight Life" back then; you'll hear it later in this set.) He wrote

"Patricia" for his daughter and recorded it on the Jazz West label in 1956 [*The Return of Art Pepper*]. He didn't play it again for more than twenty years. In 1978, he was probably thumbing through old charts, hunting for an original ballad to play at his first recording session at Fantasy Records. He saw it, brushed the dust off, and brought it to the studio. Why he didn't play it for so long, I never asked, and he never said. It must have stirred up griefs and regrets he couldn't bear to face? After that, he played it frequently in clubs and concert halls. And each performance was magnificent.

But as I said, this is the one that absolutely wrecks me. It wrecked Art, too. Listen to his ohhs and ahhs, his little mutterings of pleasure during [pianist] Milcho [Leviev]'s solo. Listen to what he says about the whole thing when it's over—the song ("there's a whole life happening in that song") and his performance, Milcho's, [bassist] Bob [Magnuson]'s, the audience response. We've all been lifted up together in an evanescent moment, by a song of love and loss, shared and transformed into something new and deep and lovely by these artists on a spring night in Atlanta, and Art's voice breaks as he says, "That's jazz."

Straight Life: The Story of Art Pepper, Cowritten with Art Pepper (excerpt)

In the [Los Angeles County Jail] tanks there was no radio, no nothing. I went five or six months without hearing a note of music before I went up to the cages. . . . So what I'd do to keep myself from going crazy, I would play my cup. We were all issued one. They give you a tin coffee cup with a little handle on it. I would hold it up to my mouth, leave a little opening at the side, and put my hands over it like you do when you play a harmonica or a Jew's harp. And I found that I could hum into the cup and get a sound sort of like a trumpet. I could do a lot with it. And in the jail, with all the cement and steel, that small sound could really be heard, especially from the corner of the cell. So I'd play to myself, and the guys would hear me. I'd look up and see that there were guys standing all around outside my cell, just digging. And I found that they got a lot of pleasure out of it, especially at night. We had one guy named Grundig, who had played drums at one time. He'd take the top from a trash can and beat on it with a spoon, and I'd play my cup, and the guys would clap, and we would have, like, a regular session. You'd have to be in that position to realize how much joy you could receive from something as crude as that.

Art: Why I Stuck with a Junkie Jazzman (excerpt)

It was horrible to watch his struggles [on the multiple takes of "The Prisoner"], but I grew merciless, because I *knew* he could do it in spite of the soupy violins behind him. He would come into the control room, listen in despair to the playback of the latest take. He'd look at me. I'd shake my head. He'd try again. Finally, he came back wanting to throw in the towel, give it up, accept it as it was. I spat into his ear, "*It stinks! It's weak. It's terrible. You've gotta give it* more." He groaned to me about the stupid, useless chart, saying that he'd done the best he could. But he went in for one last try. . . .

Who knows what mental trick Art used to wrench himself away from an improvising jazzman's lifelong understanding and to rise above it? But he did it. He dragged himself out of the quicksand of that chart, ignoring it, at last, relying just on what he heard inside. It sounded as if he was ripping his own guts out in the studio. He was magnificent, and when he heard the take he knew it. He loved it. And I still love to listen to it.

A friend recently talked about good black gospel churches, how they sometimes have nurses, even ambulances there for people who, through the preaching and singing, are kayoed by the Spirit. Art could blast you just that way, and he does it for a while, if you're at all susceptible, when he plays "The Prisoner" on *Winter Moon*.

Art: Why I Stuck with a Junkie Jazzman (excerpt)

Art became secretive and distant. He was cadging extra coke from her, stealing Lana's Valium and her other prescription medicines and hanging out with another hanger-on, a black guy who convinced Art that sniffing this heavenly stuff was wasteful and so the two of them began shooting it. I discovered all this later.

And then one day . . . I came home to a house hot as an oven and found Art shuddering and shaking on the floor, wrapped in blankets, lying beside the standup square wall heater which was on full blast. He was terrified and rambling in his speech, and his skin was icy cold. He assured me he was going to die, but commanded me not to call an ambulance. I called Art's best friend, Chris, who came and injected Art with just a little bit of heroin (an antidote, it seems, for coke O.D.). Art was restored to us. But the nightmare continued. Finally, I wrote in my diary:

4/5/80

He's been so irrational lately that earlier in the evening I'd typed up a neat plan of separation. I'm finally aware of what I really must do and can't bear to do it. . . . Every day he surprises me or dazzles me or makes me laugh and I feel such tenderness for him and leaving him will be like dying, but staying has become impossible—he's cruel and demanding and selfish and inconsiderate and false and really truly nuts, and he's killing me. And I love him.

Interview

SASCHA FEINSTEIN: If I had conducted this interview ten years ago, just about all my questions would be about the making of *Straight Life* [*The Story of Art Pepper*, 1979], a truly indispensable contribution to jazz-related literature, but you address so many of those questions in your memoir *Art: Why I Stuck with a Junkie Jazzman* [2014] and I don't want you to feel as though you're merely covering well-trodden ground.

LAURIE PEPPER: Whatever you want to talk about, I'm game.

FEINSTEIN: Thanks. That's great. You wrote that you started reading voraciously at the age of six and rather audaciously began sending poems to the *New Yorker* in junior high.

PEPPER: [Laughs.] Yes! I did.

FEINSTEIN: You called your work "pretty stuff," "lazy stuff." What did you mean?

PEPPER: I didn't know about writing in those days. I thought you were just inspired and wrote something down and it was wonderful. I didn't know how hard it was. [Laughs.]

FEINSTEIN: When did that change for you?

PEPPER: I guess when I was working on *Straight Life*—working and reworking and reworking. And that was a different writing process from when I was writing the memoir. I'm still learning; I don't think you ever realize just how much work it is, how much rewriting is required. I imagine there are some people for whom it just pours out. I've never known any.

I do *innumerable* revisions. When I got the page proofs for *Straight Life*, I kept rewriting everything down to commas. I drove them crazy because that was before computer technology. They had to set plates and whatever.

FEINSTEIN: *Straight Life* was published in 1979, and I encountered it in the winter of 1980, when I was seventeen. It was the most harrowing read of my life to that point, and one of the most harrowing reads ever since.

PEPPER: I've been reading it aloud and posting episodes online [*artpepper.bandcamp.com*]. (I'm a big audiobook fan, and I think other people should hear it, and since the publisher won't do it, I'm doing it.) A couple of days ago, I posted episode number 34 [from the chapter "Busted"], and it was like reading a novel. It was just fun. The things that were happening to Art were pretty awful, but the thing about Art is that he couldn't have lived a boring life. He wouldn't have been able to stand it; he would have just drunk himself to death or something. He *had* to suffer. He *had* to experience everything. He had to throw himself into danger. And once you get that, you realize, yes, he moans and groans and all that, but he really lived his life. He knew he was living it while he was living it. In this last chapter that I posted, you can tell how much he enjoyed retelling what had happened. So "harrowing": yeah . . . but it's not like he was in solitary being beaten every day. He was telling stories with the other convicts. He was brewing up some sort of liquor. He was engaged.

FEINSTEIN: Oh, I agree with you. I had just never read such raw accounts of drugs and prison and the like. Was it difficult for you to hear him talk about other relationships?

PEPPER: No. I felt totally secure in our relationship. It was just interesting. And I had great objectivity: I was so into the book that whatever was good for the book was good for me.

FEINSTEIN: A long time elapses between 1979 and 2014, when you published your memoir. Why did you wait that long?

PEPPER: I started writing, and then I stopped, and then I went to a writers' group to help me. [Laughs.] And one guy said, "Who wants to read about you?" I said, "I don't know," and I stopped writing for a few years. I think there are people in writers' groups who, for whatever reason, get their rocks off by being nasty. I hate writers' groups. I've only had a good experience in a general creativity group where I felt it was safe to be myself. And I started writing again.

I was really just starting because I was writing my own stuff; I wasn't dealing with Art's incredible, brilliant narrative. I mean, in the latest posted episode, he's talking about the Feds, the cops, taking him to the elevator to go up to the jail floor, and he says, "I think it was nine." That's the mind of a novelist. And I think Art—if he had had the discipline, which he never would have had—would have been a far better writer than me. He was an extremely gifted person in a lot of areas.

So I was trying to be a writer myself. And maybe if you've had work published you can go into a writers' group like that, but it was really devastating to me. But the creativity group was so encouraging in every way. Do you know *The Artist's Way* [1992] by Julia Cameron?

FEINSTEIN: Sure.

PEPPER: This group was based on that book when it first came out, so we were doing silly stuff. We were playing. I was doing Magnetic Poetry on the refrigerator. And then I went to Philadelphia to see a big Cezanne exhibit, and on my last day, when I was in a diner, I started to write. But it took being in that group for quite a while to let me do that again. I had so much belief in Art, but I didn't have any belief in myself.

FEINSTEIN: Sometimes, as adults, we have to force freedom. We don't seem to worry about that in childhood.

PEPPER: That's why *The Artist's Way* is such a terrific book: the notion of play, back to real creativity.

∽

FEINSTEIN: Three exceptional writers wrote blurbs for your memoir: the novelist Michael Connelly, the jazz critic Gary Giddins, and the poet Robert Pinsky. I'd like to hear you talk about all three of them, starting with Connelly and perhaps focusing on his book *The Black Box* [2012].

PEPPER: He talks about Art in other books as well. There's one called *Lost Light* [2003]. He's a big Art Pepper fan. A big jazz fan—period. A very sweet man.

FEINSTEIN: So you know him personally?

PEPPER: Yes. What happened was someone on the board at the Berklee School of Music who was a friend of a friend of mine (it's always that way) said I should come there and talk about my memoir and *Straight Life*. This board member also orchestrated a panel about writing and jazz, and Michael Connelly was on the panel. We had dinner together and talked and talked, and I said, "Would you give me a blurb for my book?" and he said, "Sure."

Now, Robert Pinsky was there at the same event. In fact, he was reading his poetry to jazz. We had some great conversations, and I gave him a copy of the book, and he wrote a blurb. As for Gary Giddins . . . Well, I adore Gary Giddins. I've had a crush on him ever since he wrote the first really great piece about Art ["The Whiteness of the Wail" in the *Village Voice*, 1977]. Then, when the Galaxy box came out [*Art Pepper: The Complete Galaxy Recordings*, 1989], Ralph Kaffel asked who should write the liner notes and I said, "I want Gary Giddins." Ralph said, "Well, he wants a king's ransom." (I think he wanted a thousand dollars. I don't know. Ridiculous.) And it just so happened that that month, there was a big piece by him in *Esquire* magazine, and I said, "He *deserves* a king's ransom. Look!" Then I sent Gary this endless letter—about thirty pages, single-spaced. It was really the beginning of my writing about Art and basically went over Art's whole life, so he really knew Art's story by the time he wrote those notes.

FEINSTEIN: I know, too, that you felt he was one of the few critics who fully recognized your monumental, essential work in creating *Straight Life*.

PEPPER: He got it. I think he was the only one.

FEINSTEIN: When Whitney Balliett wrote about the book for the *New Yorker*, your father was livid that your name wasn't mentioned.

PEPPER: When I read the review, I didn't even notice because it was such a wonderful review. I was so knocked out.

FEINSTEIN: Your father called him an "ignorant sexist pig who hates women." You don't contradict him in the memoir . . .

PEPPER: I didn't know him. I don't know what he was like. All I know is what he wrote, and he did neglect me. My name's right on the cover. For some reason, Gary figured it out; Balliett did not.

FEINSTEIN: I cannot, on any level, defend leaving your name out of the review, but I knew Whitney, and he did not hate women. I think it's more likely related to the same problem that Don Asher had as coauthor of Hampton Hawes's autobiography, *Raise Up Off Me*. I'm not sure Asher received enough credit.

PEPPER: *Raise Up Off Me*? Oh my god—that's a work of art.

FEINSTEIN: Are there any jazz critics, apart from Gary, whom you admire?

PEPPER: There have been reviews of Art's music by a guy in the *Irish Times*. I think the Brits and the Irish do a better job. [Laughs.] One of the things that struck me when we were on the book tour [for *Straight Life*] is we would meet a journalist or jazz critic who would talk a great game, but when it came to writing . . . Really hackneyed stuff.

C. Michael Bailey writes beautifully about music. He does a really good job because he writes from a point of view of feeling. A lot of others are so cerebral. "What are they talking about?"

FEINSTEIN: I'd like to return to Robert Pinsky for a moment. He mentions Art in his poem "The Hearts" [in *The Want Bone*, 1990]. Do you happen to know that?

PEPPER: No! That's cool.

FEINSTEIN: Do you know of other poems for or about Art Pepper?

PEPPER: I don't.

FEINSTEIN: I'll send some to you. I'm thinking immediately of "Art Pepper" by Bruce Bond [*Throats of Narcissus*, 2001] and "Art Pepper" by Ed Hirsch [*Earthly Measures*, 1994]. There's also a poem by the extraordinary poet Yusef Komunyakaa—and I mention this with some trepidation—called "Pepper" [*Testimony*, 2013], which confronts racist statements in *Straight Life*—

PEPPER: Oh, definitely—Art was a racist. There's no way to get around it. He was a creature of his time, of his parents. He was a racist. *However*: some of his best friends were black—literally. [Pianist and band member] George Cables was one of his very best friends. They talked on the phone *all* the time.

The racism was hung over from another generation, and he was from that other generation. You would never call Art an incredibly enlightened character. He was not. He was overtly racist. In fact, there are things that are not in *Straight Life* . . . and he understood that they shouldn't be. But he was talking honestly to me, vomiting out everything, and there's definite racism in the book.

It's also true that some black musicians—after the great awakening, "Black Is Beautiful"—were really nasty to him. As he said, "Somebody doesn't like you, pretty soon you don't like them." That's based on racism and there's nothing to be done about it; it's just the way it is. I mean, who says Art had to be a perfect human being, you know?

FEINSTEIN: Do you know if George Cables ever read *Straight Life*?

PEPPER: I don't know. I don't. I don't know if Carl Burnett [the African American drummer in Art Pepper's final quartet] ever read it. I don't know if David Williams [the African American bassist in that group] ever read it. But we *lived* with those guys. When you're on the road with musicians, you are living with them. David once burned Art for some cocaine, and Art was really mad—[laughs]—but that had nothing to do with race.

FEINSTEIN: Have you had a chance to read [alto saxophonist] Phil Woods's autobiography, *Life in E Flat* [2020]?

PEPPER: No, I haven't! He wrote an autobiography?

FEINSTEIN: With the critic Ted Panken. It was published posthumously.

PEPPER: Oh, man—I've gotta read it. How much truth does he tell?

FEINSTEIN: [Laughs.] I don't know, but it sure sounds legit. I never felt that Phil was lying to me, and I don't sense that in his prose.

PEPPER: Art was supposed to play with Phil at Carnegie Hall; it was scheduled for a few months after Art died [in 1982]. One of the things Art said when he was lying there, dying, was, "I've got to play at Carnegie Hall."

FEINSTEIN: There's a moment in *Straight Life* where Art is sort of yucking it up about Phil marrying Charlie Parker's widow, Chan, perhaps to get Bird's horn.

PEPPER: You know something funny? Chan was furious. She wanted to sue Art, but Phil Woods thought it was the funniest thing he'd ever heard! [Laughs.]

FEINSTEIN: Not according to Phil's autobiography . . .

PEPPER: Oh, *really*?

FEINSTEIN: It's curious how things change.

PEPPER: Yeah, because he said, "I thought it was hilarious." That's what he said to us.

~

FEINSTEIN: You've done quite a number of interviews yourself and had enough for a book, but the project got shelved.

PEPPER: I really do enjoy interviewing people. At that point in my life [in the early eighties], I was really happy on my own. Being with Art was really hard, and being alone was such a relief. So I thought, "I bet there are other women who are on their own and doing okay." I proposed it to my editor [Ken Stuart] at Macmillan, which had published *Straight Life*, and I got the go-ahead. So I started interviewing people across the United States—all ages and races. It was a fun project, and exactly the right project for me at that time. But then Macmillan fired a bunch of people, including my editor, and the woman who replaced him really hated my book. I mean, she started screaming at me at one point. She said, "These women are all oddballs!"

FEINSTEIN: That's the *point*!

PEPPER: I know! She was yelling: "I need a book that a doctor's wife in Connecticut can enjoy." Can you believe that? So that was the end of my book.

FEINSTEIN: The first ten years of *Brilliant Corners* interviews were published in a volume called *Ask Me Now*, but neither that press nor others that I've queried are interested in a subsequent collection. [Bless you, SUNY Press—SF.] I'm concerned about the disinterest in the oral tradition.

PEPPER: You should self-publish! I mean, I didn't even *try* to get an agent with my memoir. As a friend of mine said, I'm such a control freak . . .

You know, my editor for *Straight Life* said that the people at Macmillan wanted to cut the book in half. I said, "What?!" He said, "I didn't even tell you. I knew it would upset you." And as another friend of mine pointed out, *Straight Life* could not be published in this day and age. It is too politically incorrect—page after page. So when I did my memoir, I thought, "I don't want to deal with any of that." It's so easy now to self-publish. You really should!

FEINSTEIN: I know, Laurie. But I'm an old-school academic. It's hard for me to get beyond certain prejudices. That's on me!

Let me ask you about your friend Todd Selbert. [Pepper laughs heartily.] He visited you in 1977 and brought along his excellent discography of Art's work, which you included as an appendix to *Straight Life*.

PEPPER: We were *dazzled*. I mean, why did he do this? It was amazing.

FEINSTEIN: What do you think of his edited volume, *The Art Pepper Companion: Writings on a Jazz Original* [2000]?

PEPPER: Oh, I like it. I'm glad he did it. But I'll tell you something: I was really mad at him. He told me he was going to do it, and I said, "Why don't you take my liner notes that I wrote for [Art Pepper's] *The Complete Village Vanguard Sessions* [1995]?" Those were good notes.

FEINSTEIN: They're outstanding.

PEPPER: He refused.

FEINSTEIN: [Long pause.] You're *kidding* me?

PEPPER: I'm not kidding you. In fact, when I wanted to get *Straight Life* published, he read the manuscript and said, "You need an editor"—in other words, to rewrite it. It was insulting; my editor at Macmillan changed almost *nothing*. Todd's a very dismissive kind of guy.

He loved Art, but he basically only loved old Art Pepper. He did not like how Art's music changed, and that's why he didn't want to use the Vanguard notes.

FEINSTEIN: Once again, I'm floored. I thought your voice had been left out by *your* choice, that you were saving the information for your own memoir (or something like that).

PEPPER: No.

FEINSTEIN: Okay—a more positive topic: the documentary on Art, *Notes from a Jazz Survivor* [1982].

PEPPER: There's going to be an addition to that film, another piece.

FEINSTEIN: Well then, why don't you start by talking about the addition.

PEPPER: No, that's what I can't talk about! [Both laugh.]

FEINSTEIN: You've written that your favorite part of that film is when Art says, and repeats, "I'm a genius." Why?

PEPPER: [Pause.] Because it's true. And the moment that he's saying it, you can hear playing on the record player what he's talking about. In some ways, Art had been so dismissed by so many people because of his drug addiction, and because he was white, from the [West] Coast, all of that. So when he says that, it makes me happy. Yes: in that moment, he knew it.

FEINSTEIN: It's just so odd to me because from my perspective—someone who never met him but who has known his music my whole adult life—he has always been indispensable when talking about modern jazz. To quote a record album title: *Living Legend* [Contemporary Records, 1975].

PEPPER: That was the great thing about Contemporary Records and [producer] Les Koenig: he really appreciated Art. We did not get along, but I knew that Les was the guy. I mean, without Les Koenig, what would have happened to Art? So many recordings would not have been made.

FEINSTEIN: Many of the greatest of his career.

PEPPER: No doubt about it.

FEINSTEIN: The documentary is low-budget and raw—

PEPPER: The guy who made it [Don McGlynn] was at USC film school when he made that. It was his first film. He got the money from a girlfriend. [Both laugh.]

FEINSTEIN: The moment that shocks me the most is when Art exposes, fully, his inoperable hernia. I mean, from everything that you and he have written, he was painfully self-conscious about the bulging, and to be shirtless on *film* . . . Were you surprised?

PEPPER: No, I was not at all. Art was out there. Art wanted to be *known*. He wanted everyone to know who he was in all honesty, and that was part of it.

FEINSTEIN: Yet he would spend so much time strapping himself in before every performance.

PEPPER: Oh, yeah. And he hated it when people thought he was fat.

FEINSTEIN: I'm sorry that you can't talk about the addition to the movie but I'm glad that there's going to be one.

PEPPER: There is. Art talks more about music in this little addition, which is wonderful. It was very hard to get him to talk about music. And there are some clips of music that nobody has ever heard.

Feinstein: That's a mind blow. Of course, you've been doing that since 2006: giving the world unreleased recordings on your Widow's Taste label. They're extraordinary.

Pepper: I really think they are.

Feinstein: One of the gazillion reasons why I'm so grateful is that there are renditions of Art's "Patricia" [written for his estranged daughter] that are more wrenching than any other releases.

Pepper: I think so, too. I think the one in Atlanta [*Unreleased Art, Volume 11* from 1980] is beyond anything.

Feinstein: Absolutely.

Pepper: You have no idea what it's like around here when I hear something like that and say, "Oh my God!" Because nobody has heard this.

Feinstein: I don't believe in the insidious cliché that one has to suffer to create great art, but when I hear that rendition of "Patricia," I can't help but think, "He's losing his daughter." He must be experiencing love and betrayal and devastation—the gamut of emotion—as he works his way through that tune in performance. You hear it. You feel it.

Pepper: He felt such things a lot because he truly felt it would make him a better artist. It was in his head. He really believed that. For J. S. Bach, it was apparently not necessary! [Laughs.] But Art was that kind of an artist. He was all about passion. Sadness. Grief. Love. Joy. Madness.

Feinstein: You've written that after you got the large tattoo of a chrysanthemum on your chest, you were mortified, partly because of its size. The cover of your memoir presents a remarkable photo by Phil Bray where Art's pulling down your shirt to expose it. Why do you think Art did that?

PEPPER: To embarrass me. To show people what I was really like. Everybody thought that he was the crazy one and I was the good girl. So he's telling everybody, "Well . . . maybe she's not."

FEINSTEIN: You don't think there was any sense of solidarity? I love it when he writes about trying to make a move on you at the beach, and he's worried about taking his shirt off because he doesn't want to expose his hernia but he's ultimately more proud of his skull tattoo.

PEPPER: That's the best! [Both laugh.] He was such a child. And it was just childishness: "You think she's such a goody-goody: Look at this."

FEINSTEIN: So why, then, did *you* choose it for the cover image?

PEPPER: Because I love it. I *love* it. Because it's true. Exactly true—and it's our relationship. He knew me. He knew me better than anybody. He knew how crazy I was. We had this whole routine where he had to be the crazy one and I had to be the sane one, but at that moment—maybe not.

12

On the Record

Tom Piazza

Tom Piazza's thirteen books range across genres from serious literary fiction to authoritative and opinionated studies of American music. Among the latter are *The Guide to Classic Recorded Jazz* and *Understanding Jazz: Ways to Listen*, both of which won the ASCAP Deems Taylor Award for Music Writing. His album notes for *Martin Scorsese Presents the Blues: A Musical Journey* won a Grammy award, and his post-Katrina manifesto *Why New Orleans Matters* devotes much of its focus to the central place of music in that city's culture. His 2008 novel *City of Refuge* won the Willie Morris Award for Southern Fiction, and his story collection *Blues and Trouble* earned him a James Michener Award. He was also one of the principal writers for the HBO series *Treme*. His most recent books are the novels *A Free State* and *The Auburn Conference*. He lives in New Orleans.

The following excerpts from Piazza's writings have been reprinted with permission. The interview took place in my summer home in Dennis, Massachusetts, on August 1, 2014.

The Guide to Classic Recorded Jazz (excerpt)

I wish there were a way to give some sense of what it was like to see Duke Ellington rehearse his band . . . or to be sixteen and see Sonny Stitt and Dexter Gordon square off at Radio City Music Hall while two middle-aged Harlemites hollered constant encouragement and poured me shots of Tanqueray gin from a bottle they carried in a doctor's bag. I wish there were room to convey the sense of anticipation that hovers in the odd twilight of the recording studio, the strange foreshortening of sounds, the muffled quality of nearby voices, and the unexpected crispness and presence of voices from the studio as they come over the speakers. I'd love to show what certain jazz clubs are like long after closing . . .

But, finally, what lingers most for me are the occasions when I first heard something that I knew would be part of my life forever—Roy Eldridge's ecstatic solo at the end of "Let Me Off Uptown" (with Gene Krupa's band) on my grandparents' old record player, for instance, or Charlie Parker suddenly swooping out of the speakers in a used-record booth at a Long Island farmers' market when I was about twelve (it was his solo on "I'll Remember April," from *The Happy Bird*; I bought the album immediately), or the shock of hearing the urgency in John Coltrane's tenor as he peeled off chorus after chorus of "Mr. P.C." on the *Giant Steps* album. All of these recordings have become a part of my life; I revisit them regularly, and I never tire of hearing them. But the surprise, the exhilaration of hearing them for the first time, has been one of the nicest things in life.

Setting the Tempo (excerpt)

Liner notes play a special role in a jazz fan's development. They have often been the place where a new fan first begins to learn about the musicians and the repertoire of jazz. There is always that moment, which any jazz fan recognizes, of unwrapping the record, putting it on, and settling in to read the notes, to *get the word*, on the music from an expert. . . . Of course, liner notes provide factual information and are in fact the main source of printed factual data for some artists. But the best liner notes, whether historical, musicological, narrative, or impressionistic, have always provided something beyond facts; they tell the listener, in many subtle ways, what it means to be a jazz fan. They embody styles of appreciating the music, a range of possible attitudes toward it. It is in this extra dimension that the liner note as a form really distinguishes itself.

Understanding Jazz: Ways to Listen (excerpt)

Just as the literal image of a swing may be useful in thinking about the quality of swing in music, some elements of narrative technique in literature may be useful in discussing the way musicians approach improvisation.

Most jazz, with its emphasis on improvised solos, would seem, in literary terms, to be narrated in the first person. The very distinct and recognizable individual voice of the soloist inflects the material and makes that teller's version of the story distinct from anyone else's. Sonny Rollins would tell the "story" of "I Can't Get Started" in a manner very different from Stan Getz's; John Coltrane would tell it differently from their versions, as would Coleman Hawkins and Lester Young and Joe Henderson and Wayne Shorter and Ben Webster,to speak only of tenor saxophonists. It is the advancement of a personal tale told through the vehicle of a preexisting narrative skeleton.

Blues Up and Down: Jazz in Our Time (excerpt)

There is a tendency to see Thelonious Monk as a sui generis figure, barren of followers, a grand exception to the norms of jazz. Born in 1917, he had one foot planted firmly in Harlem stride piano, to which he would allude throughout his career. Whereas it is nearly impossible to find a pianist in the 1950s whose conception was not in large measure directly traceable to [Bud] Powell's, few imitated Monk directly; his influence was felt gradually, in more oblique ways.

Unlike Powell, Monk made few if any gestures in homage to the European canon of piano technique. Where Powell's intensity expressed itself through floridity and lightning-fast melodic decisions made at high speed, Monk's expressed itself through the use of space and suspense. He posed questions and answered them at the last possible moment, like a juggler with fabulous equilibrium and wit. The instrument, he seemed to imply, functioned best when emitting semaphorelike bursts of light rather than an Impressionist mist or an operatic flood. Monk's approach resembled nineteenth-century European classical piano about as much as fast-break basketball resembles the minuet.

Interview

SASCHA FEINSTEIN: You've been in New Orleans roughly twenty years, but you were born on Long Island in 1955 and raised there. How and when did you teach yourself how to play piano?

TOM PIAZZA: In high school, I played some guitar and had a basic grasp of chords and musical relationships. I also played a melodica—a wind instrument with a keyboard and harmonica reeds inside. I got one because of *The Steve Allen Show*: they'd come back from a commercial, the band would be playing, and Steve Allen would be playing the melodica. So I wanted one of those and learned how a keyboard worked from that.

When I went to Williams College, there were pianos in most of the public areas—community rooms, dining halls—so I started sitting down at them, figuring out what to do. I probably got a pretty good gear ratio in terms of a learning curve just because I had listened to so much, putting things together faster than I would have otherwise.

I've liked music as far back as I can remember. I got really turned on by The Beatles—I was eight when The Beatles came to the United States—and got all their records, but the stuff I liked the most were their versions of Chuck Berry and Little Richard tunes, stuff that really had that rock 'n' roll bottom to it. At that time, you could still find Chuck Berry and Little Richard and Jerry Lee Lewis records at the Times Square Stores on Hempstead Turnpike, or at Mays' on Sunrise Highway (department stores still had record departments then), so my mom would buy me those—she was terrific, still is—and I became a total stone, rock 'n' roll freak when I was about ten.

From there I became interested in blues because Chuck Berry talked about Muddy Waters here and there. I started buying *Down Beat* magazine when I was eleven, because they would have occasional articles on blues, and that's how I started finding out about jazz. It was a whole new continent, with extraordinary little kingdoms and fiefdoms and neighborhoods. Ecosystems within ecosystems. It was unbelievable.

At that time, if you subscribed to *Down Beat* they would send you a five-star album of your choice, and the first one that I got was *Valentine Stomp* by Fats Waller, from the RCA Vintage series. And my parents were very generous in buying me records that I wanted. I listened to Thelonious Monk early on; *Straight, No Chaser* was one of my favorite records. *The Popular Duke Ellington* on RCA was another subscription gift from *Down Beat*. And I read, of course. I'd take out books from the library and vacuum them up into my brain. So I was a confirmed jazzer by the time I was twelve, and by the time I turned thirteen or fourteen, I was way off into the woods.

FEINSTEIN: You had a piece published in *Down Beat* when you were a sixteen-year-old senior in high school.

PIAZZA: Wow—it's odd that you know that.

FEINSTEIN: What gave you the chutzpah to send them work?

PIAZZA: I had met Dan Morgenstern, the editor of *Down Beat*, because I used to go to record-collector meetings in New York City. I can't quite remember how I got conscripted into being part of that group, but every two months or so we would meet at the CBS Building. [Record producers] John Hammond and Bob Altshuler would be there. Leonard Kunstadt, who had *Record Research* magazine. Dan Morgenstern. People legendary in that field but completely unknown outside of it: Carl Kendziora, Warren Hicks (who did the Benny Goodman bio-discography), Harold Flakser. And I would also go to discographical conferences that Rutgers [University] had. I don't really know how I found out about them but I started attending when I was about fourteen. I was obviously something of a freak so I got invited along, and Dan was very friendly to me at those meetings in the CBS Building.

I was writing little articles for the high school newspaper. When Roy Eldridge played at the Roosevelt Field Shopping Center, I wrote a piece about that. Same for Teddy Wilson. Then an English teacher of mine brought me to see Mary Lou Williams at the Cathedral of St. John the Divine. (She was performing her Mass. David Amram was on French horn. It was astonishing.) So I wrote an article about that, too, which was published, I think, in the high school literary magazine. I liked seeing my words in print, so I asked Dan at one of those record meetings how one might start writing for *Down Beat*. You know Dan, right?

FEINSTEIN: Yeah.

PIAZZA: He said [Piazza imitates Morgenstern perfectly]: "Well, if you find that there's something you might like to write about, call the office and perhaps we'll give you the assignment." There was a concert coming up at Queens College, an all-star affair with Milt Hinton, Hank Jones, Ray Nance, Joe Newman, maybe Vic Dickenson. Eubie Blake played solo. I called the *Down Beat* office, and Dan's assistant Ellie, later his wife, said I could go ahead and write about it. I got off the phone and jumped around the house. I literally jumped around. I'll probably never again have any excitement comparable to that.

So I attended the event and sat in the front row, taking notes like a sixteen year old, and later mailed them my article. And I didn't hear anything for a while. This was my senior year in high school, and one day two friends came up to me in the hall with this look on their faces, as if I had won the Lottery. "Look!" And they had a copy of *Down Beat* opened to my review with my name in small italics.

For my next article, I left my high school graduation and took a train into the city to cover a memorial concert for the clarinetist Tony Parenti. And that was it; I was off.

FEINSTEIN: When you were growing up in Long Island, did you get to Manhattan much, and did you hear musicians who absolutely floored you?

PIAZZA: That's a question that makes me really happy. Sure: Manhattan was a fifty-minute train ride away. When I got a little older, it was a forty-minute car ride away; my parents *foolishly* let me borrow their car to go to the Village Vanguard and the Village Gate—sometimes to the homes of musicians. (I've got plenty of off-the-record stuff to tell you about *that*! [Both laugh.])

FEINSTEIN: Does it *have* to be off the record?

PIAZZA: Well, I guess there's a statute of limitations on some kinds of chemical use. [Both laugh.]

In terms of performances, I got so lucky. The first jazz club I ever went to was the Village Vanguard. I was on a date with a woman whom I was completely sunk in love with. I was maybe a junior in high school—fifteen or sixteen—and I don't know why they let me in. I think it was a Sunday afternoon, and it was Keno Duke and His Jazz Contemporaries. Duke was not a particularly well-known drummer, but his group included Julius Watkins on French horn and Frank Strozier. You know Frank Strozier?

FEINSTEIN: Oh yeah—he's an *incendiary* alto player.

PIAZZA: One of the very great players, and *so* little known. That whole Memphis gang with George Coleman and Phineas Newborn.

FEINSTEIN: That's right.

PIAZZA: But I walked down those narrow steps at the Vanguard and his sound just rose up, and Julius Watkins sounded wonderful. It was magic. I remember thinking that the Village Vanguard was the true heart of life, the navel of the universe. Subsequently, some of the greatest music I've ever heard—Sonny Rollins when he came back from his "exile" around '73—took place at the Village Vanguard and Village Gate. Sonny Rollins was so unspeakably brilliant, and the level of presence . . . You felt that you were on the diamond-edge of the moment with absolute lucidity. It was incredible—probably the greatest live music I've ever seen in my life.

    Slightly later I heard Monk at the Vanguard with Paul Jeffreys [on tenor] and Monk's son, Toot, on drums. I heard Dexter Gordon when he returned from Europe in the mid-1970s. And then there were all the older jazz musicians. You know, I was very fortunate in my younger years, when I was still in and just out of high school. At that time, you could still hear some of the very great musicians from the Swing era—sidemen like Dicky Wells, Rudy Powell, Buddy Tate, Milt Hinton, Taft Jordan, Sandy Williams, Budd Johnson—all these musicians who had played mainly as sidemen, and I was agape that these people were alive and that you could see them. Of course, they were happy to see this very young cat coming along, so they were as friendly and welcoming as could be.

One of the great experiences of my life was with Dicky Wells. Very few of them could make a living as a musician, and Dicky was working for a brokerage down on Wall Street. He was a *messenger*. Dicky Wells! "Between the Devil and the Deep Blue Sea." "Sweet Sue." "Taxi War Dance." He was a messenger, and he invited me to join him on his job one day. He introduced me to the people at the brokerage, and then we went out on his rounds. At one point we stopped at a Japanese restaurant. "Come on," he said. "Let's stop in and get you a calendar. Sometimes they got broads on 'em." Then we went to Merrill Lynch, and Rudy Powell, the clarinetist who played with Fats Waller, was pushing a mail cart. Julian Dash, the great tenor player with the Erskine Hawkins band, was manning a security desk. They had this whole underground of Swing-era musicians who all knew each other, and—as painful as it is to hear about it—they were fortunate to have this little network. And they were still playing gigs.

I *loved* those men so much . . . I remember one day standing in the hallway when a really attractive woman walked by. I turned to look, and they started *laughing*, and Rudy said, "You hear his neck crack?" Beautiful, man. That's just how they were.

Milt Hinton and I were very good friends, and I used to go to his house in St. Albans a lot. In fact, we did the foundation of what later became his book of photographs, *Bass Lines*, which he did with a different writer, David Berger. I was too young for the job, but I recorded *easily* fifteen or twenty hours of taped interviews with him, which I believe ended up going to the Smithsonian. But sometimes he'd invite me over just to listen to records, and sometimes Jimmy Owens would be there, or Ben Riley, or Chris White. *A Great Day in Harlem* is one of the greatest jazz documentaries ever, and I got to see a lot of the eight-millimeter color films that Milt and his wife, Mona—mainly Mona—shot at the time and which ended up in the film. We watched them in his basement. He also took a lot of still photos—candids—that day. He was a serious photographer. I thought that film was extremely moving at the end when Art Farmer says, "They're all part of us." It was very heavy. That was a wonderful film.

I met Bernard Addison, a guitarist who played with the Fletcher Henderson band in 1933 or '34, and he invited me to his house in Hempstead on Long Island. I went to Buddy Tate's house in Amityville. Budd Johnson introduced me to Jay McShann. "You should interview Jay McShann," he said. "*That's* who you need to interview. Go on!" So Jay McShann invited me to his hotel room—I have these tapes somewhere—and Al Hibbler was there, too, with a bottle of Johnny Walker Red, which they poured for me liberally. We sat there for probably two-and-a-half hours. I listened to them tell acceleratingly obscene and hilarious stories as we got fractured! I spent time with Ruby Braff, who could be a mean guy but was friendly to me off and on. I learned so much from these guys. They'd bring me around to bars in the afternoon. Those were formative experiences. I got an amazing window onto that world.

    I wrote for the *SoHo News* for a stretch in the late seventies / early eighties, and one of the articles they sent me to do was a walking tour with Art Farmer around Greenwich Village to go to the Café Bohemia and the Five Spot and all those places where he played in the 1950s and '60s. I was very, very fortunate with the situations I found myself in. I spent New Year's Eve of 1988 at Tommy Flanagan's apartment. He had a giant, black-and-white photograph of Art Tatum hanging next to his piano bench. Roy Haynes was there with a big felt hat and theatrically knotted scarf at his neck. Dexter Gordon was sitting in the kitchen, and Roy stood in front of him and sang the entire arrangement of the Billy Eckstine record *Rhythm in a Riff*. The entire thing! From the opening notes, through Eckstine's vocal [sings dramatically]: "I love the rhythm in a riff / When the music jumps I get a lift / [scats]." Then he sang the chase choruses between Dexter and Gene Ammons, and Dexter was sitting there with his eyes closed, snapping his fingers, transported. It was a beautiful thing.

~

FEINSTEIN: Of your ten books thus far, two are listening guides. Looking back at the first—*A Guide to Classic Recorded Jazz* [1995]—would you change anything now?

PIAZZA: I don't think I'd change anything much, certainly not in the choices of music. I think the template I had mind in terms of what I was and was not going to write about was valid and viable. I would just place the emphasis now in slightly different places; after all, the book came out nineteen years ago, and I'm in a different place now. At that time, as you well know, the jazz world had sunk into this fryolator of contentious discourse, and I got sucked up into that for a while. I can't say that I disagree in substance with any of the stands that I took at that time, but when I look back, there was so much negative energy generated on both sides of that whole debate about Lincoln Center, and the tradition. I certainly wouldn't get involved in that debate today. So in some places in the book, I was probably at slightly greater pains than I would be today to draw connections between the mechanics of jazz music and the mechanics of American democracy—all of which I think are interesting and, up to a point, fruitful connections to draw, but at a certain point I just got tired of having to think about American democracy every time I listened to a Sonny Rollins record.

FEINSTEIN: You and I don't agree on some jazz musicians—which simply means that we're human beings considering art—but I think one of the attractions to *A Guide to Classic Recorded Jazz* (or any well-written, interesting guide, for that matter) has to do with the discourse between the writer and the reader. Your prose is so lively and smart, and it saddened me that you faced such hostility.

PIAZZA: That book got a very odd reception. I understood it up to a point. But in the book, if I said that I wasn't thrilled by certain musicians, I tried to make it very clear that this was a matter of taste. And I got a lot of—I wouldn't call it criticism; I wouldn't dignify it as criticism—grief because I said I wasn't nuts about Bill Evans. Great as he was.

FEINSTEIN: That became the lightning rod.

PIAZZA: Yeah.

FEINSTEIN: So when did you decide to write *another* guide to jazz [*Understanding Jazz*, 2005]? [Both laugh.] Obviously, it's a very different kind of book.

PIAZZA: Well, that came out about nine years later, with a different angle of light on the same material. *The Guide to Classic Recorded Jazz* had a chronological dimension to it, in the way the first part of the book was organized; it talked about the development of the music over time. I guess if I had a model for *Understanding Jazz*, it was something like E. M. Forster's *Aspects of the Novel* [1927]: the material wasn't considered chronologically but thematically, dealing with questions of form, the nature of swing, relations between foreground and background, what have you. It was a good exercise and I'm proud of that book, but I haven't had the appetite to write another book about jazz.

FEINSTEIN: In another one of your books, *Blues Up and Down*, you're quite critical of James Lincoln Collier, and for good reason. Looking at the opposite end of that spectrum, which jazz writers have you admired?

PIAZZA: That's a fun list to try to compile—and I'm glad you said "jazz writers" and not "jazz critics" because there are so few jazz critics. Although this is in no particular order, the first person I would have to say I admire, and who is still at work today, is Dan Morgenstern. I think it's an occupational hazard for people who write about music (to say nothing about people who write about art or literature) to feel that they are in competition with the material they write about. A lot of times writers seem to be trying to outsmart the music itself. There may be a slight feeling of inferiority vis-à-vis the stuff they're writing about, so there's an odd self-advertisement that doesn't always play that well. But Dan always put the emphasis on the music in a way that showed how much love and respect he had. (This is also one of the things that I admire about Peter Guralnick's writing.) Within a sentence or two into an article, you could always tell it was Dan's writing.

FEINSTEIN: Gary Giddins said the very same thing to me.

PIAZZA: Dan was always perfectly balanced. Other writers: Martin Williams, probably the most serious jazz critic—maybe the Edmund Wilson of jazz critics. He really knew literature, art, culture as a whole, and he brought his sharp, serious mind and fine prose to considering the music in true critical fashion.

After those two, I would have to say the early [work by] Nat Hentoff. I also grew up reading Ira Gitler, LeRoi Jones / Amiri Baraka when he was still writing for *Down Beat*, Don Heckman, Don DeMichael—the whole asteroid-belt of jazz writers at that time who were all good, solid writers. Larry Kart, at least early on, was a very good writer about jazz; he focused on the so-called avant-garde and wrote some very valuable things about it. There was a wonderful writer named David Himmelstein who mainly wrote liner notes and was enormously talented. He had a wonderful edge in his voice and came up with startling figures of speech. His notes for the Booker Ervin / Dexter Gordon album, *Setting the Pace*, are fantastic, and he wrote great notes for Jaki Byard's *Out Front*. The best of Whitney Balliett is certainly among the best jazz writing you'll ever find. Whitney was a great man with a metaphor. It wasn't criticism; it was something else, but it gave you a flavor of the world of the musicians. On the prose level it is some of the best that's ever been written about jazz.

FEINSTEIN: Your book of liner notes, *Setting the Tempo*, collects about fifty wonderful pieces. Do you think—and forgive me for raising a depressing topic—that the size of CDs and, worse, information-less downloads will lead to liner notes becoming a lost art?

PIAZZA: Everything's a lost art now. I don't know. It represents a different mode of address to the person who's going to buy the music. It's a different situation. It's now dull to say it, but there used to be a romance to buying a jazz album. It was wrapped, but you could read about it on the back, read about the musicians. Mouthwatering. Leonard Feather talking about Johnny Coles on this record, Blue Mitchell on that one. Hank Mobley. You'd think, "Who the hell are these people?" Then you'd bring it home and you'd zip open the seal and pull out that record, which was beautiful and glossy. You'd put it on and get the player up to speed. And, of course, analog is always sexier than digital: that needle vibrates, and you feel a physical *connection* to something that should be unrepeatable except, guess what? Magic: it is repeatable.

So the liner note may have only been a minor art, but it was an art.

FEINSTEIN: Like a prose form, perhaps. But if CDs have notes at all, the type's so small!

PIAZZA: Oh, yeah—it's going by the boards. And, as you say, even CDs are going by the boards, and with downloads . . . It's a different game. If everything weighs the same, everything's weightless.

FEINSTEIN: I find it sad. So much of my jazz education early on came directly from the liners.

PIAZZA: Sure. Mine, too.

FEINSTEIN: You won a Grammy for your notes for *Martin Scorsese Presents the Blues*. That must have been thrilling—and a lovely endorsement for a project that must have been daunting.

PIAZZA: Oh, yes. I think I even kick off those notes with a statement about that: to compress a subject like the blues—which has so many faces, and such a history, and where so many other topics seep in—into five thousand words was a challenge. I wrote those notes in about a month at Yaddo; it was sort of fun, like gearing up for a marathon. I brought all these Document CDs—the British label with the complete recordings of Charlie Patton, Bumble Bee Slim, Bo Carter, Beale Street Sheiks—and I just thought about the blues. Whitney Balliett provided a wonderful quote that I used in those notes, taken from his notes for Joe Turner's *Boss of the Blues* on Atlantic: "Jazz would be an empty house without the blues." I loved that, and I loved him for writing that.

∼

FEINSTEIN: You're a genuine fan of classic films. Are there jazz-influenced movies—not documentary films—that you feel really capture the essence of jazz?

PIAZZA: [Pauses.] I've got to say, I'm having trouble thinking of any successful marriage of jazz and film. Plenty of films, obviously, have very successful music written for them—most obviously *Anatomy of a Murder*. That score, which was arranged as a suite for that album, is one of the very best things Ellington ever did. But the way the music's used in the film is sort of grotesque, or at least odd and arbitrary the way it crops up. *Round Midnight*? I remember enjoying the film when I saw it, and I was really happy to see Dexter Gordon receive an Oscar [nomination]—how could you not love that?—but none of it has stuck with me. Clint Eastwood's movie, *Bird*, was, of course, a travesty. *Glenn Miller Story*, *Benny Goodman Story*—those are cheesy films. *New Orleans* has a lot of wonderful moments in it but the story couldn't be more hokey.

FEINSTEIN: Let's switch, then, to TV. You were one of the writers for HBO's *Treme*, often working collaboratively with other writers. What was your greatest contribution? What did you bring to the table?

PIAZZA: That's a tricky question to answer without sounding either self-congratulatory or vague or both, because I don't know. What I might have thought I brought to the room might not have been what somebody else might have thought I brought to the room. Maybe, instead, I can give a little discourse on the way these things are written.

You have six or eight people—in season 1 there were six of us—sitting around in a room, and there's a basic template for what the two main writers (David Simon and Eric Overmyer) had in mind for the arc of the season. Basic plot points. So you sit there and collectively improvise. In effect, there's a set of chord changes laid down loosely, in terms of plot structure, and then you improvise melodies on that—and sometimes substitute changes. We'd know, say, by the end of episode 3, we'd want Sascha Feinstein to have cut his first album on saxophone, and by the end of episode 5, it's nominated for a Grammy. At the end of episode 7, he does *not* get the Grammy and decides to become an English teacher. By the end of episode 10, he's back in the studio again—or something like that. So that's, like, D minor seventh to G seventh to whatever circle of changes you want to invent. And to get from one place to another, there are trigger moments within those nodes—and that's what you improvise collectively, from signal point to signal point. In the course of doing that, the general shape may change; the form itself can mutate. It *has* to, for various reasons, among them the exigencies of casting, budget, location, availability, whatever it might be.

FEINSTEIN: So were you collectively working on all characters at the same time?

PIAZZA: Yes. Right. It's really an extraordinary process. But I never considered my main strength as a fiction writer to be plot, so that process of improvising plot to make a route through a somewhat-loose but still preexisting template was new to me. "Okay, if he's going to be making his record, how can he do that?" "Well, can he meet somebody at a club?" "Nah, that's too obvious." "What if he's at a grocery store and gets into an argument with somebody—and that somebody turns out to be a record producer?" People were constantly going, "Yes and . . ." or "How about this . . ." In that respect, it was very much like a jazz group.

But I don't think naturally in those kinds of terms. My strengths as a writer have always had more to do with mood and, especially, dialogue. So I was probably most effective in the process when it came to sitting down alone and writing the episode. As I said, we all collaborated in beating out these detailed outlines for each episode to achieve this larger outline, and then everyone's dealt an episode to write, based on the agreed-upon outline. By that time, you have a sense of all the characters, how each one talks and what makes them tick. If you're lucky, you know who the actors are and can envision them, their sound.

That first season was such a fantastic writers' group. David Simon and Eric Overmyer. A *great* writer named David Mills, a soulful cat who did some of the smartest things. (He would always ask, "If this show wasn't set in New Orleans, what would it be about? What's the *human* thing that's going on here?" Always bringing it back to that, and I found him invaluable.)

There was George Pelecanos, who's a very talented crime novelist and experienced television writer, and Lolis Eric Elie, who was Wynton [Marsalis]'s road manager; they went to NOCCA together—New Orleans Center for Creative Arts. So it was sort of like suddenly finding yourself playing in the Miles Davis sextet: Whoa! Oh man! Everybody's hearing *everything*. [Both laugh.]

FEINSTEIN: Do you feel that the show gives a fairly accurate depiction of what it's like to be in New Orleans, especially as a musician?

PIAZZA: Yes. And certainly light years better than anything else that's ever been done. No question about that, and I think the show will grow in stature in people's esteem as the years go by. If the show's considered groundbreaking or unique, it most likely will have to do with how music and narrative are integrated. In other words, the music doesn't consist (for the most part) of set pieces. Toward seasons 3 and 4, it began to move a little bit more that way when the character Annie came to the fore, but in general, the show was remarkable for the way in which music dovetailed into the narrative elements.

FEINSTEIN: You've conducted many interviews, most recently with Stanley Crouch, whom you've known for a long time, on the first volume of his Bird biography [*Kansas City Lightning: The Rise and Times of Charlie Parker*]. How did you prepare for that interview?

PIAZZA: By having a thirty-five-year friendship with the subject. [Both laugh.] After the course of thirty-five years, you anticipate somebody's moves. Stanley and I are not *as* close as we used to be, partly because of the geographical distance [between New Orleans and New York City] and partly just because way leads on to way. But there were probably twenty years when we had an extremely close, intellectual, reciprocal friendship; a lot of my mind was shaped by that friendship (and possibly vice versa—I don't know). In any case, Stanley and I have had a thirty-year conversation about that Charlie Parker material going into the publication, so I had a very good feeling for the kinds of contextualizing and sensibility that Stanley always brings to any aesthetic discussion, particularly in regard to African American aesthetic work in the United States. His understanding of the context, which has its deep roots in Ralph Ellison's and Albert Murray's work, is extremely valuable and rare, to this day. So I know that Stanley can't think about Charlie Parker and Kansas City without thinking about Buffalo Soldiers or horses coming to the Americas with Cortés. I knew that he would be thinking about that when he wrote the book, and what he came out with was pretty astonishing.

FEINSTEIN: Were you able to guide the conversation?

PIAZZA: Yeah. To a certain extent. I mean, I've had many, many hour-long, two-hour-long telephone conversations with Stanley, so I can tell when the riff is becoming a second riff and a third riff. I'm also sensitive to audiences that are general-interest audiences (not just jazz-freak audiences). I certainly don't feel intimidated to steer an interview.

FEINSTEIN: In your own fiction, which work or works have been the most influenced by the blues and jazz? *Blues and Trouble* [*Twelve Stories*]?

PIAZZA: Well, there was a scheme behind that short-story collection that was very directly related—almost mechanically as a literary conceit—to blues form: twelve stories related in a certain way that had different tonalities. My notion, at least, was that if you read the book straight through as a series, it would have a certain blues effect. Whether it did or not I really don't know; it's hard for me to imagine someone who didn't have that framework to experience the book that way.

    I don't want to say that my novels and stories are "influenced" by music; my mind was *formed* by what I got out of improvised music (most especially jazz), which is to say, I have an impatience with any mode that doesn't allow for the unexpected, for surprise, metaphor, unanticipated connection, variation.

    Let me approach this from a different entrance: I've never been the kind of writer who wanted to sketch things out in advance and execute a plan. (This is one of the things that I had to learn with *Treme*.) There wasn't a lot of reason to do this thing that was a highly risky occupation if there wasn't fun to be had in some kind of way. To me, the fun was in listening as you spoke and being alert to happy, unanticipated implications of something that had just happened. The way I write, when I feel that I'm writing well, is a very improvisatory way of working. Jazz formed my sensibility; it formed my sense of what I look for in other people's work, too.

I haven't written about jazz for about ten years. The discourse in the jazz world seemed to get so negative, and there's a spirit of community that got lost. I didn't want to be in debates about jazz anymore. I didn't want to hear, "Why doesn't Jazz at Lincoln Center hire more white musicians?" It was like having a chronic toothache. I consider myself a fiction writer. I don't know if I'll ever write fiction about jazz per se. But I do think everything that I write is saturated with a jazz sensibility.

13

The Archival Mind

Ricky Riccardi

Ricky Riccardi is the director of research collections for the Louis Armstrong House Museum and author of *What a Wonderful World: The Magic of Louis Armstrong's Later Years* and *Heart Full of Rhythm: The Big Band Years of Louis Armstrong*. He runs the online blog *The Wonderful World of Louis Armstrong* (dippermouth.blogspot.com) and has given lectures on Armstrong at venues around the world, including the Institute of Jazz Studies, the National Jazz Museum in Harlem, the Bristol International Jazz and Blues Festival, and the Monterey Jazz Festival. He has taught a Music of Louis Armstrong graduate course at Queens College, in addition to a Swing University course on Armstrong at Jazz at Lincoln Center. He has coproduced numerous Armstrong reissues in recent years, including *Satchmo at Symphony Hall 65th Anniversary: The Complete Concert*, Ella Fitzgerald and Louis Armstrong's *Cheek to Cheek: The Complete Duet Recordings*, *Pops Is Tops: The Verve Studio Albums*, two volumes of *Decca Singles*, *Columbia and RCA Victor Live Recordings of Louis Armstrong and the All Stars*, and, released after this conversation, *The Complete Louis Armstrong Columbia and RCA Victor Studio Sessions 1946–1966*, for which he won a Grammy award. A working jazz pianist, he lives in Toms River, New Jersey, with his wife and their three daughters.

The following excerpts from Riccardi's writings have been reprinted with permission. The interview took place at the Louis Armstrong Archives in Queens College on March 14, 2019.

Liner Notes for *Columbia and RCA Victor Live Recordings of Louis Armstrong and the All Stars* (excerpt)

Armstrong's small group, the "All Stars," was formed in 1947 and was a top-drawing live attraction from night one. But [manager] Joe Glaser wanted hit records and RCA Victor's few recordings with that group didn't sell especially well. In 1949, he signed Armstrong up with Decca, where Milt Gabler would oversee Armstrong's recorded output for the next five years.

Gabler, as the founder and longtime head of Commodore Records, knew and loved pure, no-frills jazz but more importantly to Glaser, he knew how to make records that sold in large quantities. Though he threw the All Stars an occasional bone—resulting in some wonderful albums, such as *Satchmo at Pasadena*, *New Orleans Days*, and *At the Crescendo*—Gabler mostly featured Armstrong covering other people's hits, backed by larger studio groups. The result was a string of commercially successful records: *Blueberry Hill*, *That Lucky Old Sun*, *La Vie en Rose*, *C'est Si Bon*, *A Kiss to Build a Dream On*, *I Get Ideas*, and more.

But it also added fuel to the flame of longstanding criticism of Armstrong, that he had "gone commercial." Armstrong liked to claim that he didn't read reviews, but clearly, he knew the cries of "commercialism" were harming his reputation as the world's greatest jazzman.

What a Wonderful World (excerpt)

After the historic *Brown v. Board of Education* decision of 1954 desegregated schools around the country, the notoriously segregated New Orleans rebelled at the end of that year by passing [as Jonathan Mark Souther has written] multiple "draconian statutes that further codified longstanding Jim Crow practices . . ."

This was too much for Armstrong, who had grown disgusted by the city's segregationist policies. The All Stars had been an integrated band from day one, something that Armstrong had always prided himself on. "Ain't nobody gonna call me intolerant," he said when asked about it in May 1956. Now the band found itself under the heel of segregation. Bitter, Armstrong vowed never to return until the city changed its racial stance. In a 1958 interview . . . Armstrong jumped in and answered, "Since [1956], in New Orleans, they don't want white and Negro musicians playing together. All I can say is, the people who made those laws, they don't know anything about music. Because in music, it doesn't make any difference. I don't run into much trouble with segregation, 'cause I don't go where I'm not wanted. And—please don't take this out, I'm going to tell this straight—I don't go to New Orleans . . . no more."

Liner Notes for Louis Armstrong's *Pops Is Tops: The Verve Studio Albums* (excerpt)

This set marks the first time the entire contents of the August 1 [1957] session tapes, previously available only as a digital release, *A Day with Satchmo*, are out in any physical form, and it's cause for celebration. For one, there's his good humor, heard immediately at the start of "Makin' Whoopee." After being told to sing the opening line, "Another bride," with "feeling," Armstrong replies, "I've felt up many-a-brides!" On some of the earlier takes of "Makin' Whoopee" and especially "Let's Do It," he bungles a word here and there; one can picture Armstrong with his black, horn-rimmed spectacles, reading the sheet music for the first time. But he keeps going, getting the mistakes out of his system.

And when he picks up the trumpet on "Willow Weep for Me," he's initially hesitant, playing around with a quote from his 1927 "Savoy Blues" solo before he abandons it and comes up with an entirely new solo steeped in the blues, giving [producer Norman] Granz his master take and giving Armstrong a chance to finally rest those abused chops.

Liner Notes for Ella Fitzgerald and Louis Armstrong's *Cheek to Cheek: The Complete Duet Recordings* (excerpt)

On July 5, 1971, Louis Armstrong spent most of his day in his den in his home in Corona, Queens, NY, copying a few of his own LPs to reel-to-reel tape. Winding down the evening, he put on *Ella and Louis*, listening until the very end, when "April in Paris" concludes with Ella Fitzgerald's aching "my heart" and a perfectly phrased trumpet coda. Gorgeous. There was still tape left on his reel but Armstrong had to get to bed.

He would never wake up, passing away in his sleep at 5:30 a.m. on the morning of July 6. Sometime later, his wife Lucille took the tape out of his Tandberg deck and wrote on its box, "Last tape recorded by Pops, 7/5/71."

Could there be any better way to go?

Interview

SASCHA FEINSTEIN: I want to begin with your Louis Armstrong "eureka" moment. It's 1995. You're fifteen years old. What on earth made you rent *The Glenn Miller Story* [1954]?

RICKY RICCARDI: [Laughs.] I was not a normal fifteen year old. [Laughs again.] I was born in 1980 and I never much enjoyed pop culture made after 1980, so old comedy was my gateway.

FEINSTEIN: Did your folks introduce you to that?

RICCARDI: I always had this part of my brain where I would discover something and then needed to know everything about it. I became a baseball fan when I was three years old. (My first memory: Dave Righetti's no-hitter, Yankees versus Red Sox, July 4, 1983. I remember my brother and father jumping on the couch, and I thought, "Alright, I'll be a baseball fan.") When I was six, my father got me the program for the 1985 World Series. On the back, it had a listing of all World Series winners and losers, and I memorized them all; that became my six-year-old party trick. They'd wheel me out for weddings and family functions. [Feinstein laughs.] People would throw dates: "1971." "Oh, that's Pittsburgh Pirates / Baltimore Orioles." So that part of my brain was always there.

When I was in first grade, before school, I'd watch *The Three Stooges* on TBS, and there was a short called "A Gem of a Jam" [released in 1943], and I thought it was the funniest thing I'd ever seen. Instead of stopping there, I then needed to see every *Three Stooges* short and read about them, and that opened the floodgate to Laurel and Hardy, Abbott and Costello, The Honeymooners, anything with Buster Keaton, black-and-white, slapstick, old, whatever—I thought it was the greatest. But I also bought texts to know the history. This took me through my elementary school years, and my family totally went down the wormhole with me: my father was a huge *Honeymooners* fan; my brother was a huge Laurel and Hardy fan. I'd bring back videos from the store and we'd laugh and laugh.

When I got to seventh and eighth grade, I started branching out into old movies in general. I went through a James Cagney phase, a Bogart phase, and then a Jimmy Stewart phase—and that's when, at fifteen, I rented *The Glenn Miller Story*.

I was not a jazz fan at that point. My brother had been a big influence and got me interested in Motown. (In first grade I was making sketches of Stevie Wonder—that was my entry.) Most of elementary school was fifties rock 'n' roll. In middle school, I leapt over jazz and ended up in ragtime and early vaudeville (Eddie Cantor and Al Jolson, obscure pop songs). So that's where I was coming from musically. I knew *of* Glenn Miller; I had heard him in countless movies. And, again, I was in my Jimmy Stewart phase, so I thought, "*The Glenn Miller Story*. Great!" Then midway through [the movie] comes Louis Armstrong, and for me he was the total combination. Because I was an ignorant Italian teenager in New Jersey, I was not viewing it with a lens of what some viewed as embarrassing about his persona—the smile, all that. I was thinking, "Geez, this guy is warm. He's funny. His voice is interesting. And when he plays [trumpet], he's a genius. I need more!"

On Columbus Day in 1995, my mom took me to the Ocean County Library where they had a whole wall [of recordings], including [a Louis Armstrong compilation titled] *16 Most Requested Songs*, with liner notes by George Avakian. Track 1 was "Mack the Knife" [1955]. Track 14 was "St. Louis Blues" [1954]—a nine-minute version; nothing had ever hit me between the eyes like that. By the end of that recording, I was a basket case: "What did I just experience?"

I go back to the library and get *All-Time Greatest Hits*, which opens with "Hello Dolly" and "What a Wonderful World." I get all these compilations and bootlegs from the fifties and sixties. He's the greatest singer, comedian, musician—I'm in heaven. So I now have to know everything there is to know and go to the books, and this is when I start reading that the young Louis Armstrong was a genius but that he gets to a certain point and sells out, goes commercial. He's a clown. He's recording pop songs. He's an Uncle Tom. And I'm thinking, "What are you telling me about this guy whom I fell in love with?" I could not justify this. (Eventually I discovered Gary Giddins and Dan Morgenstern, people who felt the same way I felt. And I later discovered early Armstrong, and it blows my mind, but certainly not enough to discount the later stuff.)

Two years go by. I've not been able to go into a record store without coming home with a CD; my collection has become quite large. Then Laurence Bergreen puts out a huge new biography [*Louis Armstrong: An Extravagant Life*, 1997], and I'm reading it, loving it. But he spent 424 pages on Armstrong's life up to '43 and 70 pages on the later twenty-eight years. James Lincoln Collier's book [*Louis Armstrong: An American Genius*, 1983] was so mean-spirited about the later years, but Bergreen's book just hit the fast-forward button: Armstrong spoke against Little Rock, then he tours the world as Ambassador Satch, records "Hello Dolly," then he dies. And that was the moment when I thought, "How is nobody taking a twenty-five-year chunk of this man's life and really examining it?" That was when the dream was born: "If no one ever wants to write that book, I want to do it."

In my senior year in high school, '99, one of my friends showed me an ad for the Rutgers University master's degree in Jazz History and Research, and I thought, "All right, I know what I need to do now!" [Laughs.] "Whatever I do in college, I need to end up there." I went to Ocean County College and ended up taking over the media. I had a radio show and played Armstrong every week, and then I became editor in chief of the paper and decided to give myself a column. (I live in the least jazz-savvy town in America. [Feinstein laughs.] Toms River, New Jersey, would not know what to do with jazz if it showed up on its front door—and I say that, by the way, as someone who has produced jazz concerts in that town. [Laughs.] It's a tough slog.) But I didn't care, so I wrote this weekly jazz column, and our newspaper advisor started submitting them to the Collegiate Press and I started winning awards for writing about Louis Armstrong. I thought, "This is pretty good!"

Two years later, I enter the program at Rutgers, and on day one they explained that everyone would have to write a thesis, and I said, "Louis Armstrong's later years," and Lewis Porter, who was my main instructor there, said, "No one has really done that before. That's a really interesting subject."

FEINSTEIN: You also, though, wrote a substantial undergraduate thesis on the topic, no?

RICCARDI: Yes—I always forget about it. I wrote a 125-page research paper, and that was only using what I had at home: books, liners, and so on. The Rutgers thesis used that as a basis, but I was then able to take advantage of the Institute of Jazz Studies, under the directorship of Dan Morgenstern.

While I was there, [Armstrong bassist] Arvell Shaw died. [Pianist] Joe Bushkin died, and I think [bassist] Jack Lesberg died—three [Louis Armstrong] All Stars died in a very short period. I thought, "Oh my God. If I'm going to do this, I've got to act fast." That's when I contacted [drummer] Danny Barcelona, [pianist] Marty Napoleon, [singer] Jewel Brown, [bassist] Buddy Catlett, and [clarinetist] Joe Muranyi.

The actual thesis was 350 pages—but it ended in 1961; Lewis Porter had to physically stop me. [Laughs.] "Save it for the book."

FEINSTEIN: Of the musicians you interviewed, who were the most helpful?

RICCARDI: Joe Muranyi was amazing. I think I earned his trust. Joe, God bless him, started writing a book about his time with Louis. (He followed Armstrong by playing with Roy Eldridge for about eight years.) He was an amazing observer. He knew these guys were important; he knew that playing in their bands was kind of, like, out of control. So he paid attention to everything. He kept audio diaries and regular diaries. And for decades he would turn down interviews because he was "saving it for the book."

When I got to him, I guess he saw that I was serious, and I passed along some bootleg recordings of him that he had never heard, so I earned his trust and he opened up. He told such *great* stories. I remember him saying in 2006, "You know, I've not told this stuff to anyone else," and I really appreciated it. Sad to say, we're sitting here in 2019 and the book has never come out. Joe died in 2012; whatever he left behind I hope sees the light of day. He was definitely the most helpful, but they were all great. Danny Barcelona was a sweetheart; Jewel Brown gave some funny stories. Buddy Catlett had some good remembrances—but at the same time, I didn't know him well and he was playing it pretty close to the vest, which I understood. Marty Napoleon also never got around to writing his book but he kept diaries from those years and was so vivacious and full of stories.

But this goes back to my reading the Collier and Bergreen books and most other stuff about Armstrong: the All Stars were all *alive*, and all well. I kept thinking, "How are these people not interviewing these folks? Trummy Young lived into the eighties. Barney Bigard. All these people. How come the people who were on the bus every day don't get a chance to tell their stories?" At least I was able to get to five of them.

For the book I'm working on now [about Armstrong's years from 1929 to 1947], a lot of those big band musicians have been dead for decades, but at least we have a number of oral histories that Rutgers did with the Smithsonian. They'll get a chance to tell their stories. But most of them have never made it into print.

∽

FEINSTEIN: One of the many things that I love about your book *What a Wonderful World* [*The Magic of Louis Armstrong's Later Years*, 2011] is your prose style. It's conversational without being casual. It's inviting. It's appealing in all ways. Now, about your master's thesis, you once said, "It's the most boring thing you've ever read in your life." [Riccardi laughs.] How did you make the leap from that kind of prose and the prose in the book?

RICCARDI: [Laughs.] I think the prose might have been okay in the master's thesis, but it was all about the research. I would write, for example, "In December 1948, Louis played the Blue Note in Chicago," and then I would quote three different reviews. "*Down Beat* said this, but *Metronome* said that, and then this person said this," and then I would move on. From a research perspective, it was fine, but not from an entertainment perspective. You felt like you were on the road. [Laughs.] Gig by gig, review by review. Still, it was so exciting to do that research.

The thesis stopped in 1961 but I kept on going. I figured if it was going to be a book, I'd write and write. I hired an agent, and we got rejected left and right. Finally I got the book deal with Pantheon. I go in to meet my new editor and sign the contract, and it says, "Manuscript should be between 105- and 110,000 words." I go home and run the word count: it was around 190,000 words.

At first the editing was agony, but then, as I cut, I realized how much better the book was because I wanted it to be accessible. I wanted anybody to be able to pick it up and be engaged. Now, I'll never put anybody down [for writing styles], but I took a course at Rutgers in jazz writing—academic writing and journal writing—and after fifteen weeks of that I said, "I don't want to write like that." Everything got so wrapped up in concepts and jargon and putting different lenses on that didn't really apply to the music. It was a tough slog, and I realized that people who write like that, God bless 'em, they can see things and hear things and describe them in ways that my brain doesn't work—but it's for a very small audience of other academics. And I wanted a book for my parents to read. You don't need to be a musicologist; Armstrong's life alone was dramatic enough: race, failing health, all the accomplishments, the humorous anecdotes—that was enough. And that's why, when the book was getting rejected like crazy, I always held out hope.

FEINSTEIN: Why do you think it was turned down?

RICCARDI: Multiple reasons. There's been a million books on Armstrong, and nobody knew who I was. So I hired my agent in 2006. He thought the idea was great, wrote a proposal, and from '06 to the middle of '07—during my house-painting years after my master's degree [laughs]—it was constant rejection, but a few things happened during that time. In '06, I came to the Armstrong Archives for the first time and started spending time with the [reel-to-reel] tapes [that Armstrong privately recorded in his study]. All of a sudden, I was hearing things that I had never read in books. Hearing him curse, hearing him angry. And he backed up my central argument. My Rutgers thesis was all my words: "Louis was still playing great in the '50s. You have to believe me!" [Both laugh.] And it was much more powerful to be able to quote Louis saying, "I'm playing better now than I've ever played in my life."

In the summer of '07, I started my blog [*The Wonderful World of Louis Armstrong*]. This was before social media, and the whole function of that was to make a name for myself. I wasn't getting published; painting was my day job. But I thought if I started to share my research maybe I could turn that into something. And oddly enough, the painting worked hand in hand with this. Painting is the most monotonous thing in the world, so I'd be on the job with my iPod. But before work, I might say to myself, "I want to write about 'Back Home Again in Indiana,'" so I'd load up the iPod with fifty-five versions of it [by Armstrong]. While rolling the walls, I'm listening. All of a sudden, I might think, "Oh! His solo changed in the summer of 1953. He's got the last eight bars down, but now he's changed it again—and there it is, in 1956: he's got the solo. It took five years." Then I'd go home, kiss my wife hello, and say, "I need to write this down." Some of my [blog] entries were tens of thousands of words with fifteen to twenty music examples. I obviously wasn't getting paid, and the first few months that I did it: not a peep. Radio silence.

The first people I heard from, God bless them, were all from Europe: the Swedish contingent (the late Gösta Hägglöf, my friend Håkan Forsberg) opened the door. But the Belgian discographer, Jos Willems, said, "Do you have my discography, 'All of Me'?" and I said, "Yes. That's my bible." He said, "Use it as a catalog. If there's anything in that discography that you would like to hear, let me know."

FEINSTEIN: Wow.

RICCARDI: So I sent him a list of five or ten things. A couple of weeks go by, and then I get a package with about twenty-five CDs of unissued Armstrong recordings. Hägglöf was the same way, and I realized there was such a *spirit* in the Armstrong community. These people were so beautiful. They saw what I was doing and opened up their collections—they didn't want anything in return—and I was then able to write about *those* recordings.

By early 2008 or so, I reconvened with my agent to rewrite the proposal, including the blog and stuff I've learned from the tapes and endorsements, and this time it worked. But that whole three-year period . . . I'll never understand why I was so calm. I look back on those years, and it's just a feeling of calmness. All these beloved people in my family circle were panicking on my behalf, but I was, like, "Relax. It's going to happen." I don't know why; it wasn't ego. I just believed so much in the importance and relevance of Louis Armstrong.

∼

FEINSTEIN: Are you comfortable speaking openly about other books on Pops?

RICCARDI: Sure.

FEINSTEIN: There is, of course, an industry of research.

RICCARDI: Yes!

FEINSTEIN: But perhaps we can begin with Thomas Brothers, since he's written three books on Armstrong.

RICCARDI: I like Tom. He got the whole ball rolling with *Louis Armstrong: In His Own Words* [2001], which was just spectacular. His book *Louis Armstrong's New Orleans* [2006] is very, very good. I did think that *Louis Armstrong: Master of Modernism* [2014] kind of missed the mark. I would not lump it in with Collier's book. I think there's some incredibly valuable stuff there. But a few different things happened. The music analysis is shaky, for one, with some unfortunate mistakes along the way, such as downplaying Armstrong's love of opera and classical music. But there's also a darkness to the narrative that paints a skewed portrait of Armstrong, bitter with white musicians stealing his music, and eventually forced to embrace what Brothers calls "The White Turn," which I found to be a curious phrase. Armstrong begins recording pop tunes, the black audience abandons him, and the book ends with this "Don't let it happen to you" kind of tone. It left a bad taste in my mouth. It became a cautionary tale.

That, indirectly, inspired the book I'm working on now because Armstrong—and many in the black community—truly loved the pop sounds of someone like Guy Lombardo, and when

Tommy Rockwell put him on [the label] OKeh [in 1929] and had him record "I Can't Give You Anything but Love," "When You're Smiling," and gave him that big band backdrop—those are recordings to celebrate. That is Armstrong embracing white popular music but bringing his own genius (which, of course, is steeped in black music) and his own unique interpretations and blowing it up from the inside. I think those recordings might be the most influential, and possibly the most important, of Armstrong's career. And black audiences also stuck with Armstrong for a much longer period of time than people assume, so I want to talk more about that relationship and how black musicians and the black press felt about him through the late forties. He was a hero.

FEINSTEIN: Terry Teachout's book [*Pops: A Life of Louis Armstrong*, 2009] came out two years before yours. Knowing your bio was in the works, how did you feel when that was published?

RICCARDI: I was actually helping Terry while he was writing the book. He was among the first people to discover my blog, and he gave me a great endorsement for my book proposal. I became almost like a research assistant: I would post something, and he would say, "Hey, that interview . . . Can you send that over?" "Sure."

His book came out in late '09, and mine was supposed to come out a few months after.

FEINSTEIN: I didn't know that.

RICCARDI: He got so much credit—deservedly so—for using the private tapes and presenting a balanced narrative and giving an equal weight to the later years, which I thought was all spectacular. So Pantheon decided to postpone mine. (It looks like a two-year difference, but we were writing and researching at the same time.) He got there first, and his became a bestseller, but the delay allowed me to get comfortable in this job [as archivist for the Armstrong Archives], and with the amount of stuff I turned up from being here, I was able to rewrite and keep adding for that full-year delay. It all worked out just fine.

Feinstein: You have frequently said that Dan Morgenstern has been a central influence in your life as a writer. How so?

Riccardi: No one has ever written better about Armstrong than Dan. From a stylistic perspective, he's such a better writer than I am, but that's what I aim for. He has such a way of describing things and making you hear them, making you feel them, but his writing has always been aimed at the general reader: he didn't dumb anything down, but it wasn't filled with anything unnecessary. "Here's what happened. I was there, and I'm going to describe it to you in the most beautiful terms imaginable." From reading his liner notes and his stories—before I discovered the [Armstrong] tapes—that was as close as I came to knowing Louis Armstrong. When I was in high school, Dan's liner notes for *The California Concerts* and *Portrait of the Artist as a Young Man* [were invaluable]. He was my idol. The first time I met him at Rutgers, I was starstruck. I sat at his table last night at Birdland, and I still have not gotten used to that. [Laughs.] He's the greatest.

Feinstein: How about Armstrong's prose style?

Riccardi: It's *so* rhythmic. Tom Brothers did a great thing in *In His Own Words* by trying to capture Armstrong's punctuation and his typewriter marks, underlining. We have all those documents here [in the archives] and you almost have to read the original versions because you see how he would go back and proofread. He would underline words and add little parenthetical expressions, and when you read it out loud, it reads like music, or at least poetry. I don't think he was squarely aiming for that; I just think everything he did was musical. Bud Freeman said he swung more telling a joke than some people did with their horns. [Both laugh.]

It's great education. There's strange grammar, spelling mistakes. He did carry around a dictionary and a thesaurus. He tried his best to eliminate what was a very minimal [formal] education, but I think his natural exuberance, his use of slang, his sense of humor (almost every letter has a joke or limerick or something to make you laugh)—like everything he did, they make you feel good. You read his letters, you read his manuscripts, you read his book—even when he's writing about his childhood in New Orleans, which was so stark and *crazy* (eating food out of garbage cans), it's never told with any self-pity. "This is reality. This is what I had to do. Now you know." Anybody else writing about those years would present something tragic, a horror story, but he always offers a little twinkle. "It was bad, but we survived." He had [his mentor] King Oliver, and he had [his mother] Mayann; he had the support of the Karnofsky family. Even with bullets whipping by his head in the honky-tonks, he had the other musicians and [drummer] Black Benny [Williams] to protect him in there. The fact that he made it out of there alive . . . I think that's why his autobiography, *Satchmo: My Life in New Orleans* [1954], ends with him joining King Oliver. Anything that followed that was gravy. Getting out of there, joining his hero in the big city—what more do you need? The fact that he goes on to change the sound of music and play for kings and the Royal Family, have hit records in every decade, make thirty-five movies, break down all these barriers: great. But he *survived* that childhood and got to play with his hero / father figure in Chicago and upset the town. That's it. Punctuation mark. That's where it ends.

∽

FEINSTEIN: Earlier you said that you and Armstrong are probably the only two people who have heard all of his 750 reel-to-reel tapes. What were some of the biggest surprises for you?

RICCARDI: The first time I came here as a researcher, they handed me a binder with all the descriptions of each tape, and I didn't know where to start. (I was also on a very short time limit; they closed at five and I got there around four.) So I didn't get very far, but I saw tape 14: Louis talking about music in 1956, and I asked for it. This was an interview that he gave from his hotel room with radio disk jockeys in Benton Harbor, Michigan, and he's talking about how he's playing better than ever before. He talks about his album *Ambassador Satch* [1956], how it's better than anything he'd done for a while. The reporter asks him about "progressive music" and he starts defending his own music. "What's any more progressive than my music? What's any more progressive than 'Blueberry Hill'? At least the public understands this. That's better than a bunch of stiff arrangements for the untrained ear." It's a short tape—around twenty-five minutes—but it offered everything I wanted to convey up to that point. For me, there was self-validation because I had made my own conclusions [about his later recordings]—not blindly, of course. (I'd read Dan Morgenstern, and interviewed the All Stars, so I kind of knew how Louis felt about these things.) But there was something about his toughness combined with his self-assuredness. That's what a lot of people don't understand. It also ties into how a lot of people view Armstrong: People who didn't get to meet him just saw the surface level. They'd see him jumping around on stage with a giant smile, and they'd think, "He's obviously a giant phony, and he's doing that so that white people applaud him. He's selling out the race and it's embarrassing to watch somebody be that fake." Then you hear the [private] tapes, and he's the life of the party. He's making all these jokes and laughing louder than anybody.

I think that was a big moment for Dizzy Gillespie. Dizzy was probably the most vocal critic until he moved around the corner [from the Armstrongs in Corona, Queens]. Then, all of a sudden, it was, "Oops. I misjudged him." That's what he wrote in his autobiography [*To Be or Not to Bop*, 1979]: nothing, not even racism, was going to take away that smile and the joy he felt for performing.

Listening to the tapes, I realized what you saw onstage is what you got off stage—ninety percent of the time. That's a lot. I mean, he is so *warm*. It's not all shtick; there's a warmth there when he's talking to fans, when he's talking to friends. He's just so positive. But the other ten percent, for me, is what *makes* the ninety percent: the toughness and the self-assurance. Knowing what a great musician he was. Knowing how proud he was of being black—how unapologetically black he was, and the racism he went through, how he carried himself. You realize he's *so* confident. Yeah, he's not Malcolm X; many people listening to these tapes try to find what's not there. But what you *do* find is someone who's comfortable in his own skin. Critics could tear him apart, but he knew who he was, he knew how people responded to him, he knew how important it was that he was a black man accomplishing what he was doing. We have all this on hundreds of tapes, which he was making for posterity.

[Trombonist] Trummy Young's daughter, Andrea Young, came here in November, and she told me that Louis would go up and down the street just giving his money away. People would come up to him with a hard-luck story, and he would smile and pass a five, pass a twenty, pass a fifty. When [his manager] Joe Glaser found out, he lost his mind: "What are you doing?!" And Louis would say, "Hey, you've got your money. I don't tell you how to spend yours, you don't tell me how to spend mine. Besides, they're gonna write about me in the history books someday." So, as down-home and humble as he is, he knows, "When the smoke clears, I'm going to be in the history books. I don't need anyone telling me how to behave, that I should do more of this or less of that. I'm going to be in the history books." That's a lot of weight.

FEINSTEIN: With your new book project, which covers Armstrong's years from 1929 to '47, do you find the challenges similar to those you faced with your first book?

RICCARDI: Yes and no. I've kind of backed myself into a hole. [Laughs.] Oxford [University Press] wants about 110,000 words, and Sascha, as I sit here today, I'm about two pages away from finishing. I'm in the epilogue; I'm just wrapping it up; I know where it needs to go.

It's 288,000 words. [Both laugh.]

I actually wrote to my editor the other day and said, "Oops . . . I think I may have written two books." So I need to have a meeting soon. Am I really going to cut 170,000 words? I think I can do it. It would be the fastest moving book in history. But there's also a perfect break in there—1929 to 1935 and 1936 to 1947. We'll see.

FEINSTEIN: Given the fact that you do like to be expansive in your research and discussions, how hard is it for you when you take on liner notes?

RICCARDI: Very hard. I've never hit my mark on the first time out. When I write liner notes for Universal or Dot Time, they usually want around three to five thousand words. My first draft is almost always ten [thousand]. It comes from knowing too much [chuckles] and wanting to get it all out. But I'm proud of the fact that I can go back and *know* when it's too much.

I'm sure when I go back to the book I'm working on right now, eighty thousand words will go right out the window without batting an eye. The other hundred thousand's gonna be tough! [Laughs.] But even if I have to cut it, this book will live on in my head. I can now talk about these years in obscene detail—but no one necessarily needs to read those details.

FEINSTEIN: Did you find it a bit more luxurious to write the liners for the Mosaic boxed set [*Columbia and RCA Victor Live Recordings of Louis Armstrong and the All Stars*]?

RICCARDI: With Mosaic, they said the booklets were usually ten to fifteen thousand words, and in five days I wrote thirty-two thousand words. I got it down to twenty-seven. Fortunately, they thought it was really good and said, "Okay, we can deal with this." I was able to push the boundaries there. And people expect it: when they pay for a Mosaic set, they want in-depth notes.

I think I learned more about jazz history from reading liner notes than from reading any textbooks, so even though CDs are dying and everything's going digital, there's something about Armstrong that they keep on making physical CDs. As long as they keep doing that and asking me to produce them and write about the music, I take the job very seriously.

FEINSTEIN: In 2003, when I was interviewing Gary Giddins for *Brilliant Corners*, he said about ninety percent of the interviews with Armstrong were purely superficial, especially those with hosts like Dick Cavett. Gary said he knew what he'd want to ask: "Basic things: Where'd you first hear the blues? Why the blues instead of these chord changes? What did you get from [King] Oliver besides phrases? How do you develop a sound—is it something deliberate, or simply a reflection of who you are?

Did you hear other sounds and say, 'That's the sound I want'?" If *you* could ask Pops any questions, what would you ask?

RICCARDI: Oh boy . . . It's a tricky question because I feel as though I've heard all of his answers by listening to all those tapes. Maybe Dick Cavett and others like him dropped the ball, but a lot of people didn't. We have a two-and-a-half-hour interview with the editors of the *Record Changer* magazine in 1950 where every question is about music—laser beam focus—and he is deadly serious. It's an interview that I don't think anyone's ever heard. (The whole prologue of my next book is going to be based on this interview because it's so great.) So my first thought is, "Is there a question I haven't heard answered?"

Jazz people view Armstrong as a trumpet genius, and some give him props as a singer, and it kind of ends there. But nobody wants to talk about him as a comedian. When they start seeing him grin—make faces, do [comical] duets with Velma Middleton—and when they watch the films, all of a sudden they start coming up with excuses: "Hollywood put him in these horrible roles, and he had to do this onstage to make the white audiences comfortable." But on tape you can hear how he is more comfortable around comedians than he is around musicians. With musicians, who want to talk about this and that, he never really gets into the technical stuff, but with comedians who want to tell jokes and play the dozens and laugh at each other, those are his people.

In the movie *Going Places* [1938] where he sings "Jeepers Creepers" to a horse: that's the example people usually hold up and say, "Poor Louis Armstrong, that he had to do this . . ." Well, we have a letter that he writes during the making of that film where he says how funny he thinks it is. "I love doing comedy in these movies." He learned everything about the stage from Bill "Bojangles" Robinson and all these black comedians, and he was *beloved* at the Apollo [Theater] until the early fifties. Then there's this split, and it's really interesting: In the late forties, the NAACP really gets vocal, and their executive secretary, Walter White, gets sent to Hollywood. "I'm going to start censoring, and get better roles [for black actors]." And the black press who covered the black actors started asking, "Why are you sending *him*? He doesn't talk to any actors and actresses. We've seen the changes; we're playing these roles. We know we're not a maid when we go home, but this is what we're doing and we're progressing." All of a sudden, you see [black actresses like] Hattie McDaniel and Louise Beavers getting hate mail because they're playing these roles, and they're like, "We won an Academy award a few years ago. We're trying our best!"

The TV cast for *Amos 'n' Andy* were all of Armstrong's friends. They were the top black comedians at the Apollo Theater, and suddenly they're being protested, and the show gets pulled off the air, and they can't get jobs. [The black comedy duo] Butterbeans and Susie: Susie's working as a domestic servant. Bill "Bojangles" Robinson dies, broke, in 1949. This whole generation of black actors, black comedians, vaudeville performers become out of favor, out of touch, while the civil rights era was gathering up steam, and a lot of those people felt hurt.

[Black actor and tap dancer] Honey Coles always said that all those acts, all that comedy, was developed in front of black audiences by black actors and comedians, but once it started reaching white people, that's when the NAACP got nervous. "You can't do that. You can't show Amos and Andy on TV; white people are going to think we're all like that." So there's just a huge transition going on between 1946 and '51, and the amazing thing is that, because Louis has that trumpet, he emerges unscathed. He has all these hit records. But every night [as heard on the private tapes], he carries himself like that vaudevillian: he's still doing the [humorous] alligator story; he's doing the duet with Velma; he's doing everything he's learned about comedy and the stage from Bill Robinson. The trumpet is where he lived. It was his most forthright way of communicating with the audiences. But he takes everything else very seriously. He's not just making faces because it's silly; he has learned the subtle way of communicating with your eyes.

So I would like to talk to him more about comedy, about timing, and about the other great black performers that he shared the stage with and learned from. He talks a lot about Bill Robinson, and [the vaudeville duo] Patterson and Jackson, and all these teams that have been completely forgotten. We have three boxes in the archives of vaudeville photos, black acts that have all been forgotten as though erased from history. The actors and dancers all have professional publicity photos signed to Louis Armstrong, "To the greatest." I would love to go through those photos with him: "What was this act like? How about that one?"

14

Don't Give It Up

A. B. Spellman

A. B. Spellman published a chapbook of poems, *The Beautiful Days*, in 1965; the following year, he published a seminal book in the history of jazz-related literature, *Four Lives in the Bebop Business*, which focused on Ornette Coleman, Herbie Nichols, Jackie McLean, and Cecil Taylor not merely as brilliant artists but as neglected (and therefore representative) jazz figures in American culture. In the late 1960s and early '70s, he wrote penetrating jazz criticism for leading publications such as *Metronome* and *Down Beat*, as well as invaluable liner notes for such seminal figures as John Coltrane, Eric Dolphy, and Ornette Coleman. He then spent thirty years (1975–2005) working for the National Endowment for the Arts, during which time he frequently spoke as a jazz commentator for National Public Radio. In 2008, he published his first full-length collection of poems, *Things I Must Have Known*. In addition to his work for the NEA, he has been a visiting lecturer at Emory, Rutgers, and Harvard universities, and has now retired to focus on his writing.

The following excerpts and poem by Spellman have been reprinted with permission. The interview itself was conducted at his home in Washington, DC, on December 18, 2008.

Introduction to *Four Lives in the Bebop Business* (excerpt)

Many currents cross in these pages, the most sinister of which is the gross indifference with which America receives those aspects of Afro-American culture that are not "entertaining." Jazz's entertainment value has decreased as black artists have conscientiously moved out of the realm of folk art and into the realm of high art; and I maintain that much of the jazz music of the last twenty years and some of the jazz of the previous thirty years is high art and should be treated with all the dignity that high art deserves. I am not suggesting that alienation, frustration, humiliation, and deprivation are the exclusive property of the jazz musicians; certainly the great majority of artists in America are poor and outcast people. But literature, classical music, and the plastic arts are taught from both the appreciative and creative viewpoints in all colleges and many of the high schools of the United States in a blind adulation of European culture, while there is little academic effort at fostering the one art form unique and indigenous to the United States. Furthermore, fortunes can be raised to sponsor prestigious symphonic and operatic societies in any sizable American city; it is of utmost importance that the rich convince themselves that they are "cultured." But serious jazz is left almost exclusively to a few out-of-the-way bars, and is given very little time on the radio and a negligible amount of time on television, so that there is nothing in the average American's life to reorient him toward this most highly developed aspect of Afro-American culture.

"On Hearing Sonny ('Newk') Rollins in the Park on a Hot Summer Night"

his worn hips barely support the horn
in his hands. it is gold & flashes under the fresnels
the sound is deep enough to live in. phrase turns to
brilliant phrase & the source never empties
i see in newk the hope of every limping
artist in the reluctant race against the slamming
of the lyric door when the senses atrophy
that dread day when a line of sound or verse
will hurt to render: the gripping eye
dims the active ear dims the trilling voice
dims such fears we can contain in the long slowdrag
to humdrum death as long as the making works
there's newk in the picture of matisse who wields
a ten-foot brush as he lay in his deathbed
newk on the bus with count basie who

could only die on the road. see newk in ghana
with du bois as he started a fifteen-volume treatise
in his eighty-fifth year. so sonny blows the final plea
of the graying work maker—let me age anywhere
but in the horn

Liner Notes for Eric Dolphy's *Out to Lunch* (excerpt)

Ever since Eric Dolphy broke up the Showplace with the Charlie Mingus group some four years ago, New York hasn't quite known what to make of him. Nobody could believe it was the same Eric Dolphy who'd been "through" the year before. Couldn't be. *That* Eric Dolphy played nice—pretty and all. This one was wild and woolly, played all kinds of unmentionable things you wouldn't say in front of your mother. . . .

His supporters, of whom Martin Williams seems to have been the first, and who've been growing in number ever since, found Eric an exciting tone colorist whose technical dexterity was practically unmatched, an imaginatively advanced improviser, and a vital alternative to the melodic clichés and rhythmic orthodoxy of the hardbop mainstream, etc. What I'm saying, if facetiously, is that Eric's career to date has been highly controversial, for reasons the listener will detect on the first playing of this particular date. This is *not* music to roller-skate by. It is the kind of muscularly individualistic stuff that will not tolerate indifference, that invokes such a strong reaction in the hearer that these essentially emotional initial responses must finally, thru qualification, be the basis of criticism. (The reader will have noticed by now that this writer's considered bias is with the musicians on this date.)

Liner Notes for John Coltrane's *Ascension* (excerpt)

To begin at the beginning, a caveat for the casual listener. Be advised that this record cannot be loved or understood in one sitting, and that there can be no appreciation at all in two minutes listening to an arbitrary excerpt in a record store. In fact, there is no casual approach to be taken to this record. It is truly modern; it is as advanced as the most advanced contemporary jazz is and, the communications scene being as retarded as it is, the kind of event which *Ascension* is will be unfamiliar to anyone who has not made it a serious avocation to search out and understand the new jazz.

What this is is a plexus of voices, all of different kinds, but most belonging to that generation which grew up on Mingus, Monk, Taylor, McLean, Coleman, Coltrane, the human rights struggle, and nuclear weapons. *Ascension* is at the same time a reevaluation of the old song formal values and a positive assertion of the heretofore unconsidered values of what is called nowadays the New Emerging Forces.

One problem for the casual listener in getting next to this record is the relatively high level of intensity at which it begins. In that respect it's like Wagner—it begins on a plane at which most performances end and builds to a higher plane than the average listener considers comfortable. As Marion Brown said, "You could use this record to heat up the apartment on those cold winter days."

Interview

SASCHA FEINSTEIN: You went to Howard University in 1952, where you met Amiri Baraka [then LeRoi Jones] and studied with Sterling Brown. How influential was Brown in terms of solidifying your understanding of relationships between music and literature?

A. B. SPELLMAN: Not much, really. It's my own fault: I didn't take advantage of him—and much of the faculty—as much as I should have. I was a pretty lazy student; I was the kind of student who read everything except what was assigned. [Both laugh.] So I wish that I could do that again. He talked about it, but I was already into the music.

FEINSTEIN: How early did your interest in music begin?

SPELLMAN: Always. I remember back home in Elizabeth City, North Carolina—up on the edge of the Great Dismal Swamp in the northeast corner of the state—there wasn't much of a jazz presence, but jazz at the time when I was growing up as a teenager in the late forties and early fifties was popular music. My father could hum Illinois Jacquet's "Flying Home" solo and Bean's [Coleman Hawkins's classic version of] "Body and Soul" and never would have thought much of it; he never would have thought he was having an art experience. They danced to Basie, and so forth. It was always in the house. But some of us [teenagers]—about a handful of us—got more interested in the music and started to collect records. (We couldn't just buy records. We had to read the magazines to find something new that was out and then order them from the local record store. We'd share them, sit around, listen to them together.) So I always had that, and I went to Howard with a love of jazz, but my knowledge was a bit skimpy. And back in Elizabeth City, on a clear night, I could get Jazzbo Collins on my radio. That was really wild to get bebop, which of course turned me on and turned my parents off. ("Get that tuneless music out of here!") But wow—that was a great mind expansion for a young kid.

At Howard, I met people who were much more exposed to the music, people like Baraka, and now had access to music from the early Brubecks—those ten-inch LPs—or [Lee] Konitz with [Lenny] Tristano, Konitz and Bill Bauer, all the Bird, all that bebop, and Miles . . . It was such new thought, such new experience, that I couldn't get enough of it.

FEINSTEIN: Did you ever play an instrument?

SPELLMAN: I used to sing some. I studied voice at Howard and sang in the choir, and I did a few club gigs as a singer. I had a really good voice, but no talent. [Chuckles.] You know how some people have the instrument but have nothing to say on it? That was me. [Both laugh.] But I used to sing at some clubs around DC, like Abarts, where [tenor saxophonist] Buck Hill had the house band.

FEINSTEIN: Dan Morgenstern once told me that he published your first piece—an essay on Archie Shepp for *Metronome*.

SPELLMAN: "Introducing Archie Shepp"—yeah.

FEINSTEIN: How influential was *Metronome* in terms of your finding a voice as a jazz critic?

SPELLMAN: It was crucial. It was the first outlet I ever had as a writer on jazz. I had never thought that I could do it; it wasn't something I had trained or prepared for. But, again, Baraka was doing it and he got me involved. He hooked me up with Dan Morgenstern, who got me involved with some of the other writers [at *Metronome*]—Martin Williams and others. So Dan published the piece, which seemed to hold its own in the magazine, and then I started writing more and more about the music.

I was insecure about my writing until John Coltrane broke out [in the 1960s] and you started getting all the anti-jazz reactions about Coltrane and Ornette [Coleman] and all the other people who were doing the jazz avant-garde. I'd go to the Village Gate or somewhere, leave feeling as though I'd just had my soul rinsed out, and [later] pick up *Down Beat* where some reviewer's written, "This is the worst thing that's ever happened to jazz." I thought, "Well, damn—these guys don't know what they're talking about. Either that or I can't hear." So that's when I got more aggressive about writing about the music.

FEINSTEIN: In fact, it's astonishing to think of the number of crucial avant-garde jazz albums for which you wrote liner notes. I'm thinking of Coltrane's *Ascension* and *Avant-Garde*, [Grachan Moncur III's] *Evolution*, [Bobby Hutcherson's] *Dialogue*, [Andrew Hill's] *Black Fire*, [Ornette Coleman's] *Ornette on Tenor*, [Eric Dolphy's] *Out to Lunch*. Even now, those albums seem unapproachable for most American listeners. But you were so *inside* the music. How did you develop such mature ears?

SPELLMAN: How old are you?

FEINSTEIN: Forty-five.

SPELLMAN: Okay . . . so you weren't around then. But [at that time in the 1960s], Lower Manhattan was the most intense laboratory of art that I've ever heard of. (There may have been periods in Paris when you had that kind of concentration of artists of all kinds in clubs and bars, hanging out together, fighting together, sharing lovers, and so forth.) But Lower Manhattan was really intense. You could have such an immersion in the music; you heard the new music before it was out, you know? It was routine [for me] to drop by Ornette's studio, and he'd say, "Oh, A. B., come on in, man. Listen to this tape. I've got a new tune I wrote; I've gotta fix some things about it, but . . ." And he'd play, you know, "Lonely Woman." Or you'd go out on the basketball court and soon you're playing basketball with several avant-garde jazz musicians. You'd talk to these guys, hear them in rehearsals warming up. There was this huge immersion in the music, and in all the arts. Painters, poets—everybody went to each other's events. It was a really great community with immense and deep exposure. Cecil Taylor lived right across the street. So this was common music to me.

I met people like [dancer/choreographer] Merce Cunningham. You'd go to parties with [pop artist] Red Grooms. So this stuff was very much in your eye and in your ear.

I was interested also in the music of people like [Karlheinz] Stockhausen and [John] Cage; those concerts would be at Cooper Union, and I knew some of the musicians who played in them. So my ear got to be very, very big.

Also, this was the time when world music began to become more and more available. You had those great UNESCO recordings, and of course Folkways was still putting out a lot of great world music records. I had a radio show, and I used to play a lot of that stuff. I had this thing about the Vietnam War when it first hit, when it was radical to oppose it—before the big movements—but if some aspect of American foreign policy resulted in some tribe getting bombed and attacked by its local dictator, I would play its music in the morning. It was a minor protest.

So there was all of this music, and it was easy to develop ears at that time.

FEINSTEIN: Easy for *you* to develop, perhaps, but even by your own admission about ten minutes ago, there were so many people at that same time who simply couldn't understand the new music, who called it "anti-jazz" and all that. Do you think one of the reasons you could hear the music so clearly had to do with the fact that you hung out with these musicians and therefore understood the humanity behind the music?

SPELLMAN: Perhaps. They were not alien to me in any way. These were my friends.

You know, somebody did a study a few years ago that determined that people after the age of about thirty-four close their ears. They then become devoted only to the music that they learned up to that point. They will listen to other expressions of that same kind of music, but anything else that's new, they don't want to hear. And I think there's some truth to that. Since the second generation of jazz musicians, there's always been an establishment that resisted the change. It happened from New Orleans to swing, and certainly from swing to bebop. I remember reading the early reviews in *Down Beat* of [Charlie Parker's] "Now's the Time" and "Billie's Bounce." The critics were saying this was absolutely corrupt music and that these musicians were absolutely deluded. And here's Max [Roach] and Miles and Bird, and they're saying that poor Miles Davis has been seduced by Dizzy Gillespie. So there's nothing new about that. It's generational. It's probably the function of young people to drive their parents crazy with their music, and this is sort of a manifestation of the same thing.

So, yeah, it's not a music that everybody will "get," because it requires a fair amount of commitment on the part of the listener. I also don't think that most people actually listen to music; I think most people have a certain *experience* of music, where they expect musicians to take all the responsibility for communicating. But if hearing music requires that you give up a great deal of whatever formulation you have of how to experience music—that you give up, for example, the anticipation of chromaticism, or of straight rhythm, or of not-too-dense rhythm, or of dynamics that you can anticipate and that are sort of developed and a sense of taking real easy care of your nervous system—then, yeah, it can be very hard.

FEINSTEIN: That reminds me of something you said in your liner notes for *Out to Lunch*: "This is *not* music to roller-skate by." [Both laugh.]

SPELLMAN: Did I say that?

FEINSTEIN: Yes, and you said similar things in notes for albums such as *Ascension*, where you wrote, in essence, "You need to prepare yourself for this." In fact, if nothing else happens today, I'm so happy to thank you for giving me an avenue into avant-garde jazz at a time [in my early teens] when I found it completely foreign. It was music from another world.

SPELLMAN: Well, thanks, man. I put a lot [of thought] into those notes; I took them seriously. I thought it was important to prepare people for the kind of experience that they could have with the music. One of my great regrets about progress is that with CDs, you can't read the damn things! Not only is the text too small, but they'll put a fuchsia on top of a green, and they'll bleed together and you can't read it. So you don't have anybody who can be an intermediary with the music.

This is also true in broadcasts. I have SiriusXM in my car, and they have fairly good mainstream taste, but the DJ presence is so minimal that you never find out, for example, who played that great piano solo on that tune. There's nobody to give you a historical context for a new musician: "This guy came out of here, and he played with these guys, and he's going there."

FEINSTEIN: When you were writing the notes for Coltrane's albums—or at any other time, for that matter—did you spend much time with him?

SPELLMAN: *Some* time. I can't say we were best friends, but he knew me.

FEINSTEIN: When you were writing notes, did you ever ask, "Is there anything that you want in here?"

SPELLMAN: Oh, yeah—for the records, of course.

FEINSTEIN: What were some of his responses?

SPELLMAN: He was a *very* nice, gentle guy—warm and generous in his explanations. He was not a voluble guy. I did one interview with him for the *Evergreen Review*, which I was proud of, and I tried to get him to let me do a book [on him and his music], but that was about the time of *A Love Supreme* [1964] and he said, "Well, I'm going through some changes now and I think it's premature."

FEINSTEIN: That's a shame.

SPELLMAN: Yeah. Then he died shortly afterward [in 1967]. I would have loved to have done it but it wasn't to be.

FEINSTEIN: What about when you were writing for Dolphy and Ornette and others—did you have conversations with them? I'm asking because so many musicians say, "I don't want to talk about the music; I want the music to speak for itself." In some ways, you had to work against that.

SPELLMAN: Right. But I don't have a lot of music theory, and I needed them to explain the music itself—what was happening [technically]—and they would do it. Also, I got to know a lot of these guys, either very well or at least well enough to be a friend in some way. I was good friends with Ornette and Cecil [Taylor]. Dolphy I was friendly with. Jackie McLean was a *very* good friend. So they would talk to me, perhaps more than they would talk to some other writers.

∽

FEINSTEIN: Are you aware that your poem for Trane ["john coltrane"] in *The Beautiful Days* may be the first published Coltrane poem?

SPELLMAN: Hmmm. No, I never thought about it.

FEINSTEIN: Your book and John Sinclair's *This Is Our Music*, which includes a Coltrane tribute, both came out in '65, and I believe those are the first Coltrane poems. In fact, very few people wrote poems for Coltrane during his lifetime. After his death, of course, there were *so* many. What did you make of the enormous swell of Coltrane elegies?

SPELLMAN: It happens. You should have seen the rush of poems after Billie Holiday died.

FEINSTEIN: Or Bird—even more so.

SPELLMAN: Exactly. It happens. My only question is, are they good? A lot of poets have difficulty—and I want to say this carefully—making the best use of music in their poems. Many poets will try to explore the hipness of the music but not the experience of the music. Again, it's the question, "Are these good poems to read?" Some poets do it well, and some don't.

FEINSTEIN: Who are some of the people who do it well?

SPELLMAN: I very much like Michael Harper; I think he does a good job. I like Paul Harding up there in Seattle, especially since I had a chance to read with him. He's a performance poet, and performance poetry can sometimes exploit music better because it has to with that immediacy; it has to do with that dimension of time that the two-dimensional, on-the-page poet can't do. Baraka's done it very well. [Pauses.] What's her name . . . ?

FEINSTEIN: Jayne?

SPELLMAN: Jayne Cortez, yeah. Thank you very much for anticipating where I was going. Jayne Cortez does it very well.

FEINSTEIN: Can you talk a bit more about how or why they succeed?

SPELLMAN: I can't say for sure as I never have done it, except for one time when Doug Carn played quietly behind me during one poem at the Gem Theater across from the Jazz Museum in Kansas City. But the ones who are best at it are, first of all, performance poets, by which I mean that they take oral presentation into consideration as they write. Second, they are deep in jazz unlike, say, Kenneth Rexroth back in the forties and fifties reciting in a manner that reflects his line breaks while somebody plucks a guitar behind him. Baraka, Cortez, and the late Sekou Sundiata share those characteristics. I think that a good portion of rehearsal with sensitive, versatile musicians would help, too.

FEINSTEIN: Jayne and Baraka, of course, were such important voices in the Black Arts Movement, which you helped to found. What do you think is the legacy of that movement?

SPELLMAN: The Black Arts Movement is more of a continuum than is normally appreciated. I mean, there's nothing that was happening in the Black Arts Movement that didn't happen in the Harlem Renaissance. Of course, the Renaissance artists were still around when the Black Arts Movement began. Nothing ever begins at a simple place in a simple time. Movements are always a bit more amorphous. But I think that several great things happened in the Black Arts Movement. There was a lot of stuff of temporal value (occasional poems that had some power for the moment), but a very large number of artists came to participate, and many of them were of enduring value.

FEINSTEIN: Who comes to mind?

SPELLMAN: The painters: James Phillips, [whose work hangs] behind you, and the artists of the AFICOBRA [the African Commune of Bad Relevant Artists] movement in Chicago (and the extensions of that movement). They were, and are still, quite wonderful artists; they produce very well. Some of the better-known poets—Sonia Sanchez, Baraka, and others—are still powerful voices in American letters. I think the relationship of music to the Black Arts Movement is underappreciated. Jazz was already *there*, but there was definitely an affinity of the jazz musicians with the black artists' expressions. So people like Jackie McLean started the Artists Collective in Hartford [Connecticut]. That's another great legacy of the Black Arts Movement: the organizations that got founded. Many have died, but some quite stellar ones have survived and are doing very well and are places where you have to go now to experience what's happening in contemporary art. The Studio Museum in Harlem, for example. For some of the activist organizations, the ones where there's this sense of art in the community, or art that can be applied to helping people who are distressed and don't have access to their own culture—many of those organizations have survived and are doing quite well. Again, Jackie McLean's Artists Collective is one of them.

FEINSTEIN: Some contemporary critics have been pretty tough on the Black Arts Movement. Stanley Crouch, for example, has said that no great books came out of it.

SPELLMAN: I'd have to argue that point. I think that Ed Bullins wrote some quite substantial plays. In fact, I think that some of the theater that was done during that movement added substantially to the literature. I think there was a great newness to the Harlem Renaissance. It was a phenomenon that America had not seen and that America had to deal with: black intellectuals. It wasn't something that broader America—mainstream America, white America—had given any thought to at all. But at least the liberal side of mainstream America did take it upon itself to recognize it. (In many ways, a lot of writing, when we read it now, seems kind of patronizing, even demeaning, but in the context of the times it was worthy of acknowledgment.) The publications that came out at the time struck a certain kind of curiosity: What is this new phenomenon of black intellectuals, of black artists? Also, there were influences of the Harlem Renaissance that extended beyond the African American community; the kinds of iconographic art that was produced resonated with some breadth. The interest in primitivism, where rather sophisticated artists such as [Horace] Pippin and Jacob Lawrence would get cast, took over in society, even though, as I said, these artists were much too sophisticated to be so reviewed.

    I think the Black Arts Movement was largely seen in the popular press as an expression of black anger, and I don't know if it ever got serious critical attention. But there are poems, plays, and fiction that stand up from that period.

FEINSTEIN: Were there figures from the Harlem Renaissance—and now I'm thinking of obvious choices like Langston Hughes and Sterling Brown—who became more important to you as you found your voice as a writer, or were you really focused on the contemporary scene?

SPELLMAN: It was the contemporary scene for the most part. I mean, I was very much aware of Langston Hughes. I knew him; he was always very supportive of me and Baraka and others who came along. He was a very accessible guy. But he wasn't stylistically influential to me. Sterling Brown as a poet was perhaps more important. In the period when I went from a very strong [Robert] Creeley influence—around the time of *The Beautiful Days* [1965], when I really worried about enjambment and double meanings and line breaks—to the time when I tried to find a voice that was more expressive of the culture without whoring my integrity, I went back and read Sterling Brown. He was very successful at exploiting, say, the black toasts in a poem like "The Ballad of Joe Meek"—black toasts like "Signifying Monkey" and "Shine." For a sort of an imagist integrity for writing about things as they are, the poet Fenton Johnson—who is not very well recognized—was one of the best poets of the period. He was really quite important for me to read. Jean Toomer's *Cane*—another underappreciated American masterpiece, for a real sense of modernism, for writing from a black stance—was very interesting to me.

FEINSTEIN: Unlike all the other poets you've mentioned today, Fenton Johnson was a formalist, and I found it very interesting to learn that after your hiatus from writing—a span of about thirty years—you turned to formal verse to get your pen moving. Do you think there's any connection between, say, a poet working within a strict form and a jazz musician playing against set changes?

SPELLMAN: Perhaps. I went back to the forms primarily as exercises. I don't even *have* those sonnets that I wrote. They were sheer doggerel. [Both laugh.] I just tried to make them funny. But after thirty years of not writing, I couldn't just pick up the pen and have my chops back. Your chops really go down. It's a matter of reordering your brain and, primarily, reordering your senses: the ear is gone, the eye is gone. So I wrote sonnets to try to get my ear back and deal with sound, and also the fact that the form would force word combinations you wouldn't make when writing prose. That helped with getting language back. Villanelles . . . Oh, God . . . I did publish one villanelle.

FEINSTEIN: "Villanelle for the Hell of It" [from *Things I Must Have Known*].

SPELLMAN: Yeah, right. But it was *way* more trouble than it was worth. [Both laugh.] I had another villanelle, and when I got to the last line of it, I said, "Just *fuck* it, man!" [Both laugh.] "Why am I forcing this sentence together just to fit this stupid form?" I'm not really a formal guy, but, of course, there's so much great literature in form that you have to acknowledge it.

Maybe for some poets there's a connection to be made between the form and a jazz musician playing a tune, and there probably is a real connection, now that you mention it. I haven't really thought about it before. I suppose that's one of the things about staying within a given structure. But it *all* needs structure, no matter what you do. It has to hang together, and that is structure. You know, a few years ago, when I was preparing an introduction for Ornette (when he got an award from the Association of Performing Arts Presenters), it occurred to me that the discipline of freedom is much more rigorous than the discipline of regimentation. It's just *harder* to make something hold together if the bones aren't imposed on you. That's why Ornette had to workshop for so very long—you know, with Charlie [Haden] and Billy Higgins and Don [Cherry]—because it's much, much harder when you have to make up a structure as you go along.

FEINSTEIN: Earlier you mentioned the influence of Robert Creeley, who felt he'd been strongly influenced by jazz. What do you think of the relationship between jazz and his work?

SPELLMAN: I met Creeley a couple of times, but I never got any insights into that. I mean, I knew he liked jazz, but I expected people in poetry and in the arts to like jazz; in the late fifties and sixties, it was a common denominator. If you ask me if I can detect a jazz influence in reading Creeley, I'd have to say no. Do you?

FEINSTEIN: I don't hear it, no.

SPELLMAN: I don't hear it and I don't see it in the way the poems are made. But I'm sure it helped to tune him up for expression, you know?

FEINSTEIN: *He* felt he heard it, and maybe that's more important—using whatever you need to make your poems—because I respect and enjoy his poetry. Just because I don't hear Charlie Parker in a Parker-influenced poem doesn't mean the poem doesn't work.

SPELLMAN: Right, of course.

FEINSTEIN: Let's turn to jazz critics. You mentioned Martin Williams and Dan Morgenstern. Do you respect their work?

SPELLMAN: Very much. I've learned a great deal from them. Gunther Schuller [too]. We don't always agree on everybody, but for the people we *do* agree on, the kind of penetrating analysis that someone like Martin could give to the music was really quite educational.

FEINSTEIN: How about books? If someone asked you to recommend great books on jazz, what would you suggest?

SPELLMAN: I still send people who are trying to get a sense of the history of jazz to Marshall Stearns's old book [*The Story of Jazz*, 1956]. I don't think anybody has ever done that more economically—up to bebop. He fails at bebop. [Both laugh.]

I send people to a lot of the autobiographies because the stories are so helpful in getting people into music of different periods.

FEINSTEIN: Which ones come to mind?

SPELLMAN: Well, Jelly Roll's [stories in *Mister Jelly Roll* by Alan Lomax, 1950]; those are great stories that Jelly Roll has to tell.

Danny Barker has great stories [in *A Life in Jazz*, 1986]. Even Pops Foster's book [*The Autobiography of Pops Foster: New Orleans Jazz Man—As Told to Tom Stoddard*, 1971]. I like the book Dizzy [Gillespie] did with Al Fraser, *To Be or Not to Bop* [1979]; there's a lot of good stuff in there that you don't get when people have written about the musicians, like Dizzy talking about how his first piano teacher couldn't read music and how valuable that was because it helped him develop rhythm and ear. He makes a fundamental point about how jazz *was* learned, and the difference between the way jazz is learned now versus in Dizzy's day.

I had the pleasure of reviewing George Lewis's *A Power Stronger than Itself* [subtitled *The AACM and American Experimental Music*, 2008], and that's a very, very good book. It's a little long, and it's a little repetitious, and there are times when he doesn't write for a year or two and you can see those breaks in style, and occasionally it's pedantic—but it's a really good rendition of the history of AACM and how these musicians made themselves, the way of working collectively, and of intellectually insisting that this music be put in the center of any conversation about contemporary music. You don't discuss, say, the music of Cage without discussing AACM, and I think that's a very good insistence. That book over there—*Cuba and Its Music* [*From the Earliest Drums to the Mambo*, 2004] by Ned Sublette—is a *great* book. It may be the greatest book of social history that I've ever read.

FEINSTEIN: I'm interested in your recommendations because—and I mean this very sincerely—your *Four Lives in the Bebop Business* makes my shortlist.

SPELLMAN: Thank you.

FEINSTEIN: It's partly for some of the reasons that you've mentioned. The stories *are* so important. And I think appreciating the humanity behind the art is also important—to have some understanding of the human experience that takes place offstage, that there are, in fact, lives behind the business. I'm so glad the book's been reprinted [as *Four Jazz Lives*].

It is a bit bewildering, of course, to know your lovely first book of poems, and your crucial book of prose, and then see nothing for forty years! [Both laugh.]

SPELLMAN: I actually am very hard on myself for that.

FEINSTEIN: You now have a second book of poems [*Things I Must Have Known*]. What about critical work? Have you considered, for example, compiling your liner notes and essays?

SPELLMAN: [Smiles.] Huh . . . Actually, I never thought of that.

FEINSTEIN: I think that would be wonderful.

SPELLMAN: I've become pretty evangelical about people [like myself] who get involved with arts administration and give up [making] art, because it's too hard to master an art's discipline to give it up for a job or family and kids. I mean, I certainly don't minimize the pressures of those commitments, but it's too hard to learn how to take a blank space and put something in it—whether it's music or words or colors—and bring it to life, and then just give it up. I keep telling people, "Look, just practice the piano. Find a group of other musicians who maybe aren't doing it for a living and just jam with them, or something—but keep it up. Don't give it up. Bring your sketchbook to work, but don't give it up."

∼

FEINSTEIN: One of my favorite poems in your new collection is your poem for Sonny Rollins ["On Hearing Sonny ('Newk') Rollins in the Park on a Hot Summer Night"]. Would you talk about the making of that poem?

SPELLMAN: As the title says, I was in the park over here listening to him playing. I was watching the guy hobble out on stage—you know his hip is bad—and he had a hard time raising his leg for the stairs. Struggled to get to the mike. And then, *Pow!* you know? All this horn gets out, and it's wide open.

I was watching Clark Terry a couple of years ago at one of the NEA Jazz Masters ceremonies. He's rolled onto the stage in a wheelchair. He struggles to sit on the stool. Next thing you know, he's got two trumpets in his mouth! [Both laugh.] And he's dealing. So it occurred to me that these guys age, but they don't age in the horn. It's very inspiring for me as I get older—I'm seventy-three now—and I'm trying to keep my chops up, too. Let me age any way except in the horn. You start thinking about all the other artists you have known over time and how they still made work up until the end. There's Matisse with that enormous brush on a stick, doing the work. It's the thing about how art keeps you alive, keeps you strong. I remember interviewing [Count] Basie—I happened to be the emcee of his last concert in Washington—and I asked him, "You've been out here for so long, wouldn't you rather just go home and not be on the road all the time?" and he looked at me like I was crazy. He said, "Well, what else would I do?"

I remember reading about [W. E. B.] Du Bois in Ghana. Here's a man who was eighty-five years old and started a fifteen-volume history of Africa. [Both laugh.] I think that's the way you have to live. And that's why retirement was so good for me: I had something to do in retirement, and I think it's a mistake to just watch TV or putter around the house. That's just waiting to die.

FEINSTEIN: Do you think you'll write another critical book?

SPELLMAN: I've been trying to focus almost exclusively on poetry. I really want to make poems more than anything else. One thing about being at the Endowment is that it made me a little bit too much of a generalist. I was responsible for expression in all the arts and so I had to have scope, but I think I lost some depth in certain areas. It would be hard for me now, for example, to teach a literature course because my reading is so broad that there's no area I could focus on without years of preparation. So I'm contented right now to try to make the poems. That's what I really want to be remembered as: a poet.

FEINSTEIN: At the Endowment, how responsible were you for the Jazz Masters program?

SPELLMAN: I never had primary responsibility for it. The program was created back in the early eighties. The person who built it up was the late Antoinette Handy. She was the director of music and an authority on International Sweethearts of Rhythm. But it was Dana [Gioia] who pumped it up and made it into an award that had the stature of the big awards in America—Grammys and Pulitzers and so on. I was deputy chairman at the time and given some responsibility for developing that, but the person who did most of the work was Wayne Brown, who was the director of music.

It was very nice of Dana to name an award after me when I retired [the A. B. Spellman NEA Jazz Masters Award for Jazz Advocacy]. It caught me entirely by surprise.

FEINSTEIN: It must be satisfying to have started out as an advocate for musicians who weren't being praised or recognized—quite the opposite, actually—and to now have major awards for innovators like Ornette Coleman. We've made *some* change, at least.

SPELLMAN: Yeah. I mean, it's been a hard change. I used to go around saying that America had never forgiven jazz for its origins—which was true. It took a long time for America to shake off that image of the underground life. I think that was probably one of the reasons why jazz never got appreciated to the degree that it later did in America as an art expression. The French and Europeans were more accustomed to a bohemian life; they were accustomed to looking into the slummy underground for artists. But America, with its strong sense of social conservatism that is always at war with the more progressive forces in the country, had it held back.

That's why the anti-jazz movement in the twenties was so interesting. Almost every religious denomination had an anti-jazz society. These were really powerful organizations that made the front page of the *New York Times* every week—the greatest censorship movement in the country—to try to stamp out jazz. There was a doctor who "proved" that pregnant women listening to jazz gave birth to deformed children, and another who "proved" that syncopation impeded digestion so one should not play jazz anyplace where food was being served. There were laws passed forbidding the playing of drums and saxophones after dark. People tried to stamp it out, but it was too strong, and it became the music of America.

When it moved into the art phase—after bebop, when it had to be talked about as art—the art world very much resisted it because it had been seen as commercial music. I remember Gian Carlo Menotti, who swore that jazz would never be played at Spoleto. He changed that before he left Spoleto, but he was adamant that it didn't belong in an arts festival. Even at the Endowment, there were people when I first went there [in 1975] who didn't believe that jazz deserved to be funded at an arts agency. Jazz has a history that America hasn't wanted to forget, but it now has. It has. And now this migration from a poor commercial economy to a poor nonprofit economy has occurred. [Chuckles.] I don't know if that's an economic advancement at all, but it has happened.

I wish I could project and see what it's all going to look like twenty years from now. For one thing, I keep wondering what jazz is going to *sound* like. I mean, here we have more good musicians playing jazz than ever before. These are people who know more music, more theory, they've got way better technique, they know the history better. But this is the longest we've ever been without a genius. This is a period when the music needs a genius, and it needs somebody to pull all this great technique and knowledge together and make this big powerful thing out of it. I keep thinking it may be a composer's music; maybe some great [Billy] Strayhorn-like person will emerge. But I haven't seen it.

FEINSTEIN: It's hard to imagine any art form being expanded once it's been broken apart as far one can break it. I mean, you're not going to find someone who's going to make jazz more abstract.

SPELLMAN: No.

FEINSTEIN: So I'm curious, too, but I'm also content if what we have—in terms of jazz styles—remains a twentieth-century music. It's just that jazz progressed at such speed, faster than any form of music that I can think of.

SPELLMAN: Jazz in the twentieth century is pretty much a recapitulation of all of classical music history. You had this Baroque period in New Orleans sound, then you get Romanticism in swing . . . But then classical music hasn't moved much, either.

FEINSTEIN: True, but unlike jazz, classical music isn't often tagged as being "dead."

SPELLMAN: That's because it has institutions, and an art form without institutions is defenseless. That's the importance of Jazz at Lincoln Center and some museums that are trying to get their feet on the ground now. Somebody has to be there to say, "This is important. This needs preserving and developing." Of course, the bigger the institution becomes, the more preservationist it becomes; institutions are not notorious for forwarding new art.

FEINSTEIN: It's so warming to have institutions like Jazz at Lincoln Center preserving and supporting jazz, but I must say I *much* prefer the intimacy and ambiance of small clubs.

SPELLMAN: Oh yeah. That's still the best way to hear music. In my poem "The First Seventy," where I recapitulate the decades of my life, I was surprised when I was going over the poem that the longest section was [about] hearing John Coltrane at the Five Spot. It was like that was the most important thing that ever happened to me. And in a way, it might have been. To be in a room with Trane when he was wide open, and you're sitting twenty feet from him, was an experience I wish you could bottle and transmit to everybody. God, it was transforming.

FEINSTEIN: Is that what you meant when you wrote [in the poem "Did John's Music Kill Him?"], "Trane's horn had words in it"?

SPELLMAN: I guess. [Laughs.] Whenever there's a transformation . . . I mean, when you say, "This spoke to me," it has to mean something. It would strike your consciousness in a way that mere words couldn't. That's why all the poets I know envy musicians so much: they cut straight through to the core.

FEINSTEIN: That's one of the reasons why your line ["Trane's horn had words in it"] interests me: we *can't* translate music exactly into words, and yet we often have passionate, linguistic responses to sound.

SPELLMAN: Right. Exactly. Sound has that immediacy.

In the online interview that I did for Coffee House Press [to promote *Things I Must Have Known*], Pearl Cleage asked me, "If you could give up these lines of poetry for lines of music, would you do it?" and my answer was, "In a syncopated heartbeat!"

Index

AACM (Association for the Advancement of Creative Musicians) tribute, 163, 277
A. B. Spellman NEA Jazz Masters Award for Jazz Advocacy, 145, 280
abstract jazz, 17, 32, 281–82
Adderley, Cannonball, 32, 145, 153–54
Addison, Bernard, 230–31
Aebersold, Jamey, 166
African Commune of Bad Relevant Artists (AFICOBRA), 272
African Rhythms (Jenkins), 145, 146, 152, 153, 154–56, 166
Africa Speaks, America Answers (Kelly), 166
Afrocentrism and African history, 65–68, 107–8
Aftermath, 102
"After You've Gone," 8
Ain't But a Few of Us series / *Ain't But a Few of Us* (Jenkins), 145, 148, 156–61
Albertson, Chris, 194
Aldana, Melissa, 77
Ali, Rashid, 182–83
Allen, Geri, 76, 109, 113–14
Allen, Steve, 226
All Music Guide to Jazz, 36–37
"All of Me" discography (Willems), 250
All-Time Greatest Hits (Armstrong), 245
Altshuler, Bob, 227
American Singers (Balliett), 5, 9, 16
Ammons, Gene, 231
Amos 'n' Andy, 259
Amram, David, 188
"AM/TRAK" (Baraka), 119–20
Anatomy of a Murder, 236
Andrews, Dwight, 114
Apollo Theater, 170, 258
apologies and ethnic hostility, 68
"April in Paris" (Gordon), 101, 102–3
Armstrong, Louis: All Stars group of, 242, 247–48; *All-Time Greatest Hits*, 245; books written about, 61–62, 246, 248; *Cheek to Cheek*, 241, 243; *Columbia and RCA Victor Live Recordings of Louis Armstrong and the All Stars*, 241, 242, 257; comedy and film roles of, 259–60; criticism about commercialism of and selling-out by, 242, 245–46, 255–56; Crouch on, 60–61; death of, 243; *Ella and Louis*, 243; evolution of career and style of, 245–46, 249–50, 251–52, 254–55; genius of and

Armstrong, Louis *(conitnued)* learning to play by ear and imagination, 60–61; Hasse on, 129; "Hello Dolly," 245, 246; influence and importance of, 103, 127; interviews with, 257–58; "Jeepers Creepers," 258; Middleton relationship with, 105, 258, 259; Morgenstern's writings on, 253; musical perspective of, 52; on *The Playboy Jazz All-Stars*, 22; pop music recording by, 251–52; *Pops Is Tops*, 241, 243; prose style of, 253–54; reel-to-reel tapes of, 254–56; Riccardi's book on later years of, 241, 242–43, 248–51, 252; Riccardi's thoughts on other books about, 251–53; *Satchmo: My Life in New Orleans*, 254; *16 Most Requested Songs*, 245; "Some of These Days" recording by, 7–8; variations of style of, 54; warmth and generosity of, 255–56

Armstrong, Lucille, 243

Armstrong, Maryann, 254

art, Lower Manhattan as laboratory for, 266–67

Art Ensemble of Chicago, 42, 60

Arthur Pepper Music Corporation, 207

Articulation (Jones), 152

Artificial White Man, The (Crouch), 49, 51, 52, 66

Artists Collective, Hartford, 272, 273

Artist's Way, The (Cameron), 212–13

"Art Pepper" (Bond, *Throats of Narcissus*), 215

"Art Pepper" (Hirsch, *Earthly Measures*), 215

artpepper.bandcamp.com website, 211

Art Pepper Companion (Selbert), 218

Art Pepper: The Complete Galaxy Recordings (Pepper), 213–14

Arts Midwest, 145, 158, 159

Art: Why I Stuck with a Junkie Jazzman (Pepper), 207, 209–10, 212, 218

ASCAP / Deems Taylor Award, 140, 223

Ascension (Coltrane), 263–64, 266, 269–70

Ashbery, John, 181–82

Asher, Don, 214

Ask Me Now (Feinstein), 2, 217–18

Ask Your Mama (Hughes), 64

Aspects of a Novel (Forster), 233

Association for the Advancement of Creative Musicians (AACM) tribute, 163, 277

Atlantic, 10, 13, 19

Atlantic (Pepper), 207–8

Auden, W. H., 51

Autobiography of Pops Foster, The (Foster), 277

Avakian, George, 245

Awakenings, 97

Ayler, Albert, 42, 65, 178, 182–83

"Back" (Balliett), 14

Bacon, Paul, 194

Bad Dream Notebook, The (Dahl), 71, 72–73, 83

Bailey, C. Michael, 215

Baker, Chet, 22, 29, 129

Baker, David "Dave," 138–39, 160–61, 167

Baldwin, James, 63, 87–88, 95

Balliett, Whitney, 5–18; *American Singers*, 5, 9, 16; art and sculpture interests of, 11; on biographies and autobiographies, 12; on boundaries of jazz and younger musicians, 17–18; *Collected Works*, 5, 13, 17; on Coltrane, 17; connection between writing and music for, 11;

Crouch on, 55, 67; drum playing by, 10–11; "The Duke's Party," 5–6; on Ellington and experience of hearing him live, 15–16; on Feather, 11–12; interview style of, 8–9; introduction of author to writings of, 2; on Marsalis and Lincoln Center orchestra, 12–13; on Mary Lou Williams, 9; on Monk, 11–12; "The Natural," 7–8, 17; on O'Meally's CD collections, 16–17; overview of career of, 5; Piazza on, 234, 235; poetry writing by, 13–14; "The Prince of Jazz," 7; *Straight Life* review by, 214; on Taylor, 14–15; "Three Pianists," 6–7; White House concerts attended by, 15; writing career of, 10–11, 13–14, 17, 234, 235

Bang, Billy, 102

Baraka, Amiri (LeRoi Jones): "AM/TRAK," 119–20; *Black Music*, 177; *Blues People*, 176–77; *Cricket*, 148, 157; criticism and reviews by, 26, 67, 234; Ed Dorn's correspondence with, 178; Jenkins on, 157–58; Jones marriage to, 171, 176; "The Lady," 118; as Lifetime Achievement Award recipient and presenter, 157; Monk relationship with, 198; relationship with music of, 122; Roach book by, 106; role in writing *Clawing at the Limits of Cool*, 119–20; Spellman on and relationship with, 264, 266, 271–72; writings of, 148

Barbieri, Gato, 168

Barcelona, Danny, 247–48

Barker, Danny, 277

Barron, Kenny, 7

Basie, Count, 97, 279

Bass Lines (Hinton), 230

Baudelaire, Charles, 53

Beale Street Sheiks, 235

Bearden, Romare, 122

Beatles, The, 226

Beautiful Days, The (Spellman), 261, 270, 274

bebop, 21, 42, 61, 88–89, 122, 142, 147, 183, 265, 268, 276, 281

Bell, Hugh, 123

Beneath the Underdog (Mingus), 2

Benny Goodman Story, 236

Berendt, Joachim, 2

Berger, David, 230

Bergreen, Laurence, 246, 248

Berklee College of Music, 77, 163–64, 213

Berlin Jazz Festival, 94

Berman, Paul, 59

Bernal, Martin, 68

Berry, Chuck, 226

Beyond Category (Hasse), 125–26, 133–38

Bigard, Barney, 248

Big Star Fallin' Mama (Jones), 169, 179

Billie Holiday (Szwed), 115–16

bipolar disorder (manic depression), 82

Bird (movie), 236

Bird (Reisner), 2, 29

Birdland, 91

Bird Lives! (Russell), 62

Black Arts Movement, 63–66, 106, 150–51, 272–73

Black Athena (Bernal), 68

Black Box, The (Connelly), 213

Blackburn, Julia, 115, 116, 118

Black Music (Baraka), 177

black musicians: jazz started by, 12; magician-perspective of musicians, 52, 58–59; paying scale at Hughes's funeral, 156

Black Nationalism, 65–68

Black Panthers/Black Panther Party, 106, 150
black people/African Americans: Armstrong's pop music recordings and response of black audience, 251–52; audiences for jazz and losing music of, 159–60; black studies programs and interest in black American culture, 55–56; jazz as part of the culture of African American families, 38–39; music sounding like the way black people talk, 153
Black Power period, 67–68
Black Pow-Wow (Joans), 181
black radio station, 22, 24, 54–56
black toasts, 274
Black United Students (BUS), 150–51
black writers/African American writers: Crouch on, 63–69; Hughes's contributions to *Uhuru Afrika*, 155–56; Jenkins's writings about, 145, 147–48, 156–61; publishing business and opportunities for, 38–39
Blake, Eubie, 228
Blakey, Art, 1, 24, 26, 87, 91–92, 186
Blesh, Rudi, 130
Blessing the Boats (Sundiata), 197
Blood on the Fields, 7, 12–13
Blowin' Hot and Cool (Gennari), 38
Blue Monk (Ponzio and Postif), 195
Blue Note Records and RVG reissues, 19, 20–21, 32–33, 45, 94, 112
blues, 226, 235, 239
Blues and Trouble (Piazza), 223, 239–40
Blues People (Baraka), 176–77
Blues Up and Down (Piazza), 225, 233
Blumenthal, Bob, 19–47; advice on writing liner notes, 44–47; book idea to make people comfortable listening to jazz, 39–41; borrowing records from the library, 22–24; on Coltrane, 19–20, 32, 35, 46; connection between writing and music for, 26–27; on Crouch, 39; on Davis, 46; on evolution of jazz, 41–44; Grammy awards received by, 19, 31, 32; introduction to jazz, 22–27; law career of, 19, 29–30; liner notes written by, 19–22, 31–35, 45–46; listening project of, 37; on McLean, 21; most challenging project of, 31; nightclubs in St. Louis visits by, 24–26; overview of career of, 19; radio station routine of, 24; on relationship and experience with current music, 34; on Silver, 20; writing career of, 27–36
Bohemian Caverns, 157, 163, 164
Bohemian Caverns Jazz Orchestra, 163
Bohn, Roger, 168
Bond, Bruce, 215
Boomers club, 94
BOPland, 88–89
Boss of the Blues (Turner), 235
Boston After Dark/Boston Phoenix, 19, 28, 29–30, 45
Boston Globe, 19, 28, 29–30
Braff, Ruby, 231
Braxton, Anthony, 42
Bray, Phil, 221
breath and finding own rhythm, 173
"Brilliant Corners" (Monk), 203
Brilliant Corners: A Bio-Discography of Thelonious Monk (Sheridan), 196–97
Brilliant Corners: A Journal of Jazz & Literature, 2, 13, 27, 38, 95, 101, 104, 180–81, 184, 198, 217–18
Britt, Stan, 100
Brodeur, Paul, 10
Bronx African American History Project, Fordham, 102

Brother Ray (Ritz and Charles), 9
Brothers, Thomas, 251, 253
Brown, Clifford, 1, 24
Brown, Frank London, 196, 204
Brown, Jewel, 247–48
Brown, Marion, 183, 264
Brown, Ray, 147
Brown, Sterling, 264, 273–74
Brown, Tina, 13, 14
Brown, Wayne, 280
Brown, Wesley, 95
Brubeck, Dave, 23, 265
Bullins, Ed, 273
Bumble Bee Slim, 235
Burma (Myanmar), 77
Burnett, Carl, 216
Bushkin, Joe, 8, 9, 247
business side of jazz, 77
Byard, Jaki, 129–30, 138

Cables, George, 215–16
Cage, John, 267, 277
Calhoun, Chris, 106–7
Caliman, Hadley, 103
Camargo, Summer, 77
"Canary" (Dove), 117
Cane (Toomer), 274
CapitalBop, 163
"Caravan," 8
Carmichael, Hoagy, 135, 140–41
Carn, Doug, 271
Carnegie Hall, 216
Carney, Harry, 94
Carrington, Terri Lyne, 77, 106, 109
Carroll, Jon, 73
Carter, Bo, 235
Carter, Jimmy, 15
Carter, Ron, 130
Cassidy, Sharel, 77
Catlett, Buddy, 247–48
Catlett, Sid, 8
Cave Canem, 181

Cavett, Dick, 257–58
Cecilia, Saint, 72
Celebration of Hoagy Carmichael, A, 140–41
Chambers, Paul, 27
Charlap, Bill, 7, 8, 17
Charles, Ray, 9, 22
Charlie Parker Story, The (Parker), 40
Charlie Parker with Strings, 29
Charters, Ann, 179
Chase, J. Newell, 188
"Chasin' the Trane" (Coltrane), 24
Cheek to Cheek (Armstrong and Fitzgerald), 241, 243
"Cherokee" (Parker), 41
Cherry, Don, 25–26, 275
Chicago Jazz Festival, 159
Child Is Born, A (Allen), 113
Chilton, Karen, 84
civil rights movement, 106
Clapton, Eric, 141
classical music, 142, 143, 282
Classic Hoagy Carmichael, The (Hasse), 125, 140, 141
Clawing at the Limits of Cool (Griffin and Washington), 109, 110, 119–20
Cleveland Plain Dealer, 149, 151
Cleveland State University, 165–67
Clifford's Blues (Williams), 83
clubs/nightclubs: Blumenthal's visits to, 24–26; Gordon's visits to, 91, 92–93, 94; Hasse's visits to, 130; Jones's visits to and writers she would hang with at, 181–82; *The Ordinary* piano gigs of Hasse, 139; Piazza's visits to, 228–29; Smiling Dog Saloon visits of Jenkins, 149–50, 152, 167–68; Spellman on listening to jazz in, 282–83
Cobb, Jimmy, 27, 32
Cohen, Anat, 77
Cohen, Harvey, 137

Cole, Richie, 75
Coleman, Denardo, 62
Coleman, George, 229
Coleman, Ornette: anti-jazz reaction to, 266; family of, 62; Lyons variations on, 7; *Ornette on Tenor*, 266; *The Shape of Jazz to Come*, 23; Spellman on and relationship with, 267, 270, 275; "Turnaround," 8
Coles, Honey, 259
Coles, Johnny, 234
Coles, Robert "Bob," 28, 29
Collected Works (Balliett), 5, 13, 17
Collector's Jazz, The (Wilson), 26
Collier, James Lincoln, 135–36, 233, 246, 248, 251
Collins, Jazzbo, 265
Colombi, Chris, 151
Colomby, Harry, 205
Coltrane, Alice McLeod, 24
Coltrane, John: *Ascension*, 263–64, 266, 269–70; Balliett on, 17; Blumenthal on, 19–20, 32, 35, 46; "Chasin' the Trane," 24; club performances of, 24–25, 26; death of, 270; Ellington work with, 17; evolution of career and style of, 42, 266; Gordon on, 92–93; Griffin on and writings about, 110, 119–20; "Impressions," 24; intellect, sophistication, and vision of, 110, 161; "It's Easy to Remember," 24–25; Jones on, 183; on knowing how to stop, 189; Lyons variations on, 7; *Miles Davis & John Coltrane*, 19, 31, 32, 40; Monk's work with, 203; *My Favorite Things* / "My Favorite Things," 25, 183; poems about, 270–71, 282–83; political environment inhabited by, 110, 120, 161; quartet music of, 19–20, 31–32, 92–93; Spellman on and relationship with, 269–70; Spellman on listening to in a club, 282–83
Coltrane Live at the Village Vanguard, 24
Coltrane: The Classic Quartet, 19–20, 31–32
Columbia and RCA Victor Live Recordings of Louis Armstrong and the All Stars (Armstrong), 241, 242, 257
Columbia Records, 112, 191–92
Columbia University, 66, 109
Commodore Records, 242
Common, 163
Complete Argo / Mercury Art Farmer / Benny Golson / Jazztet Sessions, The, 21–22, 46
Complete Blue Note Lou Donaldson Sessions 1957–60, The, 46
Complete Clifford Jordan Strata-East Sessions, The, 152
Complete Village Vanguard Sessions, The (Pepper), 218–19
Congress of Racial Equality (CORE), 204
Connelly, Michael, 213
Considering Genius (Crouch), 49, 55, 62, 66–67
Contemporary Records, 220
Cookers, The, 162, 163
Cooper Union, 267
Copley Plaza, 140
Cortázar, Julio, 198
Cortez, Jayne, 62, 198, 271
Coss, Bill, 27
Council on Interracial Books for Children, 174–75
Cowell, Stanley, 152–53
Crease, Stephanie Stein, 84
Creeley, Robert, 180, 274, 275–76
Cresman, Natalie, 77

Cricket (Baraka), 148, 157
Crime Story, 97–98
Crouch, Stanley, 49–69; on Armstrong, 60–61; *The Artificial White Man*, 49, 51, 52, 66; on Balliett, 55, 67; on Black Arts Movement and Afrocentrism, 63–66, 273; on black studies programs and interest in black American culture, 55–56; Blumenthal on writings of, 39; *Considering Genius*, 49, 55, 62, 66–67; dismissal from *Jazz Times*, 147–48, 159; *Don't the Moon Look Lonesome*, 49, 50, 51–52; focus of writing career of, 49–52; on going own way and believing in what you do, 68–69; Griffin on, 120; on Harper, 62; on iconographic status of jazz musicians and American's perspective on jazz, 57–59; on impact of Black Nationalism, 65–68; on improvisational aspect and understanding how to make music, 52–54, 58–59; on jazz-related fiction, 51–52, 62–64; Jenkins on, 159, 161; *Kansas City Lightning*, 59, 103, 120, 238–39; on limitations of intellectual approach taken by critics and reviewers, 52–54; on magician-perspective of musicians, 52, 58–59; on Martin Williams, 54–55, 66; on Morgenstern, 55; overview of career of, 49; Parker biography by, 59–62, 103, 120, 238–39; Piazza on, 238–39; poetry writing by and thoughts on poetry, 50–51; on popularity of music and support for jazz, 56–59; "Putting the White Man in Charge," 66–67; role in writing *Clawing at the Limits of Cool*, 119–20; on successful criticism, 54–55; team effort of jazz and value of playing in a band, 60–61; on white writers of jazz criticism, 55–56; writings of, 148
Cuba and Its Music (Sublette), 277
cubism, 53
culture/American culture: black studies programs and interest in black American culture, 55–56; communal events and the collective experiences, 43–44; iconographic status of jazz musicians and American's perspective on jazz, 57–59; improvisation as heroic virtue, 66; jazz as American music, 179; jazz as culture and self-definition, 122; jazz as indigenous to, 3; jazz as part of culture and importance of survival of jazz, 142–43; jazz as part of the culture of African American families, 38–39; social conservatism and anti-jazz and censorship movement, 280–81; value of slowing down in current fast-information and sound-bite culture, 190
Cunningham, Merce, 267
Cuscuna, Michael, 45–46, 152

Dahl, Linda, 71–85; aspiration to write about Nica, 82–83; author's appreciation for work of, 84–85; *The Bad Dream Notebook*, 71, 72–73, 83; on decision to write as a career, 74–75; early life and education of and decision to move to New York City, 74–75; fiction writing by and favorite jazz-related fiction, 71, 72–73, 77, 83–84; on Gordon, 84; on Griffin, 84; Griffin on, 120–21; *Gringa in a Strange Land*, 71, 77; *Haunted Heart*, 71, 73, 80–82; on Liston, 76; *Morning Glory*, 71, 72,

Dahl, Linda *(continued)*
    77–80, 84, 120–21; overview of career of, 71; *Piano Girl*, 80; *Stormy Weather*, 71–72, 75–77, 84, 121; *An Upside-Down Sky*, 71, 77; on women writing about jazz, 84
Dash, Julian, 230
David Baker (Jenkins's contribution to), 160, 167
Davis, Angela, 84
Davis, Chuck, 200
Davis, Miles: Blumenthal on, 46; Cleveland concerts of, 168; details about making music from, 59; evolution of career and style of, 42, 183–84, 268; Griffin on and writings about, 110, 116, 119–20; Griffin's fascination with, 110, 112; intellect and sophistication of, 58–59, 110; Jones on, 183–84; on knowing how to stop, 189; *Miles Davis & John Coltrane*, 19, 31, 32; *Miles Davis at Carnegie Hall*, 27, 40; *Milestones*, 40; on notes you don't play, 84; on *The Playboy Jazz All-Stars*, 22; political environment inhabited by, 110, 120; *Porgy and Bess*, 23; racism, reverse racism, and, 12; *Sketches of Spain*, 183–84; "Straight, No Chaser," 40; writings about and opinions about writings, 115–16
Davis, Richard, 130
Dawson, William, 114
"Day Lady Died, The" (O'Hara), 117–18, 177
DC Jazz Festival, 145, 161–65
Dear John, Dear Coltrane (Harper), 64
DeCarava, Roy, 122
Decca, 242
DeJohnette, Jack, 162, 163
DeMichael, Don, 234
Denver, Bob (Maynard G. Krebs), 23
de Paris, Sidney, 8
Desmond, Paul, 15, 23
de Wilde, Laurent, 196
Dexter Gordon (Britt), 100
Dexter Gordon Society, The, 87
"Dexter Leaps In" (Harper), 101
Dial Records, 103
Dickenson, Vic, 8, 228
"Did John's Music Kill Him?" (Spellman), 282–83
"Digesting Dexter Gordon at 80" (Harper), 101
DiNicola, Dan, 81
Discover Jazz (Blumenthal, Smithsonian), 42
Discover Jazz (Hasse), 125, 128
Divine Days (Forrest), 63
Dizzy's Big 4 (Gillespie), 146–47, 153
Document CDs, 235
Dodds, Baby, 129
Dodgion, Dottie, 75
Dolphy, Eric, 7, 205, 261, 263, 266, 270
Donaldson, Lou, 1, 46
Donleavy, J. P., 96
"Don't Explain" (Sholl), 118
Don't the Moon Look Lonesome (Crouch), 49, 50, 51–52
Dørge, Pierre, 166
Dorn, Ed, 178–79
Dorn, Helene, 178–79
Dorn, Joel, 191
Douglas, Dave, 33–34
Dove, Rita, 117
Down Beat magazine, 12, 26, 129, 131, 142, 168, 180, 204, 226, 227, 234, 266, 268
Drop of Patience, A (Kelley), 63
drumming, 10–11, 39, 93
Du Bois, W. E. B., 279
Duke Ellington (Collier), 135–36

Duke Ellington and His World (Lawrence), 137
Duke Ellington's America (Cohen), 137
"Duke's Party, The" (Balliett), 5–6
Dyani, Johnny, 166

Eady, Cornelius, 181
East River Jazz Festival, 162
Eastwood, Clint, 236
Eckstine, Billy, 97, 231
Edison, Harry "Sweets," 97
Edwards, Brent, 99, 121–22
Eldridge, Roy, 23, 224, 227, 247
Elias, Elaine, 77
Elie, Lolis Eric, 238
Eliot, T. S., 51, 182
Ella and Louis (Armstrong and Fitzgerald), 243
Ellington, Duke: *Anatomy of a Murder* score by, 236; archives of, 133–35; birthday party for and concert at the White House, 5–6, 15; books written about, 84; "Caravan" recording by, 8; Coltrane work with, 17; denial of Pulitzer for, 7; Hasse's biography on, 125–26, 133–38; influence and importance of, 136; as inspiration for Jungle Orchestra, 166; introduction of author to music of, 1; Monk's lack of familiarity with music of, 193; "Mood Indigo," 133; movie with Welles, 57; musical perspective of, 52; *Music Is My Mistress*, 2; *The Popular Duke Ellington*, 226; Presidential Medal of Freedom award ceremony, 5–6; taxes owed by estate of, 134; writings about, 135–37
Ellington, Mercer, 133–35
Ellington at Newport, 23
Ellington Reader, The (Tucker), 137
Ellington: The Early Years (Tucker), 137

Ellison, Ralph, 148, 239
embassies, concert series held at, 163–64
Emory University, 114
emotional center of jazz, 7–8
Empyrean Isles (Hancock), 33
Encyclopedia of Jazz (Feather), 2, 26, 38
Epistrophies (Edwards), 121–22
Erickson, Erik, 28–29
"Eronel" (Hakim and Sulieman), 186–87, 192
Ervin, Booker, 234
ethnic hostility and apologies, 68
Evans, Anita, 92
Evans, Bill, 130, 232
Evans, Gil, 23, 84, 87, 93–94
Everett, Percival, 84
Expansion Arts program (NEA), 158–59
ExtraOrdinary Ragtime (Hasse), 139

Fantasy Records, 47, 208
Farmer, Art, 230, 231
fate and fame, 7
Faulkner, William, 51
Feather, Leonard: Balliett on, 11–12; *Encyclopedia of Jazz*, 2, 26, 38; Jenkins on, 158; liner notes written by, 234
"February in Sydney" (Komunyakaa), 101–2
Feidt, Thorpe, 1–2
feminists, 179
Ferrante & Teicher, 129
Fields, Joe, 152
Fifty-First (Dream) State, The (Sundiata), 197–98
"First Seventy, The" (Spellman), 282
Fishman, Charlie, 163
Fishman Young Artist Embassy series, 163–64

Fitterling, Thomas, 196
Fitzgerald, Ella, 1, 16, 22, 52; *Cheek to Cheek*, 241, 243; *Ella and Louis*, 243
Fitzgerald, F. Scott, 51, 126
Five Spot, 6–7, 173, 184, 231, 282
Flack, Roberta, 94
Flakser, Harold, 227
Flanagan, Tommy, 89, 231
Fleming, Robert, 148
"Flying Hawk" (Monk), 187
Flying Toward the Sound (Allen), 113
Folkways music records, 267
Forrest, Leon, 63, 64
Forsberg, Håkan, 250
Forster, E. M., 233
Foster, Pops, 277
Four Lives in the Bebop Business (Spellman), 158, 261–62, 278–79
Fowler, William L., 168
Franklin, Aretha, 105
Fraser, Al, 277
Freedom Dreams (Kelley), 185, 197, 201
freedoms, four, 6
Freeman, Bud, 253
Fuller, Curtis, 21–22
"Funky Blues," 8

Gabler, Milt, 242
Gallagher and O'Brien, 91
García, Yissy, 77
Garland, Red, 40, 91
Garner, Erroll, 28
Garrison, Jimmy, 20, 92
Gennari, John, 38
George, Don, 136–37
George, Nelson, 148
Getz, Stan, 22, 146–47
Ghana, 93
Gibbs, Terry, 24
Gibbs, Vernon, 148

Giddins, Gary, 27, 55, 213–14, 233, 246
Gillespie, Dizzy, 15, 24, 52, 92, 145, 146–47, 187, 255, 268, 277
Gillis, Frank, 139–40
Ginger Man, The (Donleavy), 96
Ginsberg, Allen, 178, 180, 181–82
Gioia, Dana, 280
Gitler, Ira, 38, 234
Glaser, Joe, 242, 256
Glasper, Robert, 163
Gleason, Ralph, 38
Glenn Miller Story, The, 236, 244–45
Gnawa World Music Festival, 154–55
Golson, Benny, 21–22, 46
Gonsalves, Paul, 1, 8
Goodman, Benny, 227
Gordon, Dexter: Academy Award nomination for, 95; "April in Paris," 101, 102–3; autobiography manuscript written by, 95–97, 103, 104; *Awakenings* acting role of, 97; Baldwin relationship with, 87–88, 95; biography about and writing about his life having a happy ending, 84, 87–88, 89, 94–97, 99–100; books written about, 100, 108; Chino prison time of, 103–4; *Crime Story* acting role of, 97–98; darker times of life of, 103–5; Europe years of, 88; *The Ginger Man* as a favorite book of, 96; marriage to Maxine, 87, 92; meeting Maxine, 94; Piazza on, 231; poems written about, 100–103; *Round Midnight* acting role of, 89, 95, 97, 98, 236; *The Saga of Society Red*, 97; on separation of personal and public personas, 96–97; *Setting the Pace*, 234; *Tokyo*, 90; on work to be a jazz musician but also feeling fortunate, 97
Gordon, Leonard, 192

Gordon, Max, 14, 91

Gordon, Maxine, 87–108; Accra visit and listening to jazz records residents, 93; biography about Dexter and writing about his life having a happy ending, 84, 87–88, 89, 94–97, 99–100, 103–5; Blakey relationship with, 87, 91–92; book about women in jazz, 105–6; on Coltrane, 92–93; Dahl on, 84; delay in getting Dexter biography published, 106–7; *Dexter Calling*, 99; early life of, listening to jazz with a group of kids, and having a life focused on jazz, 90–92; on Elks Club concert, 88–89; feelings about Dexter biography, 107–8; graduate school and research assistant work of, 99–100; on importance of everyone in a band, 107; on index of Dexter biography, 107; interviews with women or African Americans by, 107; on jazz police and opinions about Dexter biography, 107–8; on Jones, 92–93; on Kelley, 99–100; liner notes written by, 88–89, 90; marriage to Dexter, 87, 92; meeting Dexter, 94; on Morgenstern, 100; *Norway* experience of, 89; overview of career of, 87; road manager for Evans, 87, 93–94; *Sophisticated Giant*, 87–88, 89, 94–97, 99–100

Gourse, Leslie, 84, 195–96

Grackle, The (Welburn), 148

Grammy awards: Blumenthal's award, 19, 31, 32; Hasse's nomination for, 125, 141; Piazza's award, 223, 235; Riccardi's award, 243

Granz, Norman, 146–47, 243

Grauer, Bill, 194–95

Gray, Vernard, 162

Gray, Wardell, 98

Great Day in Harlen, A, 230

Great Gatsby, The (Fitzgerald), 51

Green, Benny, 153

Greenlee, Sam, 160–61

Griffin, Farah Jasmine, 109–24; Allen collaboration with, 109, 113–14; *Clawing at the Limits of Cool*, 109, 110, 119–20; on Coltrane, 110; Columbia University positions of, 109; course on biography and autobiography taught by, 116–17; on Crouch, 120; on Dahl, 120–21; Dahl on, 84; on Davis and writings about Davis, 110, 116; Davis as special interest after death of father, 110, 112; early life of and immersion in jazz after father's death, 109–10, 111–13; Gordon relationship with, 99; *Harlem Nocturne*, 109, 111, 120–21, 123; on Holiday and books about Holiday, 84, 109–10, 111–12, 114, 115–16, 117, 118–19; Holiday as special interest after death of father, 110, 112; *If You Can't Be Free, Be a Mystery*, 109–10, 111–12, 114, 115–16, 118–19, 123; *Lady Day*, 117; "Literary Lady," 110–11; overview of career of, 109; *Read Until You Understand*, 112; *Uptown Conversations*, 122

Griffin, Johnny, 87

Grimes, Henry, 26

Gringa in a Strange Land (Dahl), 71, 77

Grooms, Red, 267

Grove Press, 176

Grundig, 208

Gruntz, George, 94

Guide to Classic Recorded Jazz, The (Piazza), 223–24, 231–33

Guralnick, Peter, 233

Hackett, Bobby, 11, 12
Haden, Charlie, 150, 275
Hadlock, Dick, 179
Hägglöf, Gösta, 250
Hajdu, David, 138
Hakim, Sadik, 186–87, 192
Half Note club, 92
Hall, Jim, 12, 15
Halvorson, Mary, 77
Hamilton, LisaGay, 203
Hammond, John, 30, 227
Hampton, Lionel, 97, 103
Hancock, Herbie, 33, 130
Handy, Antoinette, 280
Hanna, Roland, 129–30, 131
Harding, Paul, 271
Harlem Nocturne (Griffin), 109, 111, 120–21, 123
Harlem Renaissance, 272–74
Harper, Billy, 94
Harper, Michael, 2–3, 62, 64, 101, 116, 271
Harrell, Tom, 7
Harris, Barry, 187–88
Harrison, Jim, 148
Hartman, Johnny, 17
Harvey, John, 104
Hasse, John Edward, 125–43; on Armstrong, 129; on audience for jazz and need for more audience, 141–43; *Beyond Category*, 125–26, 133–38; on Carmichael and writings about Carmichael, 135, 140–41; *The Classic Hoagy Carmichael* LP set, 125, 140, 141; as curator of American Music, National Museum of American History, 125, 133; *Discover Jazz*, 125, 128; early life and introduction to jazz, 128–31; *ExtraOrdinary Ragtime*, 139; *Indiana Ragtime* album and booklet, 139–40; Indiana University graduate school attendance by, 138–40; *Jazz: The First Century*, 125, 126–27, 131–33; *Jazz: The Smithsonian Anthology*, 125, 141–42; overview of career of, 125; piano gigs and recording and album in Indiana, 139; piano study by, 129–30, 131; public radio station work of, 130–31; *Ragtime: Its History, Composers, and Music*, 138; on Strayhorn, 137–38; on teaching jazz and jazz textbook, 131–33, 143; "We Saw Jazz through His Lens," 127
Haunted Heart (Dahl), 71, 73, 80–82
Hawes, Hampton, 214
Hawk Flies High, The, 1
Hawkins, Coleman, 1–2, 22, 54, 65, 103, 187
Hawk Relaxes, The (Hawkins), 1–2
Hayden, Robert, 51
Hayes, Elaine, 84
Hayes, Louis, 94
Haynes, Roy, 7, 231
Hear Me Talkin' to Ya (Shapiro and Hentoff), 2
"Hearts, The" (Pinsky, *The Want Bone*), 215
Heath, Jimmy, 108
Heckman, Don, 234
Heineman, Alan, 158
Hellman, Daphne, 10
"Hello Dolly" (Armstrong), 245, 246
Hemingway, Ernest, 51, 129
Henderson, Fletcher, 38, 230–31
Henderson, Joe, 20
Hendricks, Jon, 40
Hentoff, Nat, 2, 38, 158, 179–80, 196, 234
Heywood, Eddie, 11
Hibbler, Al, 231
Hicks, Warren, 227
Higgins, Billy, 26, 105, 275

Hill, Andrew, 53, 266
Hill, Constance Valis, 84
Hill, Theo, 84
Himmelstein, David, 234
Hinte, Terri, 47
Hinton, Milt, 228, 229, 230
Hinton, Mona, 230
Hirsch, Ed, 215
Hoagy Carmichael Jazz Society, 140–41
Hodeir, André, 21, 37–38, 43
Hodge, Derrick, 163
Hoffman. Stanley, 28
Holiday, Billie "Lady Day": Griffin on and books about, 84, 109–10, 111–12, 114, 115–16, 117, 118–19, 123; Griffin's fascination with, 110, 112; influence and importance of, 110–11; influence of Mercer on, 16; introduction of author to music of, 1; Jones on, 177; poems about, 271; tapes of rehearsal session with Rowles, 123–24; understanding music by and talent for making music, 53–54; victimization of, 112, 116; writings about, 103, 110–11, 115–16, 117–18
Honorable Amendments (Harper), 101
Hopps, Jimmy, 105
Horne, Lena, 156
How I Became Hettie Jones (Jones), 169, 172–76
Hughes, Langston, 51, 64, 155–56, 273–74

"I Didn't Know What Time It Was" (Parker), 183
If You Can't Be Free, Be a Mystery (Griffin), 109–10, 111–12, 114, 115–16, 118–19, 123
I Hate to Talk about Your Mother (Jones), 174–75

Iliad, The, 51
"Impressions" (Coltrane), 24
improvisation: as heroic virtue, 66; teaching concept of, 166; understanding how to make music and improvisational aspect of jazz, 52–54, 58–59
"In" Crowd, The (Lewis), 129
Indiana Ragtime album and booklet (Hasse and Gillis), 139–40
Indiana University, 138–39
Ingalls, Ann, 80
Ingham, Keith, 81
Institute of Jazz Studies, Rutgers University, 78, 79, 100, 106, 180, 195–96, 201
interracial children's books, 174–75
It's All True, 57

"Jackie-ing" (Monk), 199
Jackson, Mahalia, 173
Jackson, Milt, 156
Janis, Harriet, 130
Jarrett, Keith, 150, 168
jazz: as American music, 179; anti-jazz reaction to avant-garde musicians, 266; audience for and need for more audience for, 141–43, 159–60, 167–68; blues as important to, 235; boundaries on, 17; as culture and self-definition, 122; definitions of, 162–63; evolutions of careers, changing styles of jazz, and has jazz run its course, 41–44, 54, 266, 267–69, 280–82; humanity behind and understanding, 267–69; improvisational aspect and understanding how to make music, 52–54, 58–59; as indigenous to American culture, 3; introduction of author to, 1–2; as language and language of the spirit, 184; Lower

jazz *(continued)*
  Manhattan as laboratory for art, 266–67; mechanics of and mechanics of American democracy, 232; as part of the culture of African American families, 38–39; on popularity of music and support for, 56–59; recordings of other people and learning to play, 60–61; relationship and experience with current music, 34; social conservatism and anti-jazz and censorship movement, 280–81; spiritual dimension of from suffering, 111, 123; teaching jazz and jazz textbooks, 131–33, 143, 165–67; team effort of, 60–61; terms for jazz styles, 281–82
Jazz Advance (Taylor), 14
Jazz Appreciation Month, 125, 142
Jazz at Lincoln Center, 12, 67, 77, 232, 240, 282
Jazz Book, The (Berendt), 2
Jazz Girl (Kelly), 80
Jazz: Its Evolution and Essence (Hodeir), 37–38, 43
Jazz Journalists Association, Lifetime Achievement Award, 157
Jazz Magazine, 75
Jazz Messengers, 24, 91–92
Jazz Spotlite News, 148
Jazz: The American Theme Song (Collier), 135
Jazz: The First Century (Hasse), 125, 126–27, 131–33
Jazz: The Smithsonian Anthology, 125, 141–43
JazzTimes magazine, 142, 147–48, 159
Jazz Tradition, The (Williams), 37–38
Jazz West label, 208
Jeanty, Val H., 77
"Jeepers Creepers" (Armstrong), 258

Jeffreys, Paul, 229
Jenkins, Willard, 145–68; *African Rhythms*, 145, 146, 152, 153, 154–56, 166; Ain't But a Few of Us series / *Ain't But a Few of Us*, 145, 148, 156–61; Arts Midwest role of, 145, 158, 159; audience for and need for more audience for jazz, 159–60, 167–68; on Baker, 160–61, 167; on Baraka, 157–58; on Black Arts Movement, 150–51; on Crouch, 159, 161; DC Jazz Festival role of, 145, 161–65; early life and introduction to jazz, 148–50; edits to *African Rhythms* by Weston, 155; on Feather, 158; Kent State education of, 148–49, 150–51; Lifetime Achievement Award presented to, 157; liner notes written by, 145, 146–47, 152–54; on Morgenstern, 158; Northeast Ohio Jazz Society role of, 168; OpenSkyJazz website, 145, 156; overview of career of, 145; on race and racism, 159–61; radio work of, 145, 157, 160; Smiling Dog Saloon visits of, 149–50, 152, 167–68; on Spellman, 158–59; teaching jazz courses by, 165–67; writing career of, interest in writing, but never making a living writing, 149, 151, 156
Joans, Ted, 181, 198
Jobim, Antonio Carlos, 31
Johannessen, Joy, 75
"john coltrane" (Spellman), 270
John Coltrane and Johnny Hartman, 35
Johnson, Budd, 229, 231
Johnson, Fenton, 274
Johnson, James P., 8
Johnson, Joyce, 177, 179
Johnson, Robert, 16, 118

Jones, Elvin, 20, 92–93, 152
Jones, Gayl, 110
Jones, Hank, 147, 228
Jones, Hettie, 169–84; on Ali, 182–83; on anger, 176; apartment of, 170–71, 183; on Ayler, 178, 182–83; Baraka marriage to, 171, 176; *Big Star Fallin' Mama*, 169, 179; *Blues People* editing by, 176–77; club visits by and writers she would hang with at clubs, 181–82; on Coltrane, 183; on Davis, 183–84; early life and introduction to jazz, 172–73; editing and freelance work of, 175, 176–77; encouragement for women writers, 172; family of, 171, 176; favorite jazz musicians of, 182–84; on feminists, 179; Helene Dorn's correspondence with, 178–79; on Hentoff, 179–80; on Holiday, 177; on Joans, 181; on Kerouac, 180; kids' books written by, 174–75; memoir of, 169, 172–76; on Monk, 173–74; on Morgenstern, 180; music as first written language of and language of the spirit, 172, 184; on O'Hara, 177–78; overview of career of, 169; piano in family home and piano lessons of, 172–73, 174, 184; poetry writing by, 178, 182; on poets influenced by jazz, 180–81; reading aloud as valuable to writer, 174; *Record Changer* work of, 179; on Shepp, 171–72, 182–83; on suburban women, 178–79; on Sundiata, 170; on Taylor, 182; teaching and lecture work of, 169–70, 181, 182; on Williams, 179–80
Jones, LeRoi. *See* Baraka, Amiri (LeRoi Jones)
Jones, Philly Joe, 32
Jones, Rodney, 152
Jones, Thad, 130, 131
Joplin, Scott, 130, 138–39
Jordan, Clifford, 145, 152–53
Jordan, Sandy, 153
Jordan, Taft, 229
Josephson, Barney, 10–11, 14
Jungle Orchestra, 166
Just Above My Head (Baldwin), 63

Kaffel, Ralph, 213–14
Kansas City Lightning (Crouch), 59, 103, 120, 238–39
Kart, Larry, 234
Kaufman, Bob, 181
Keepnews, Orrin, 153–54, 192–95
Keepnews, Peter, 75, 193
Keith Jarrett quartet, 150
Kelley, Robin D. G., 185–206; academic background of, 190; access to archives for research on Monk, 190–92, 202; adversities in life of while writing biography, 200–203; *Africa Speaks, America Answers*, 166; car accident of, 201–2; on Dolphy, 205; *Freedom Dreams*, 185, 197, 201; on Gourse, 195–96; on Keepnews, 192–95; on material cut from manuscript, 192; Monk family's feelings about writing biography, 198–200; musical background of and introduction to jazz, 188–89; musical cadence to writing style of, 189; Nellie Monk's interview and relationship with, 196, 199, 201–2; overview of career of, 185; piano playing by, 188–89; on Ponzio, 196; on Sheridan, 196–97; on Sundiata, 197–98; *Thelonious Monk*, 99–100, 185–88, 198–206; thoughts on other biographies about Monk, 195–97; value of slowing down in current fast-information

Kelley, Robin D. G. *(continued)*
  and sound-bite culture, 190; on writing another biography, 205
Kelley, William, 63
Kelly, Sarah Bruce, 80
Kelly, Wynton, 27, 91
Kendziora, Carl, 227
Kennedy, Roger, 133
Kent State University, 148–49, 150–51, 165–67
Kernodle, Tammy, 80, 121
Kerouac, Jack, 179, 180
Kinard, John, 133
Kirk, Rahsaan Roland, 24
Koch, Kenneth, 181–82
Koenig, Les, 220
Koenigswarter, Baroness Pannonica "Nica" de, 82–83, 186, 187, 191
"Ko Ko" (Parker), 41, 61
Komunyakaa, Yusef, 101–3, 215
Krebs, Maynard G. (Bob Denver), 23
Krivda, Ernie, 152
Kuehl, Linda, 115
Kulik, Gary, 133
Kunstadt, Leonard, 227
Kuti, Femi, 163

"Lady, The" (Baraka), 118
Lady Day (Griffin), 117
Lake, Oliver, 163
"Lament for M" (Schuller), 8
Larkin, Philip, 14
Las Vegas Jazz Society, 168
Lateef, Yusef, 166
Lawrence, Austin, 137
Lawrence, Jacob, 273
Lawrence, Vera Brodsky, 138
Lee, Julia, 16
Leonard, Herman, 127
Lesberg, Jack, 247
Let Freedom Ring (McLean), 21

Let's Get Lost (Weber), 29
Letters to Theo (Van Gogh), 53
Levertov, Denise, 181
Leviev, Milcho, 208
Lewis, George, 277
Lewis, Jerry Lee, 226
Lewis, Mel, 130, 131
Lewis, Ramsey, 69, 129
library, borrowing jazz records from, 22–24
Liebman, Dave, 130
Life in E Flat (Woods and Panken), 216–17
Life in Jazz, A (Barker), 277
Life Time (Williams), 33, 42
Lila Wallace Reader's Digest Fund, 136
Lilly Endowment grant, 139
Lincoln Center Orchestra and Jazz at Lincoln Center, 12, 67, 77, 232, 240, 282
liner notes: Blumenthal's writings, 19–22, 31–35, 45–46; with CDs, 269; as connection between writing and music for Blumenthal, 26; Feather's liner notes, 234; Giddins's liner notes, 213–14; Gordon's liner notes, 88–89, 90; Jenkins's writings, 145, 146–47, 152–54; Morgenstern's liner notes, 253; Pepper's liner notes, 207–8, 218–19; Piazza on, 224, 234–35; Riccardi's liner notes, 242, 243, 256–57; Spellman's liner notes, 2, 261, 263–64, 266, 268–70, 278; writing advice from Blumenthal, 44–47
Liston, Melba, 76, 105, 106
"Literary Lady" (Griffin), 110–11
literature and writing: biographies and autobiographies of musicians, 2, 12, 116–17; book idea to make people comfortable listening to jazz, 39–41; books about jazz out of date by

the time of publication, 41; books to make people interested in jazz, 37–38; criticism and reviews of jazz, 26–30, 34–41, 54–56, 233–34, 265–66; crossover between writing and music, 11, 172; introduction to and influence on author, 2; jazz-related fiction, 51–52, 62–64, 71, 72–73, 77, 83–84; limitations of intellectual approach taken by critics and reviewers, 52–54; need for literature on jazz, 141; Piazza on jazz writers, 233–34; women writers, 84, 172

Little Piano Girl, The (Ingalls and Macdonald), 80
Little Richard, 226
Living Legend (Pepper), 220
Lloyd, Charles, 184
Lomax, Alan, 276
Lombardo, Guy, 251–52
Lorenz, Lee, 10
Lost Chords (Sudhalter), 12
Lost Light (Connelly), 213
Loueke, Lionel, 163
Louis Armstrong: An American Genius (Collier), 246, 248, 251
Louis Armstrong: An Extravagant Life (Bergreen), 246, 248
Louis Armstrong: In His Own Words (Brothers), 251, 253
Louis Armstrong: Master of Modernism (Brothers), 251
Louis Armstrong's New Orleans (Brothers), 251
Lourie, Charlie, 45
Lovano, Joe, 7, 8, 145, 152
Lovano, Tony, 152
Lucas, John S. (Jax Lucas), 129
Lurie, Thea, 81
Lush Life (Hajdu), 138
Lyons, Jimmy, 7

Macdonald, Maryann, 80
Macero, Teo, 191–92
magician-perspective of musicians, 52, 58–59
Magnuson, Bob, 208
Malone, Leonard "Skip," 104
manic depression (bipolar disorder), 82
Mann, Michael, 98
Man Who Cried I Am, The (Williams), 83
"Maple Leaf Rag" (Joplin), 130, 138–39
Marsalis, Wynton, 7, 12–13, 52, 67, 147, 238
Marsalis Music, 34
Martin Scorsese Presents the Blues album notes (Piazza), 223, 235
Mary Lou Williams (Witkowski), 80
McBride, Christian, 17, 184
McCorkle, Susannah, 73, 80–82
McDonough, Chris, 51
McDuff, Jack, 105
McGlynn, Don, 220
McKenna, Dave, 11, 140
McLean, Jackie, 21, 33, 270, 272, 273
McLeod Coltrane, Alice, 24
McPartland, Marian, 10–11, 72
McPherson, James, 64
McShann, Jay, 231
Meditations in an Emergency (O'Hara), 178
Mehegan, John, 40
Mehldau, Brad, 7, 17
Menotti, Gian Carlo, 281
Mercer, Mabel, 16
Merkerson, S. Epatha, 113–14
Metheny, Pat, 35
Metronome magazine, 26, 180, 265–66
Micheline, Jack, 181
Middleton, Velma, 105, 258, 259

Miles Davis & John Coltrane, 19, 31, 32, 40
Miles Davis at Carnegie Hall, 27
Miles: The Autobiography (Troupe), 116
Milestones (Davis), 40
Miller, Glenn, 245
Miller, Warren, 10
Mills, David, 237
Mingus, Charles, 2, 23, 150
Mister Jelly Roll (Lomax), 276
Mitchell, Blue, 234
Mobley, Hank, 27, 234
Modern Jazz Quartet (MJQ), 91
Monk (de Wilde), 196
Monk, Barbara "Boo Boo," 186, 199–200
Monk, Nellie: care for and as foundation for Monk, 187–88; caring nature and healing work of, 201–2; income of and covering expenses by, 186; interviews given by, 196; Kelley's interview and relationship with, 196, 199, 201–2; recordings made by, 191; seamstress work for and opinion about Mary Lou Williams, 201, 202
Monk, Thelonious: acid bath treatment of pop songs by, 21; adversities in life of, 200, 202–3; archives and other records for research on, 190–92, 202; Balliett on, 11–12; Baraka relationship with, 198; "Brilliant Corners," 203; car from Nica for, 186; Coltrane's work with, 203; death as important and hard for, 189; details about making music from, 58; Ellington's music as unfamiliar to, 193; "Eronel" composition credits, 186–87, 192; fire in apartment and loss of papers and manuscripts, 190–91, 200; "Flying Hawk," 187; functional idealism of, 69; influence and importance of, 225; "Jackie-ing," 199; Jones on, 173–74; Keepnews's relationship with, 192–95; Kelley's biography of, 99–100, 185–88, 198–206; Kelley's introduction to music of, 188–89; Kelley's thoughts on other biographies about, 195–97; money and financial problems of, 185–86, 191–92; Monkisms and Monkish introductions, 187; *Monk Plays Ellington*, 193; "My Ideal," 187–88; Nica's support of, 83, 186, 187, 191; "On the Bean," 187; Overton's work with and responsibility for decision making, 194; on playing slow and learning a song a day, 190; PSA read by, 131; racial politics and resistance to talk about race by, 203–5; *Straight, No Chaser*, 226; sword in cane carried by, 173; "Whispering," 187
Monk, Thelonious, Jr. "Toot," 189, 198–99, 229
Monk Plays Ellington, 193
Monterey festival, 164–65
Montgomery, Monk, 168
Montgomery, Wes, 168
Montreal festival, 164–65
"Mood Indigo" (Ellington), 133
Moran, Jason, 184
Morehouse, Paul, 188
Moreira, Airto, 150
Morgenstern, Dan: on covering festivals, 165; Crouch on, 55; Gordon on, 100; Institute of Jazz Studies role of, 100, 247; Jenkins on, 158; Jones on, 180; liner notes written by, 253; Piazza on, 227–28, 233; Riccardi on, 246, 253; Spellman on and relationship with, 265–66, 276; Spellman piece

published by, 265–66; writings about Armstrong by, 253
Morning Glory (Dahl), 71, 72, 77–80, 84, 120–21
Morningside Community Center, 205
Morocco, 154–55h
Morrison, Toni, 84, 123
Morton, Jelly Roll, 276
Mosaic Records, 45–46, 152–53, 257
Moses, Bob, 68
Moten, Fred, 99
Motian, Paul, 150
"Moulin Rouge" (*Crime Stories*), 97–98
Mozart, Wolfgang, 83
Mulligan Gerry, 15
Muranyi, Joe, 247
Murray, Albert, 51, 54–55, 148, 239
Music from "The Connection" (Redd), 21, 33
Music Is My Mistress (Ellington), 2
Myanmar (Burma), 77
My Favorite Things / "My Favorite Things" (Coltrane), 25, 183
"My Ideal" (Monk), 187–88

Nadler, Mark, 81
Nance, Ray, 228
Napoleon, Marty, 247–48
National Endowment for the Arts (NEA): anti-jazz sentiments and funding for jazz by, 281; A. B. Spellman NEA Jazz Masters Award for Jazz Advocacy, 145, 280; Expansion Arts program, 158–59; Jazz Masters program at, 280; Spellman's work with, 279–80
National Jazz Service Organization (NJSO), 145
"Natural, The" (Balliett), 7–8, 17
Neidlinger, Buell, 188
Nelson, Oliver, 27
Neon Vernacular, 102

Nero, Peter, 129
Newborn, Phineas, 229
Newman, Joe, 228
New Orleans, 236
New Orleans, segregation in and vow of Armstrong to not return to, 242–43
New Orleans Center for Creative Arts (NOCCA), 238
Newport Jazz Festival, 1, 43
New Republic, 62
New School, The, 169–70
New Thing, 17
Newton, Frankie, 10
New Wave in Jazz, The, 42
New Yorker: Balliett's writings for, 2, 5, 10–11, 13–14, 17, 214; Crouch's writings for, 49; Pepper's poems submitted to, 210
Nicholas Brothers, 84
Nichols, Herbie, 46, 194
Nicholson, Stuart, 147–48
Nielsen, Lotte, 104
Night at Birdland, A (Blakey), 1, 24
Night at the Village Vanguard, A (Rollins), 45
nightclubs. *See* clubs/nightclubs
"Night in Tunisia, A," 1
Night in Tunisia, A (Blakey), 26
Nixon, Richard, 5–6, 15
Nonesuch Records, 138
Norgran label, 146
Northeast Ohio Jazz Society, 168
Norton Anthology of African American Literature, The, 16–17
"Now's the Time" (Parker), 39–40, 268

O'Brien, Geoffrey, 91
O'Brien, Joel, 91–92
O'Brien, Peter, 78, 79, 120–21
O'Day, Anita, 84
Odyssey, The, 51, 66

O'Hara, Frank, 117–18, 122, 177–78, 181–82
Oliver, King, 129, 254, 257–58
Olivier, Laurence, 54
Olson, Charles, 182
O'Meally, Robert "Bob," 16–17, 122
"Omega" (McLean), 21
One for Me (Scott), 105
"On Hearing Sonny ('Newk') Rollins in the Park on a Hot Summer Night" (Spellman), 262–63, 278
"On the Bean" (Monk), 187
OpenSkyJazz website, 145, 156
Open University, 165
Ornette on Tenor (Coleman), 266
Ory, Kid, 1
Osborne, Mary, 76
Out to Lunch (Dolphy), 263, 266, 268
Overmyer, Eric, 236, 237
Overton, Hall, 194
Owens, Jimmy, 188, 230

Padgett, Ron, 181–82
Painter of Modern Life, The (Baudelaire), 53
Palmer, Don, 148
Panken, Ted, 216
Parenti, Tony, 228
Parker, Charlie: bebop work of, 147; Blumenthal's writing about, 28–29; books written about, 61–62, 103; *The Charlie Parker Story*, 40; *Charlie Parker with Strings*, 29; "Cherokee," 41; Crouch's biography about, 59–62, 103, 120; death of and interest in horn of, 216–17; drug addiction of, 103; evolution of career and style of, 42, 268; fiction about correlatives between Mozart and, 83; "Funky Blues" recording by, 8; "I Didn't Know What Time It Was," 183; influence and importance of, 103; interviews about in *Bird*, 2, 29; Kelley's introduction to music of, 188; "Ko Ko," 41, 61; learning jazz by, 61; "Now's the Time," 39–40, 268; opinions about music of, 52; poems about, 271; variations of style of, 54; "Warming Up a Riff," 41; wives of, 60
Parker, Leon, 7
Parlato, Gretchen, 163
Pat Metheny Group, 35
"Patricia" (Pepper), 207–8, 221
patron saint of music, 72
Patton, Charlie, 235
Payton, Nicholas, 162, 163
Pelecanos, George, 238
Pellegrinelli, Lara, 84
Penguin Guide to Jazz, The, 36–37
"Pepper" (Komunyakaa, *Testimony*), 215
Pepper, Art: addiction of, 209, 211; *Atlantic*, 207–8; *The Complete Village Vanguard Sessions*, 218–19; documentary about and additional footage added to, 219–21; hernia of, 220; "I'm a genius" quote of, 219; influence and importance of, 219–21; Laurie's relationship with and feelings about leaving, 209–10, 221–22; Laurie's tattoo and pulling down shirt to expose it, 221–22; *Living Legend*, 220; "Patricia," 207–8, 221; poems for and about, 215; "The Prisoner," 209; prison time of and playing cup while in jail, 208, 211; racism of, 215–16; relationships of, 211–12; *The Return of Art Pepper*, 208; "Straight Life," 207; *Straight Life*, 2, 12, 207, 208, 210, 211–12, 215–17, 218–19; *Straight Life* review by Balliett, 214; *Unreleased Art Pepper, Volume 11*, 207, 221; *Winter Moon*, 209

Pepper, Laurie, 207–22; Art's relationship with and feelings about leaving Art, 209–10, 221–22; *Art: Why I Stuck with a Junkie Jazzman*, 207, 209–10, 212, 218; on blurbs, criticism, and reviews, 213–15; book idea about women on their own, 217; on Connelly, 213; on documentary about Art, 219–21; on Giddins, 213–14; influence of *The Artist's Way* on writing of, 212–13; liner notes written by, 207–8, 218–19; overview of career of, 207; on Pinsky, 213–14, 215; poetry writing by, 210; *Straight Life*, 2, 12, 207, 208, 210, 211–12, 215–17, 218–19; *Straight Life* readings by and online access to episodes, 211; *Straight Life* review by Balliett, 214; tattoo on chest of and cover photo on memoir, 221–22; Widow's Taste record label of, 207, 221; on Woods's interest in Parker's horn, 216–17; writing approach and process of, 210–11
Petry, Ann, 121
Phillips, Harvey, 140–41
Phillips, James, 272
Piano Girl (Dahl), 80
Piano Jazz, 72
Piazza, Tom, 223–40; on Balliett, 234, 235; *Blues and Trouble*, 223, 239–40; *Blues Up and Down*, 225, 233; classic film interests and opinion about jazz-related films, 235–36; on Collier, 233; on Crouch, 238–39; *Down Beat* submission from, 227–28; early life of, introduction to jazz, and experiences being around musicians, 223–24, 225–31; on Evans, 232; fiction writing by, 239–40; on Gordon, 231; Grammy award received by, 223, 235; *The Guide to Classic Recorded Jazz*, 223–24, 231–33; on jazz writers, 233–34; on liner notes, 224, 234–35; love for and appreciate of relationships with musicians, 229–31; *Martin Scorsese Presents the Blues* album notes by, 223, 235; on Martin Williams, 233–34; melodica playing by, 226; on Morgenstern and encouragement to write from Morgenstern, 227–28, 233; overview of career of, 223; on Rollins, 229; *Setting the Tempo*, 224, 234; *Treme* writing by, 223, 236–38; *Understanding Jazz*, 223, 224–25, 232–33; on Wells, 230; writing career of, 227–28, 231
Picasso, Pablo, 52–53, 58, 129
Pinsky, Robert, 213–14, 215
Pippin, Horace, 273
Playboy Jazz All-Stars, The, 22
Pleasure, King, 17
Poet in New York (Lorca), 62
poetry: about Coltrane, 270–71; about Dexter Gordon, 100–103; about Holiday, 117–18; Balliett's poems, 13–14; Crouch's poems and thoughts on writing poetry, 50–51; jazz as inspiration for, 2; Jones on poets influenced by jazz, 180–81; Jones's poems, 178, 182; Kerouac's poems, 180; Pepper's poems, 210; poets' envy for musicians, 282–83; Spellman on success of poets, 271–72; Spellman's poems, 261, 262–63, 270, 274–75, 278, 279; spoken word from, 182; Sundiata's projects uniting jazz and, 170; Taylor's poems, 14; understanding with knowledge of jazz, 3
Ponzio, Jacques, 195, 196

Pops: A Life of Louis Armstrong (Teachout), 252
Pops Is Tops (Armstrong), 241, 243
Popular Duke Ellington, The (Ellington), 226
Porgy and Bess (Davis and Evans), 23
Porter, Bob, 141
Porter, Lewis, 246–47
Porter, Tom, 157
Postif, François, 195
Powell, Bud, 147, 188, 225
Powell, Rudy, 229, 230
"Powerhouse" (Welty), 62–63
Power Stronger than Itself, A (Lewis), 277
Previte, Bobby, 33
Primus, Pearl, 121
"Prince of Jazz, The" (Balliett), 7
"Prisoner, The" (Pepper), 209
Pulitzer Prizes, 7, 13, 280
Pure Jazz, 148
Purim, Flora, 150
"Putting the White Man in Charge" (Crouch), 66–67

"Quadrangle" (McLean), 21
Queens College concert, 228
Quinn, Alice, 13–14

race and racism: apologies and ethnic hostility, 68; Black Nationalism impact on, 65–68; criticism of Armstrong about commercialism and selling-out, 242, 245–46, 255–56; Jenkins on, 159–61; Monk's attitude toward racial politics and resistance to talk about race, 203–5; New Orleans segregationist policies and vow of Armstrong to not return to, 242–43; Pepper's racism, 215–16; racist assumptions about Marsalis, 67; reverse racism, 12; Smiling Dog Saloon closure based on, 167–68

radio: black radio station, 22, 24; Blumenthal's radio show, 27–28; Jenkins's work on, 145, 157, 160; no radio in jail, 208; public radio station work of Hasse, 130–31; Spellman's radio show, 267
ragtime, 130, 138–40
Ragtime: Its History, Composers, and Music (Hasse), 138
Raise Up Off Me (Hawes and Asher), 214
Ramsey, Guthrie, 173
Ray Charles: In Person, 22
reading aloud as valuable to writer, 174
Read Until You Understand (Griffin), 112
Record Changer, 179
Record Research magazine, 227
Redd, Freddie, 21, 33
Redd, Vi, 76
Redman, Dewey, 150
Reeves, Dianne, 109
Rei, Sofia, 77
Reid, Tomeka, 77
Reisner, Robert, 2, 29, 60
religion, jazz is my, 43–44
"Rene" (McLean), 21
Return of Art Pepper, The (Pepper), 208
Return to Forever, 150
Rexroth, Kenneth, 271
Rhythm in a Riff (Eckstine), 231
Riccardi, Ricky, 241–60; archivist work at Armstrong Archives, 241, 252; Armstrong Archives research by, 249; Armstrong community support for Armstrong research by, 250; baseball interests of, 244; blog about Armstrong, 241, 250; early life and introduction to jazz, 244–46; focus of writing about Armstrong, 246–47; Grammy award received by, 241;

house-painting jobs of, 249, 250; interviews with All Stars members, 247–48; liner notes written by, 242, 243, 256–57; on listening to Armstrong's reel-to-reel tapes, 254–56; on Morgenstern, 246, 253; new book project of, 256; overview of career of, 241; start of interest in Armstrong, 245–46; thoughts on other books about Armstrong, 251–53; undergraduate and graduate theses on Armstrong, 246–49; *What a Wonderful World*, 241, 242–43, 248–51, 252; writing style of, 248
Richardson, Chan, 60, 216–17
Rifkin, Joshua, 138
Riley, Ben, 230
Ritz, David, 9
Riverside Records, 192–95
Roach, Max, 60, 69, 106, 147, 268
Roach, Robert "Bob," 151
Robinson, Bill "Bojangles," 258, 259
Rockwell, Tommy, 252
Rolling Stone Jazz Record Guide, The, 35–36
Rolling Stone Record Guide, The, 35–36
Rollins, Sonny, 12, 24, 25, 26, 45, 229, 232, 278
Rosnes, Renee, 76, 77
Round Midnight, 89, 95, 97, 98, 236
Rouse, Charlie, 203
Rowles, Jimmy, 53, 123–24
Ruffing, Rebecca, 60
"Rush Hour," 8
Russell, Ross, 62
Rutgers University: discographical conferences at, 227; Institute of Jazz Studies at, 78, 79, 100, 106, 180, 195–96, 201, 247; jazz writing course at, 249; oral histories program with Smithsonian, 248; Riccardi's master's degree from, 246–48, 249

"Salt Peanuts" (Gillespie), 15, 187
Sanborn, David, 94
Sanchez, Sonia, 64, 272
San Juan Hill, 100
Satchmo: My Life in New Orleans (Armstrong), 254
Saturday Review, 10
Scascitelli, Patrizial, 77
Schaap, Phil, 180
Schlitz Salute to Jazz, 131
Schneider, Maria, 77
Schuller, Gunther, 8, 276
Scott, Geraldine, 60
Scott, Hazel, 84
Scott, Shirley, 87, 105
Scott Joplin: Complete Piano Works (Lawrence), 138
Selbert, Todd, 218–19
Setting the Pace (Ervin and Gordon), 234
Setting the Tempo (Piazza), 224, 234
Shakespeare, William, 125–26
Shange, Ntozake, 110–11
Shape of Jazz to Come, The (Coleman), 23
Shapiro, Nat, 2
Shaw, Arvell, 247
Shaw, Woody, 87
Shaw, Woody Louis Armstrong, III, 87, 92–93
Shawn, William, 10
Shepp, Archie, 166, 171–72, 182–83, 265
Sheridan, Chris, 196–97
"Shield of Achilles, The" (Auden), 51
Sholl, Betsy, 118
Shorter, Wayne, 97
Silver, Horace, 20
Simon, David, 236, 237

Simone, Nina, 28
Sinatra, Frank, 16
Sinclair, John, 270
16 Most Requested Songs (Armstrong), 245
Skea, Danny, 168
Sketches of Spain (Davis), 183–84
Smiling Dog Saloon, 149–50, 152
Smith, Bessie, 27
Smith, Evelyn, 186
Smith, Howie, 166
Smith, Jabbo, 9, 23
Smith, Jimmy, 105
Smith, Judith "Muffin," 186
Smith, Lonnie, 33
Smith, Sean, 7
Smithsonian Collection of Classic Jazz (Williams), 12, 43, 142, 179
Smithsonian five-CD collection of jazz singing (O'Meally), 16
Smithsonian Institution: acquisition of collections by and acquisition of Ellington archives, 134–35; Artifact Wall, 135; audience for jazz and role in getting more audience, 141–43; Hasse as curator of American Music, National Museum of American History, 125, 133; oral histories program with Rutgers, 248
Smithsonian Jazz Masterworks Orchestra, 125, 136
SNCC (Student Nonviolent Coordinating Committee), 67–68, 204
Snyder, Doris, 60
SoHo News, 231
"Some of These Days," 7–8
Something to Live For (van de Leur), 138
Sonata for Jukebox (O'Brien), 91
Song for My Father (Silver), 20

"Sonny's Blues" (Baldwin), 63
Sophisticated Giant (Gordon), 87–88, 89, 94–97, 99–100
Soul on Soul (Kernodle), 80, 121
So What (Szwed), 115
Space Is the Place (Szwed), 115
Spalding, Esperanza, 76, 163
Spears, Britney, 56–57
Spellman, A. B., 261–83; on aging and retirement, 278–79; on Baraka and relationship with, 264, 266, 271–72; *The Beautiful Days*, 261, 270, 274; on Black Arts Movement, 272–73; book recommendations, 276–77; on Brown, 264, 273–74; on clubs as best place to experience jazz, 282–83; on Coleman and relationship with, 267, 270, 275; on Coltrane and relationship with, 269–70; on Creeley, 274, 275–76; criticism and review writing by, 265–66; "Did John's Music Kill Him?," 282–83; early life and interest in music, 264–65; on evolutions of careers and changing styles of jazz, 266, 267–69, 280–82; Expansion Arts program role of, 158–59; "The First Seventy," 282; *Four Lives in the Bebop Business*, 158, 261–62, 278–79; on Harlem Renaissance, 272–74; "On Hearing Sonny ('Newk') Rollins in the Park on a Hot Summer Night," 262–63, 278; Howard University education of, 264, 265; on Hughes, 273–74; Jenkins on, 158–59; "john coltrane," 270; liner notes written by, 2, 261, 263–64, 266, 268–70, 278; on Lower Manhattan as laboratory for art, 266–67; on making time for art, 278; on Morgenstern and

relationship with, 265–66, 276; NEA award named in honor of, 145, 280; NEA work of, 279–80; overview of career of, 261; poetry writing by, 261, 262–63, 270, 274–75, 278, 279; radio show of, 267; on social conservatism and anti-jazz and censorship movement, 280–81; on success of poets, 271–72; on terms for jazz styles, 281–82; *Things I Must Have Known*, 261, 275, 278, 283; on transformative experience listening to music, 282–83; "Villanelle for the Hell of It," 275; on Williams and relationship with, 266, 276; writings of, 148
spoken word, 113, 170, 173, 182
Spoleto, 281
Spook Who Sat by the Door, The (Greenlee), 160
sporting events, 43–44
Stearns, Marshall, 276
Sterne, Teresa, 138
Stewart, Chuck, 123
Stewart, Jimmy, 245
Stites, Tom, 75
Stockhausen, Karlheinz, 267
Stompin' the Blues (Murray), 55
Stormy Weather (Dahl), 71–72, 75–77, 84, 121
Story of Jazz, The (Stearns), 276
"Straight, No Chaser" (Davis), 40
Straight, No Chaser (Gourse), 195–96
Straight, No Chaser (Monk), 226
"Straight Life" (Pepper), 207
Straight Life (Pepper and Pepper), 2, 12, 207, 208, 210, 211–12, 214, 215–17, 218–19
Strata-East Records, 105, 152
Stravinsky, Igor, 58, 83
Strayhorn, Billy, 6, 137–38, 281

Student Nonviolent Coordinating Committee (SNCC), 67–68, 204
Students for a Democratic Society (SDS), 151
Sublette, Ned, 277
Sudhalter, Dick, 12
Sulieman, Idrees, 186–87
Sullivan, Maxine, 105, 106
Sundiata, Sekou, 170, 197–98, 271
Sung, Helen, 76
Sun Ra, 115, 168
SUNY Press, 218
SUNY Purchase, 182
Sweet Man (George), 136–37
Swenson, John, 35–36
Swing-era musicians, 229–30
Szwed, John, 115–16

Tate, Buddy, 229, 231
Tate, Greg, 148
Tatum, Art, 52, 61, 231
Tavernier, Bertrand, 98
Taylor, Billy, 130
Taylor, Cecil, 6–7, 14–15, 17, 42, 182, 267, 270
Tazi, Neila, 154–55
Teachout, Terry, 147, 252
Teagarden, Jack, 12
Temperly, Joe, 67
Terry, Clark, 89, 279
Thelonious Monk and Sonny Rollins, 25
Thelonious Monk: sein Leben, seine Musik, seine Schallplaten (Fitterling), 196
Thelonious Monk: The Life and Times of an American Original (Kelley), 99–100, 185–88, 198–206
They All Played Ragtime (Blesh and Janis), 130
Things Are Getting Better (Adderley), 153–54

Things I Must Have Known (Spellman), 261, 275, 278, 283
This Is Our Music (Sinclair), 270
Thompson, Bob, 177
"Three Pianists" (Balliett), 6–7
Thurman, Camilla, 77
Timeless Muse, 152
Time Out, 23
To Be or Not to Bop (Gillespie and Fraser), 277
Tokyo (Gordon), 90
Toomer, Jean, 274
transformative experience listening to music, 282–83
Treme, 223, 236–38
Troupe, Quincy, 116
Tucker, Mark, 137
Tucker, Sherrie, 84
"Turnaround" (Coleman), 8
Turner, Joe, 16, 235
"27 Cooper Square" (Brown), 183
Tyner, McCoy, 20, 24–25, 92

Uhuru Afrika (Weston), 155–56, 166
Understanding Jazz (Piazza), 223, 224–25, 232–33
University of New Mexico Press, 178
Unreleased Art Pepper, Volume 11 (Pepper), 207, 221
Upside-Down Sky, An (Dahl), 71, 77
Uptown Conversations (Griffin, Edwards, and O'Meally), 122
Urban Word, 170
Use Trouble (Harper), 101

Valentine Stomp (Waller), 226
Van Clief-Stefanon, Lyrae, 180–81
van de Leur, Walter, 138
Van Gogh, Vincent, 53
Vaughan, Sarah, 84
Vick, Harold, 105

View from Within, The (Keepnews), 193
Village Gate, 130, 228–29, 266
Village Vanguard, 91, 130, 200, 228–29
"Villanelle for the Hell of It" (Spellman), 275

Walcott, Derek, 64
Waller, Fats, 226, 230
Wall Street, musicians working in firms on, 230
"Warming Up a Riff" (Parker), 41
Warner Brothers, 31
Washington, Salim, 109, 110, 119–20, 121
Waste Land, The (Eliot), 51
Waters, Muddy, 226
Watkins, Julius, 188, 229
Watts, Marzette, 171
Weather Report, 42, 150
Webb, Chick, 84
Weber, Bruce, 29
Webster, Ben, 8
Wein, George, 43, 158
weird, not thinking jazz people are, 92
Welburn, Ron, 148, 158
Welles, Orson, 57
Wells, Dicky, 229, 230
Wellstood, Dick, 9, 10
Welty, Eudora, 62–63
"We Saw Jazz through His Lens" (Hasse), 127
West, Cornell, 68
West, Mike, 165
Weston, Randy, 100, 145, 146, 152, 153, 154–56, 166, 200
What a Wonderful World (Riccardi), 241, 242–43, 248–51, 252
"What'd I Say" (Charles), 22
"What's Your Take" (Jenkins), 147–48

Where's the Melody? (Williams), 39, 54–55
"Whispering" (Monk), 187
Whitaker, Popsie, 11
White, Chris, 230
White, William, 177
White House concerts, 15
white musicians: elevation of, 147–48; Lincoln Center Orchestra musicians, 12, 67, 240; slighting in books on jazz, 12
white writers of jazz criticism, 55–56
Widow's Taste record label, 207, 221
Wilder, Billy, 58
Wiley, Andrew, 62
Willems, Jos, 250
Williams, David, 216
Williams, John A., 83
Williams, Martin: Crouch on, 54–55, 67; *The Jazz Tradition*, 37–38; Jones on, 179–80; mentorship of Tucker by, 137; Piazza on, 233–34; *Smithsonian Collection of Classic Jazz*, 12, 43, 142, 179; Spellman on and relationship with, 266, 276; support for Dolphy by, 263; *Where's the Melody?* 39, 54–55
Williams, Mary Lou: Allen's work with, 76; autobiography manuscript written by, 79–80; Balliett on, 9; Dahl's biography about, 71, 72, 77–80, 84, 120–21; early life of, 79; Griffin on and writings about, 120–21, 123; Kelley's research in papers of, 201; Nellie Monk's seamstress work for and opinion about, 201, 202; papers and private journals of, 78–79; Piazza performance review written by, 227; spiritual dimension of jazz and zodiac interests of, 111, 123; White House concert performance of, 15; writings about, 80, 120–23
Williams, Sandy, 229
Williams, Tony, 33, 42, 54
Wilmer, Val, 204
Wilson, Cassandra, 13
Wilson, Edmund, 10, 233–34
Wilson, John S., 26
Wilson, Steve, 7
Wilson, Teddy, 227
Winter Moon (Pepper), 209
With Billie (Blackburn), 115, 116, 118
Witkowski, Deanna, 80
women in jazz, 71–72, 75–82, 84, 105–6, 120–21
Wonderful World of Louis Armstrong blog (Riccardi), 241, 250
Woods, Phil, 216–17
"Work," 25
world music, 267
World Trade Center attack, 201

Young, Andrea, 256
Young, Larry, 105
Young, Lester, 61, 89
Young, Trummy, 248, 256
Young Man with a Horn, 57–58

Zappa, Frank, 158
Zarra, Malika, 77
"Zoning Mary Lou Williams Zoning" (Edwards), 121–22